道可道非常道名可名非常名無名萬物之始

有名萬物之母故常無欲以觀其妙

常有欲以觀其所徼此兩者同出而異名

同謂之元元之又元眾妙之門

The Tao that can be told is not the invariant Tao
the names that can be named are not the invariant Names.

Nameless, it is the source of the thousands of things
named, it is 'Mother' of the thousands of things.

Yes:
Always: being desireless,
    one sees the hidden essentials.
Always: having desires,
    one sees only what is sought.

These two lines are about The Merging—
it is when things develop and emerge from this
that the different names appear.

The Merging is something mysterious—
mysterious, and more mysterious,
the abode of all the hidden essences.

The Tao of the
Tao Te Ching

SUNY Series in Chinese Philosophy and Culture
David L. Hall and Roger T. Ames, editors

The Tao of the
Tao Te Ching

A Translation and Commentary

Michael LaFargue

State University of New York Press

The excerpt on page 209 from THE FIRST TIME EVER I SAW YOUR FACE, by Ewan MacColl, is reprinted by permission of STORMKING MUSIC INC., © Copyright 1962 (renewed) by STORMKING MUSIC INC. All Rights Reserved.

An excerpt from 'The Man with the Blue Guitar' is reprinted by permission of Random House and Faber and Faber Ltd. from COLLECTED POEMS by Wallace Stevens.

Calligraphy for chapters 1 and 81 from the *Tao Te Ching* is reprinted from *Tao Te Ching: A New Translation* by Gia-fu Feng and Jane English, Vintage Books, ©1972 Gia-fu Feng and Jane English.

Cover illustration courtesy of The Gichner Foundation for Cultural Studies.

Published by
State University of New York Press, Albany

For information, address State University of New York
Press, State University Plaza, Albany, N.Y. 12246

Production by Dana Foote
Marketing by Dana E. Yanulavich

Library of Congress Cataloging-in-Publication Data
Lao-tzu.
[Tao te ching. English]
The tao of the Tao te ching : a translation and commentary /
Michael LaFargue.
p.   cm. — (SUNY series in Chinese philosophy and culture)
Includes bibliographical references.
ISBN 0-7914-0986-4 (alk. paper)
I. LaFargue, Michael. II. Title. III. Series.
BL1900.L26E5   1992
                                                              91–18284
                                                              CIP

10 9 8

*This Book is Dedicated
to My Students*

Contents

How to Read This Book

This book can be read in several ways.

The reader may simply want to read the text of the *Tao Te Ching* itself, printed throughout on the left-hand pages of this book. For an explanation of a few *Chinese words left untranslated* in the text, such as *Tao* and *Te,* consult the alphabetically arranged "Topical Glossary" at the end of the book.

The reader interested in a brief account of my interpretation can read the first paragraph at the top of the right-hand pages, where I impersonate an ancient Taoist paraphrasing the text in modern terms, and suggest the relevance of the *Tao Te Ching* for today.

Other features of this book are designed to aid the reader interested in a more careful study of the *Tao Te Ching*. This requires understanding a few more facts about how this book is arranged and printed:

The traditional text of the *Tao Te Ching* consists of eighty-one very brief, numbered "chapters," arranged in no readily apparent order. As an aid to the modern reader, *I have rearranged the chapters of the* Tao Te Ching *in a topical order* and given each chapter a corresponding additional new number, enclosing the old number in brackets. For example, 1[24] indicates Chapter 24 in the traditional arrangement, which is Chapter 1 in my new arrangement. Readers wishing to read the chapters in their traditional ordering will find on the last page of this book a list of chapters in this order, matched with my new numbers and with page numbers where they are found in this translation.

In my reconstruction, each "chapter" is made up primarily of sayings that originally were independent of each other, each saying part of the oral tradition of a small ancient Taoist community which I refer to as the "Laoist" School (see p. 195). These sayings were artfully arranged in "sayings collages" by Taoist teachers whom I refer to as the *composers* of the chapters. Sayings I believe to stem from this oral tradition are printed in plain print in the translation.

I believe that sometimes the composers alter these oral sayings or add to them, and I indicate this by printing suspected alterations and additions *in italics*. Finally, I think the composers sometimes use sayings borrowed from outside their own community; I indicate this by enclosing such sayings in double quotes.

The first part of the commentary on each chapter consists of a paraphrase representing my view of how a Taoist would present the message of this chapter in modern terms.

The second part of the commentary on each chapter is more analytical. It is also designed to be used as a study guide. It gives cross references to other passages in the *Tao Te Ching* that shed light on the passage being commented on. *Asterisks* in this analytical commentary indicate words or ideas explained more fully in the Topical Glossary located at the end of this book. Topics in this Glossary are listed alphabetically.

The translation divides each chapter into several sections, and each section is given a number (placed in braces in the right margin), so that the commentary can refer to sections by number. References to other chapters use square brackets and colons: For example, 28[16] refers to Chapter 16 in the traditional arrangement, which is Chapter 28 in my new rearrangement, and 28[16]:1 refers to the first section of this chapter. (28[16]:1:2 refers to the second line of the first section.)

A chapter on "Hermeneutics" following the translation sketches the approach to interpretation followed here, including an outline of the sociohistorical background of the *Tao Te Ching,* my hypothesis about its composition, and some thoughts on how to interpret the enigmatic sayings in it. The Topical Glossary following this gives my interpretation of various key Laoist themes in more synthetic form, and also serves as an index, giving all the passages on a given theme.

Sometimes in discussions I find it helpful to give Chinese words along with their English equivalents. In doing this I have adopted a modified version of a format now being used by some sinologists:[1] The Chinese word is placed first, followed by a slash and then an English equivalent. Where it is helpful to give two or more English equivalents, these are separated by colons. For example, *hsiao*/small:insignificant includes first the Chinese word *hsiao,* then two English equivalents *small* and *insignificant,* separated by a colon. Where an English *phrase* is being used to translate a Chinese word or phrase, I mark the boundaries of the English phrase by enclosing the whole phrase in quotation marks following the slash, as in *wu wei*/"not doing."

Acknowledgments

Peggi Erickson introduced me to the *Tao Te Ching*, and I hope some of her spirit lives in these pages. I owe a very great deal of what I know about interpretive theory and practice to several years participation in seminars led by Dieter Georgi. My ideas on the relevance of sociohistorical research to textual interpretation were developed in conversation with Dick Horsley. Russell Kirkland gave me encouragement and advice, without which this project would not have reached publication. Jessica Gill helped greatly in preparing research materials. The final three years of concentrated work on this book would not have been possible without the warm support and personal sacrifice of my wife Hilda Dorgan. The development of my understanding of the *Tao Te Ching* is due above all to my students, both at the Cambridge Center for Adult Education and at the University of Massachusetts/ Boston, to whom it is dedicated. I am sure many of my interpretations derive ultimately from some student's remarks, as well as some lines like, "Man runs to escape what he has forgotten" (p. 79), coined by a student whose name I wish I could remember. I would especially like to thank Beth Barth, Nancy Borofsky, Susan Graesser, Dorothy Lindsay, Carol Sipe, Kristina and Robert Snyder, Donna Ulrici, and Phil Walcutt—the interest and support they showed in faithful attendance for several years at weekly discussions of the *Tao Te Ching* are responsible for my own perseverance in this study, and much of my understanding stems from conversations with them.

Introduction

The *Tao Te Ching* stems from the early formative period of Chinese thought (c. 500–200 B.C.). It is one among a small number of books from this period that have a place in Chinese tradition roughly similar to that of the Greek classics, the Bible, and the Koran in the Judeo-Christian and Islamic traditions, and to the Upanishads and the Pali Canon in the Hindu and Buddhist traditions. In this century, the *Tao Te Ching* has become immensely popular in Western countries as well, reputedly having been translated more than any other book in the world except the Bible and the *Bhagavad Gita*.[1]

The approach of this book to interpreting the *Tao Te Ching* differs in many respects from its predecessors. If there is any merit in these differences, this derives primarily neither from new spiritual or philosophical insights, nor from new historical or linguistic research. It comes rather from an attempt to develop and apply some facets of modern "hermeneutics"—the theory and practice of trying to recover the original meaning of written texts.[2] Hermeneutics has been the subject of intense discussion in areas such as biblical studies (my own original field of study), but only recently has begun to be discussed in an explicit and extensive fashion among Western interpreters[3] of the Chinese classics. Despite its origin in scriptural study, modern hermeneutics in its best moments has striven to *overcome* many tendencies ordinarily associated with the interpretation of "scriptural" writings. One resultant principle, of special importance in the present study, is that the ideas we find in scriptural writings did not fall from the sky. They grew out of human experiences—often extraordinary experiences, to be sure, but experiences that are not radically different from experiences we ourselves might have or imagine ourselves having.[4] One of the main reasons that writings like the *Tao Te Ching* are so interesting is that they stand at the origin of a tradition, and reflect the originating human experiences that under-lie ideas that later became dogmas and doctrines separated from experiential roots. To understand the words in such writings, we must try to enter vicariously into the historical world, and the way of experiencing that world, that the words reflect. An impor-tant key to doing this is to try to find analogies in our own experi-ence and extrapolate from them. A further outline of the hermeneutic principles underlying this approach to the *Tao Te Ching* will be found in the essay "Hermeneutics" that follows the translation and commentary.

The *Tao Te Ching* has the reputation of being a vague and ambiguous book, containing almost as many meanings as there are readers. I believe, on the contrary, that the book had a quite definite meaning to its original authors and audience, that this meaning is worth trying to recover, and that careful attention to interpretive method can help us get closer to it—though all such attempts will be rough approximations based on educated guesses.

Translation and Commentary

1

Excellence That Is Not Outstanding

1[24]

"A person on tiptoe is not firmly planted   {1}
a person in a rush will not go far."

One who shows off will not shine   {2}
one who promotes himself won't become famous
one who boasts of himself will get no credit
one who glorifies himself will not become leader.

In Tao   {3}
this is called 'stuffing oneself,' 'overdoing it.'

Things seem to detest this,   {4}
so the ambitious man does not dwell here.

(Paraphrase:)[1] Some people try to manufacture increased public stature for themselves by deliberate attention-getting tactics {2}.[1] This is like a simpleton who is on tiptoe because she[2] thinks that standing higher must necessarily be standing better {1}. Such a manufactured image, like standing on tiptoe, is precarious, an "excess" {3} added above and beyond any solid grounding in reality. Such a person cannot have any genuine success. It is as though her pretentious claims are detested by "things," by reality itself {4}.

(Analysis:) Saying {1}[1] looks like a common proverb against overextending oneself. Saying {2} is a Laoist* saying[4] countering[3] the tendency of *shih**[4] toward self-promotion*,[4] by posing the image[3] of the person whose deliberate efforts to impress only turn people off and inhibit his success. Saying {4} is a Laoist saying that could apply to many areas of life, depending on the context in which it is said.

Sections {1} and {3} implicitly characterize the "showing off" of {2} as an "excess." This implies a background view of reality in which there is a "normal" amount of importance and recognition given to each individual, based on true substantive worth and the part each plays in an organic social whole. The self-promoting person is "excessive" in trying to get more for himself above and beyond this. The rejection of the show-off by "things*"[4] {4} is related to this same idea: *Things* here refers to normative reality as seen from a Laoist perspective, that is, reality as an organically*[4] ordered whole. This is the reality that "detests" the show-off who violates this organic order by deliberate attempts to "stand out." Compare the occurrence of {4} in 67[31]:2.[1] "Things detest" weapons of war, and so the soldier out for personal glory by killing others "cannot achieve his purposes in the world" (67[31]:6). This has a quasi-superstitious*[4] basis. In the Laoist view, people in various ways put themselves out of joint with reality, and reality in turn turns against them. *Tao**[4] in {3:1} has an adjectival sense, referring to the specifically Laoist way of looking at things.

---

1. For the arrangement, numbering system, and typographical conventions followed in the translation and commentary, see "How to Read This Book," pp. ix–x.

2. Paraphrases are partly intended to indirectly suggest the modern relevance of the *Tao Te Ching*, so I freely use *she* in the paraphrases (to counterbalance *he* in the analysis). So far as I know it is unlikely that members of the Laoist school included women.

3. Terms like *counter, criticize, directed against*, etc. indicate that the saying being commented on is a Laoist polemic aphorism. The target of the aphorism is being countered by "posing an image." On these elements of the meaning-structure of aphorisms, see pp. 201–05.

4. Asterisks mark topics explained and discussed further in the Topical Glossary, where the key words so marked are listed in alphabetical order.

2[9]

In filling, if you keep on and on—   {1}
better to have stopped.
In sharpening, if you keep trying—
the edge won't last long.
When gold and jade fill the halls,
no one can guard it all.
Rich, famous—and conceited:
leading to a downfall self-caused.

Achieve successes,   {2}
win the fame,
remove yourself:
Heaven's Way.

A person who gets caught up in the quest for wealth and fame is like a person who keeps pouring after the jar is full, or who keeps filing after the blade is sharp {1}. Such a person is fooled by the momentum of her attraction, pursuing what is attractive beyond the point where it is still really useful. So likewise, when you distinguish yourself in public service, don't avidly capitalize on this for self-promotion. The highest Way is to do a great job and quietly move on {2}.

Saying {1} is a rhymed saying presenting both accumulated wealth and pride in one's success, as a kind of "excess" that is precarious (similar to the Greek concept of hubris. Compare 1[24]). Saying {2} counters the tendency toward self-promotion* by posing the image of the *shih** who quits his government post just when he is becoming successful. The contrast between the two sayings has a specific basis in Laoist thought: Real worth is typically hidden worth, whereas those qualities that win public recognition typically are less solid and genuine. A person who tries to capitalize on the attention-getting aspect of his accomplishments to further his career {2} is relying on the *less* solid part of what he has done. The person who gets his self-esteem from being rich and famous {1} is a more extreme example of this same tendency and so puts himself in an even more precarious position.

The first three chapters in this Section 1 (1[24], 2[9], 3[67]) all have to do with precarious "excess." (See also 19[44]:2, 62[29]:4).

3[67]

Everyone in the world says of me: {1}
    'great—but doesn't seem normal.'
It's just 'greatness'—
    that's why it does not seem normal.
If I were normal,
I'd have been of little worth for a long time now.

I have three treasures,   {2}
I protect and keep hold of them.
The first is called 'gentleness'
the second is called 'frugality'
the third is called 'not presuming to act
    like leader of the world.'

Gentle, so able to be bold
frugal, so able to be lavish
not presuming to act like leader of the world,
    so able to become head of a government.

Now:
To be bold without being gentle
to be lavish without being frugal
to act like leader without putting oneself last:
This is death.

Yes, gentleness: {3}
"Attack with it and you will win
defend with it and you will stand firm."

When Heaven wants to rescue someone,   {4}
it surrounds him with a wall of gentleness.

There are loud and outgoing qualities (being bold, lavish, self-assertive), and there are quiet and retiring ones (being gentle, frugal, self-effacing). When outgoing qualities exist by themselves, they are typically the result of artificial effort, and so lack grounding in reality. An identity founded on this is precarious, insecure, "death" inviting. But the outgoing qualities are not wrong in themselves. One whose basic identity resides in the quiet virtues has a safe and solid basis for herself. Such a one can be bold and lavish on occasion, or occupy the highest social positions, without danger {2}. Quiet virtues like gentleness have a quality about them that acts as a magical protection, whatever situation one is in {3–4}.

Quiet virtues intensely cultivated—"taken to an extreme" by normal standards—make one appear not only quiet but odd {1}. But it is normal standards that are at fault in this: "Extremism" in the service of what is truly good is the right way. There is reason to worry if one is *not* a little odd.

Saying {1} is related to sayings countering the tendency to admire only impressive appearances*. The "I" is anonymous, but the image of the "great but not normal" person probably has primary reference to teachers* in the Laoist school, held up as models for others (compare 45[70]:2–3). Saying {2} is a saying against the tendencies of the upper classes toward assertiveness, conspicuous consumption, and self-promotion*. "Death" is hyperbole, portraying the "dangerous" precariousness of this. There seems no *practical* basis for the implication that the quieter virtues give one's life a "safe" foundation. The most likely basis is rather the one suggested in 1[24]: Loud self-assertion is precarious because it lacks a firm basis in (normative) reality.

In juxtaposing {1} and {2}, the composer draws on the Laoist association between personal qualities that attract little notice at all {2} and qualities that make one appear positively odd or disreputable {1} (see 4[22]). Saying {3:2–3} looks like it could be a common saying applicable to a variety of things. In their thrust, both {3} and the composer's addition in {4} function as celebratory sayings that portray the marvelous benefits of the quality "gentleness," which Laoists cultivate. (See "Benefits*" for further notes on this genre of sayings.)

4[22]

"Bent—then mature."   {1}

Compromised—then upright   {2}
Empty—then solid
old and spent—then young and sprightly.

A little—then a gain   {3}
a lot—then confusing.

And so the Wise Person: {4}
Embraces The One Thing,
and becomes the Shepherd of the World.

He does not show off, so he shines   {5}
he does not promote himself, so he becomes famous
he does not boast of himself, so he gets the credit
he does not glorify himself, so he becomes leader.

He just does not contend   {6}
and so no one can contend with him.

What the ancients said: "bent—then mature,"   {7}
is this an empty saying?
This is true maturity, turn back to it.

There are two parts to human goodness: The part that makes a good impression in the social world, and the part that is simply good. The part that makes a good impression is easily counterfeited. So the "purest" image of goodness is found in those persons who are good but do not appear so: A person who has great integrity but who appears compromised, a person of substance who appears "empty," and so on {1–2 and 7}. One who rests in this kind of goodness does not join the social competition for high status {5–6}. She realizes, for example, that a little bit of knowledge deeply understood may not impress others, but is actually more valuable than simply memorizing a lot of information {3}. Quantity impresses, but what one needs is only to turn back to the One Simple Thing, a certain quality of mind embodying pure but hidden goodness—this is the Center of the World {4}.

I believe {1} is a folk proverb to the effect that the negative, "bent" appearance of old people is a sign of something positive, their maturity. Saying {2} is a Laoist saying against admiring only impressive appearances*, posing the counterimage of fine qualities that appear negative on the surface. (Some of the wording, such as "compromised/upright," recalls similar sayings in 5[45]:1–2, see comments there). Confusing in {3} suggests that, despite the parallelism with {2}, this saying is on a different topic. It criticizes the view that gaining understanding* consists in widespread study or information gathering, posing the counterimage of the person whose multifarious knowledge only confuses him (compare 41[47]:2). Saying {4} celebrates the cosmic* importance of Laoist self-cultivation, described here as "embracing* the One* Thing." ("Shepherd of the World" is a traditional designation of the Emperor*.) Sayings {5} and {6} are sayings against self-promotion*. Saying {5} (a version of 1[24]:2) evokes the image of the person whose self-effacing manner elicits the admiration of others and wins influence. Saying {6} (= 55[66]:4) expresses the Laoist view that the ideal person, by refusing to compete (contend*) for social status, becomes in fact superior to all.

The image evoked in {2}, of great qualities hidden under negative appearances, expresses in more extreme fashion the advocacy of a self-effacing attitude in {5} and {6}. "The One Thing" that Laoists cultivate in themselves was felt by them to be something conventionally looked down upon (see 14[23]:3, 35[39]:2), and this association connects {2} and {4}. A connection between embracing this One Thing ("a little"), on the one hand, and having a multifarious store of impressive knowledge on the other {3} also may be intended. The composer frames* the chapter with a reference to the same traditional saying in {1} and {7}.

5[45]

The greatest perfection will seem lacking in something   {1}
but its usefulness never ends.
The greatest solidity will seem Empty
but its usefulness is inexhaustible.

The greatest uprightness will seem compromised   {2}
the greatest ability will seem clumsy
the greatest eloquence will seem tongue-tied.

"Agitation overcomes cold   {3}
Stillness overcomes heat."

Purity and Stillness are the Norm of the World.   {4}

Cultivating personal qualities that impress others takes constant effort, and so is mentally tiring. And in the absence of an audience, what good are they really? Look within for qualities of mind that are inherently satisfying to yourself, and cultivate these instead. These qualities will always appear in the conventional world as something worthless or not quite right {1–2}. But they sustain themselves, and so will be an inexhaustible source of real satisfaction to you {1}. In them your mind can find rest and stillness—that Stillness which is the Center of the world {4}.

Sayings {1} and {2} counter the tendency to admire only impressive appearances*, posing contrasting images of a kind of true internal greatness that, however, has a negative external appearance. *Perfection* in {1} is more literally "completeness," that is, a personal character "brought to completion" (see 10[7]:3, 44[41]:4, 65[51]:1:4, 71[63]:5). *Solidity** is more literally "fullness": I take it to describe a person whose presence seems "substantial," in contrast to someone who appears worthless, Empty* (see 6[15]:2 and 4). The Laoist contrast to the showiness of fine appearances is "usefulness," which probably refers to a concrete sense of personal satisfaction in one's own being. (Compare the image of inexhaustibly useful Emptiness in 16[5]:2, the useful Nothingness in 15[11], and the fruit/flower image in 11[38]:7). *Upright/compromised* in {2} is more literally "straight/bent," but the *Mencius*[1] uses these same words to describe moral integrity and moral compromise, respectively. Saying {3} is a celebratory* saying borrowed from contemporary speculation about the "conquest cycle," concerning which physical/psychic energy "overcomes" ("conquers") which other. Here a two-line saying is quoted from this speculation, of which only the second line—about how the energy Stillness* conquers its opposite, agitation*—is relevant to Laoist thought (see "Conquest*"). Saying {4} is celebratory, celebrating Stillness as a cosmic* norm.

The composer's associations between {1–2} and {3–4} here probably depend on the fact that achieving an impressive appearance requires "working*" (see 11[38]:2–3), that is, a mind stirred into activity, as opposed to the deep mental Stillness Laoists associate with a more "natural*" (but less impressive) way of being. This same association underlies the juxtaposition of sayings in 6[15]:2–3.

Three chapters grouped together here (4[22], 5[45], and 6[15]) urge cultivation of good personal qualities that appear negative or Empty*/worthless from a conventional point of view.

---

1. 3B/1.

6[15]

The Excellent *shih* of ancient times {1}
penetrated into the most obscure,
    the marvelous, the mysterious.
They had a depth beyond understanding.

They were simply beyond understanding, {2}
the appearance of their forceful presence:
Cautious, like one crossing a stream in winter
timid, like one who fears the surrounding neighbors
reserved, like guests
yielding, like ice about to melt
unspecified, like the Uncarved Block
all vacant space, like the Valley
everything mixed together, like muddy water.

Who is able, as muddy water, {3}
    by Stilling to slowly become clear?
Who is able, at rest,
    by long drawn-out movement to slowly come to life?

Whoever holds onto this Tao {4}
does not yearn for solidity.

He simply lacks solidity, and so {5}
what he is capable of:
Remaining concealed, accomplishing nothing new.

Cultivating mental depth {1} means fostering a deep Stillness {3}, and coming to exist at a level of mind that, from a conventional perspective, seems to have no existence {4–5}. It appears vacant, unspecific, un-definite {2:7–9}. The person who has it has a magically forceful presence, which however typically presents an appearance of hesitance and timidity {2:3–6}. Her great achievement is to blend in perfectly, to do nothing that appears strikingly new and different {5}.

Saying {1} reflects one of the ideals of Laoist *shih**: To become a person who understands* things "in depth," which for them meant primarily cultivating the depths of one's own mind (see 43[1]:5). Here this ideal is projected onto an idealized ancient* time, when immensely "deep" *shih* advised the legendary great emperors. Saying {2:3–6} is related to sayings against self-promotion*, countering the common admiration of an aggressive and forceful presence by posing somewhat exaggerated images of the opposite kind of person. Lines {2:7–9} are probably added by the composer. (They interrupt a rhyme scheme, and they switch from describing external appearances to describing an internal state and from everyday metaphors to the more technical Laoist terms, *Uncarved* Block* and *Valley**. Line {2:9} may be a connective* link to {3}. My translation of *ch'iang wei* [lit. "strong working"] as "forceful presence" in {2:2} [and in 39[25]:2:3] is new. Others translate "[I will] *ch'iang*/try to *wei*/render their appearance....") Saying {3} is meditation* instruction: One first brings the mind from a state of busy-ness to Stillness*, and then gradually returns to being mentally active (see comments on 33[55]:2.) Saying {4} (a version of 31[4]:1) is an instructional saying giving a normative* description of what one is like who embodies Laoist Tao*—he will not yearn for a "solid*" (lit. "full") social presence.

The juxtapositions here suggest that "not...solid" in {4} is a description of the person of shy and retiring presence described in {2} and the person who remains unnoticed in {5}. *Concealed* also seems connected with the image of the ancient *shih* in {1}, whose minds existed on such a mysterious and deep level that no one could understand them. This is the state of mind and hidden/Empty way of being aimed at by one who cultivates Stillness {3–4}. The sayings in this chapter connect the internal state of the ideal person {1, 3, 4, 5} to a certain kind of external appearance {2:3–6}.

7[8]

The highest Excellence is like water.   {1}
Water, Excellent at being of benefit
    to the thousands of things,
does not contend—
it settles in places everyone else avoids.
Yes, it is just about Tao.

Excellence in a house: the ground   {2}
"Excellence in a mind: depth
Excellence in companions: Goodness
Excellence in speaking: sincerity
Excellence in setting things right: good management
Excellence on the job: ability
Excellence in making a move: good timing."

Simply do not contend   {3}
then there will be no fault.

What makes for a good house is not what gives it a striking appearance, but the solidity of the unseen foundation. Look out for this in other areas of life as well: For example, sincerity in speech and depth of mind do not get as much attention as eloquence and brilliance, but they are more solid {2}. Cultivating truly solid qualities means forgoing social competition and a willingness to accept the lowest rung on the social ladder. But these also are the qualities of most actual benefit to others. Cultivating these should be the main business of anyone truly devoted to helping others in public service, rather than just making a name for herself {1}.

Saying {1} is a saying against self-promotion*, using a nature image as an extended metaphor*. The fact that water flows downward and nourishes plants serves as an image illustrating the Laoist ideals of (a) not contending* with others for high social status, (b) willingness to accept being in a low* and unnoticed position ("which all others avoid"), and (c) devoting oneself to public service ("benefiting the thousands of things") as a *shih** in government office. To act like this is to identify with the role of Tao* in the world. Saying {2:2–6}, in its idealization of *jen*/Goodness,[1] sincerity, and "good timing,"[2] reads best as a rhymed saying from some school with a Confucian* bent. Saying {3} is a saying using an oracle* formula to present not-contending* as a "lucky" way to act.

Because the first line of {2} alone is metaphorical, and because it does not rhyme with the rest, I mark it a connective* addition by the composer. The "lowness" of the house's foundation connects this saying to the theme of lowness (water flowing downward) implicit in {1}. (Compare the low foundation image in 35[39]:2). The composer probably sees the virtues praised in {2} as examples of good qualities that are relatively unimpressive externally (as in the paraphrase). This is why he associates this saying with the Laoist polemic against contending for high social standing {1 and 3}, and with the advice to accept a social position low and unnoticed {1}. He "baptizes" this Confucian saying by relating it to the Laoist theme of "lowness*," an association facilitated by the occurrence of "depth" in {2:2}.

The same associations apparent in this chapter—criticism of fine appearances, devotion to public service, and "not contending"—also link sayings in the next chapter, 8[81].

---

1. Words printed in this format represent a Chinese word (*jen*) and an English equivalent ("Goodness"). For further explanation see pp. x–xi.

2. See *Mencius* 5B/1,5.

8[81]

Sincere words are not elegant   {1}
elegant words are not sincere.
Excellence is not winning arguments
winning arguments is not being Excellent.
Understanding is not wide learning
wide learning is not understanding.

The Wise Person does not store up for himself.   {2}

By working for others   {3}
he increases what he himself possesses.
By giving to others
he gets increase for himself more and more.

"Heaven's Way: to benefit and not to harm."   {4}
The Way of the Wise Person: to work and not contend.

People pretend to be striving for Excellence when they are really just egotistically trying to store up points for themselves by impressing others. These are the people who value elegance over sincerity in speech, and prefer impressive learning to real understanding {1–2}. But the real route to personal worth is not storing up points for oneself in social competition. It lies in selflessly trying to be of service to the people {3–5}.

Saying {1} is a saying against admiring only impressive appearances*, countering this tendency with a series of contrasting images: good qualities that are not impressive on the one hand, and impressive qualities that are empty show on the other. (Saying {1:5–6} is also related to sayings about true understanding*.) Sayings {2} and {3} are sayings against self-promotion*, countering the tendency of shih* toward a self-centered focus on their own personal ambitions. The contrasting image posed in {3} is that of the shih who perfects his own being by selfless service to his society. (The first line of {4} looks like a common saying: Its sentiment is not specifically Laoist, and the parallelism with the last line is very rough.)

In the composer's final line, wei/work* is an elliptical reference to "working for others" in {3} (compare the similar ellipsis in 51[75]:2]). And "not contending*" is a reference back to the polemic against impressive qualities in {1}. As in 7[8]:1, the contrast is between cultivating impressive qualities with the intention of self-promotion, on the one hand, and self-effacing public service, on the other.

9[79]

"When great hostilities are smoothed over   {1}
there is always some hostility left."
How could this be considered good?

And so the Wise Person: {2}
"Keeps hold of the left-hand contract tally,
and doesn't make demands on others."

One who has Te is concerned with fulfilling his contract   {3}
one who does not have Te concerns himself
   with collecting his due.

Heaven's Way: {4}
Not to have personal favorites,
but to be invariably good to all.

Even when people make up after a fight, hurt and hostile feelings remain. How can the cycle of hurting be broken? The person concerned about her self-importance will always insist on her rights. The person secure in herself can afford to be generous all the time—careful of her responsibilities, but willing to overlook what others owe her. So she can be an agent of peace.

Saying {1}, and possibly {2}, appear to be common sayings, used by the composer as take-off* points for more specifically Laoist ideas. Commentators generally interpret "holding the left-hand tally" to mean being mindful of one's own obligation. (Contracts in ancient China were sometimes sealed by breaking a tally, each partner keeping one half.) Saying {3} is a normative* description of what one is like who has Te*/virtue:charisma,[1] related to sayings against self-promotion*. The tendency to insist on one's own rights is countered by the image of the ideal person whose behavior expresses the Te he has inside. Te is associated with self-forgetting generosity with no thought of reciprocation also in 60[49]:2 and 71[63]:3. This idea seems to be the connecting thread throughout for the composer here as well. (Most other translators understand *t'ien heng yü shan jen* in {4} to mean something like "Heaven is always *yü*/with the *shan*/good man." I understand *yü* in the sense of "bestow" and *yü shan jen* as "bestow kindness on [all] others," connecting this line to *shan*/good in {1:3} and the theme of unreciprocated generosity to all in {2–3}.)

Three chapters are grouped here (8[81], 9[79], 10[7]) that share the theme of selflessness.

---

1. Words printed in this format represent a Chinese word before the slash, followed by two or more English equivalents, separated by colons. See pp. x–xi.

10[7]

Heaven is lasting, Earth endures.   {1}
What enables Heaven and Earth to last and endure?
Because they do not live for themselves—
so it is that they can live so long.

And so, the Wise Person: {2}
Puts himself last, and so finds himself in front.
Puts himself in the out group, and so maintains his place.

The personal does not exist for him—   {3}
isn't this how he can perfect
    what for him is most personal?

A person focused on furthering her own interests has to do it all herself, with constant effort. This produces a sense of precariousness—if she rests, everything will fall down. The person who can be unconcerned about whether she is "getting hers" can also realize the natural goodness in her being {3}. And she can rest secure in something that is just there, lasting all by itself, like the earth and the sky {1}. Give up trying to be recognized, and others will recognize it {2}.

Saying {1} is a saying using a metaphorical* nature image. "Heaven* and Earth" sometimes serve as quasi-divine cosmic powers in the *Tao Te Ching,* but here the image may well mean to evoke also a concrete sense of the still permanence of the physical sky and the ground underneath us. In content all three sayings are aphorisms against self-centeredness and self-promotion*. "Perfect what for him is [most] personal" probably describes perfecting one's character through self-cultivation (see 5[45]:1). For Laoists, to achieve the kind of selflessness described in {2} *is* to perfect one's character.

Saying {2:3} reads literally "outs his *shen*/self but *shen*/self preserves." In the context, this seems to mean that he preserves his social standing by, paradoxically, being willing to be considered someone in the "out" group. The use of *shen* here to refer to a person's social standing is the basis for my similar interpretation of *shen*/self in 18[13]:3. Note that, as in the case of many other words, *shen* has no uniform meaning consistently adhered to in the *Tao Te Ching.* For example, in 19[44]:1 and 23[26]:2 *shen* has a positive ("Yangist*") sense, referring to one's own basic being as something to which one ought to pay primary attention, in contrast to fame, wealth, and exciting things in the world. But 18[13]:3 and 28[16]:6 speak of *losing* one's *shen*/self as something positive—in these latter passages *shen* seems to refer to one's "sense of self" as a socially acknowledged participant in the ongoing life of the world. This "inconsistent" use of terms is a common characteristic of everyday conversational speech, in contrast to the more specialized and technical use of language by philosophers intent on grasping reality by means of a comprehensive and consistent conceptual system. See further comments under "Naming*."

11[38]

The finest Te is not Te-like, so it is Te	{1}
the poorest Te never leaves off being Te-like, so it is not Te.	

The finest Te: no working at it, no goal in mind {2}
the poorest Te: people work at it, with a goal in mind.

The finest Goodness: People work at it, {3}
    but with no goal in mind
the finest Morality: People work at it,
    with a goal in mind
the finest Etiquette: People work at it,
    and, when none pay attention,
    they roll up their sleeves and go on the attack.

Yes: {4}
Losing Tao, *next comes Te*
losing Te, next comes Goodness
losing Goodness, next comes Morality
losing Morality, next comes Etiquette.

And now Etiquette is loyalty and sincerity spread thin {5}
    and the first sign of disorders.

Foreknowledge is the flower of Tao {6}
and the beginning of folly.

And so the great man: {7}
Resides with the substance
does not stay with what is thin.
Resides with the fruit
does not stay with the flower.

Yes: {8}
He leaves 'that' aside and attends to 'this.'

Some human qualities are like flowers: They are striking and attract a lot of attention, but they are thin on substance and so bring no real satisfaction to the one who has them {7}. They are really pseudo-virtues, just the product of conscious efforts to impress other people {2–6}. Other qualities are like fruit, dull and uninteresting in appearance, but deeply nourishing to the possessor. These need to be cultivated for their own sake, with no hope to "get something out of it" {2–3}.

Saying {1} is a saying against impressive appearances*. Saying {2} is about cultivating Te*/virtue in oneself and contrasts the spirit of Laoist self-cultivation with the spirit of other *shih** schools who also cultivated Te. Sayings {3–5} are sayings against schools of a Confucian* bent. (Sayings {2} and {3} are separate sayings; there is no implication that "poorest Te" is equal in rank to "finest morality.") That the goal others "work" at is public impressiveness comes out in {3:7}, an exaggerated image of the person who does not get the recognition from others he wants and so turns nasty. "Not working" describes the *spirit* of Laoist self-cultivation—getting in touch with and drawing out one's own inherent "natural*" goodness, rather than "working" according to conscious ideals. Saying {4} denigrates Confucian virtues by presenting them as the result of the progressive decline from an ancient* Utopia (compare 12[18]). In {6} "foreknowledge" refers to extraordinary powers to see into the future, a result of intensive mental self-cultivation.[1] The saying recognizes that this might happen, but criticizes the tendency to make much of it. Saying {8} (= 21[12]:3 and 53[72]:4) advocates attending to the quality of one's own being ("this"), in contrast to a concern for the external impression one makes on others ("that"). (See "This*.")

The composer's comments in {7} pick up the words *thin* and *flower* from {5} and {6}. The association flower/thin and fruit/substance is important because it suggests the *positive* basis of Laoist thought about good-but-unimpressive qualities: Showy qualities ("flowers") are associated with lack of substance ("thin"), whereas substantive worth ("fruit") lies in what does not attract much attention. The "fruit" image probably also means to evoke the "usefulness"—that is, the satisfying quality—of unimpressive virtues, mentioned also in 5[45] and 15[11]. Showy-but-thin qualities must be "worked" at, whereas the useful-but-unimpressive ones are associated with "not working." This is in accord with the underlying Laoist assumption that the "natural*" goodness organic to one's being is more real and substantial, whereas virtues imposed by a planning mind out of touch with this organic* goodness are less real and "thin."

---

1. Compare *Doctrine of the Mean* 24.

12[18]

When Great Tao vanished   {1}
we got 'Goodness and Morality.'

When 'Wisdom and Know-how' arose
we got the Great Shams.

When the six family relationships fell into disharmony
we got 'Respect and Caring.'

When the states and the great families
    became all benighted and disordered
we got 'Loyal Subjects'.

Some people try to be virtuous only because they sense the need to have some qualities that will gain the respect of others, qualities that they now lack. But instead of turning back to the neglected goodness inherent in their being, they try to go forward, to "make progress" in applying their know-how to developing qualities that everyone admires. This will succeed only in producing artificial substitutes of no real worth. So when people start *talking* a lot about "Goodness," you know something is wrong. Run the other way.

Couplets 1, 3, and 4 here criticize Confucian* self-cultivation, which focused on the virtues mentioned in the second line of the first, third, and fourth couplets. As in 11[38]:4, these sayings evoke the image of an ideal ancient* Golden Age when everyone was "naturally*" good. (The "six [main] relationships" are father/son, husband/wife, elder-brother/younger-brother. "Respect" and "caring" are the virtues proper to children and parents respectively.)

Because of the lack of parallelism, I believe that the second couplet was added by the composer: The virtues Confucians cultivate are a product of calculating reason ("know-how") pressed into the service of self-interest in impressing others and hence are "Shams," artificially created to cover up for the lack of the more real and natural, "original" state of being Laoists cultivate.

This is one of three chapters criticizing Confucianism, grouped together here (11[38], 12[18], 13[20]).

13[20]

Break with Learning, and there will be no trouble.   {1}

'Yeah' and 'yes sir'—   {2}
is there a big difference between them?
'Excellent' and 'despicable'—
what's the real difference between them?

"What others hold in respect, we can't fail to respect."   {3}
Craziness. Aren't we over this yet?

"All the others are beaming and beaming   {4}
like people enjoying a great ceremonial feast,
like people climbing an overlook tower in the spring.
I am alone still—
no indications at all yet
like an infant who hasn't yet even smiled.
So sad. Like someone with no place to go home to.

All the others have a superabundance
I alone seem to have missed out.
Oh my simpleton's mind! So confused.

Ordinary men are so bright
I alone am so dull.
Ordinary men are so sharp
I alone am so stupid.
Churned up like the ocean,
blown about, like someone with no place to rest.

All the others all have their function
I alone am thick-headed,
     like someone from the back country."

I am alone, different from others—   {5}
treasuring the nourishing Mother.

There is an ongoing vibrancy to the social life that everyone wants to be a part of. But it is sustained by the constant effort of everyone to be "up" and outgoing {4} and to show off their refined manners {1–3}. One who cultivates the hidden substance of goodness inside has to accept often appearing and feeling "out of it." But there exists a nourishing and sustaining internal presence one can feel inside, that substitutes for the loss of a feeling of social support {5}.

Sayings {1} and {2} criticize Confucian* self-cultivation. Saying {1} uses an oracle* formula to picture the abandonment of Confucian Learning as a very "lucky" thing to do. Saying {2} refers to one of the main objects of such Learning, knowing proper *li*/Etiquette—how to distinguish proper from improper conduct and when to use formal or informal ways to say "yes." Saying {3:1} is probably a Confucian saying advising respect for accepted social conventions. (Compare the similar saying in the *Great Learning*,[1] "What ten eyes behold, what ten hands point to, is to be regarded with reverence.") The composer follows it here with a sarcastic rejection. Section {4} is uncharacteristically lyrical. I suspect it is from a non-Laoist source, perhaps a popular song, or a lament like those found in a roughly contemporary book called the *Ch'u Tz'u*.[2] Laoists like it because it mirrors an important aspect of their own experience—feeling "left out" of normal life because the quality of being which they value most highly seems like "nothing" from a conventional point of view. It is "left out" of the conventional world, as the next chapter 14[23]:2 describes it. (This in contrast to the Confucians, whose Etiquette seems to Laoists to be itself part of conventional society. Hence the connection between the first and last parts of this chapter.) Note the important twist in the composer's line at the end, showing that in his mind the lament is not a real lament. It only pictures the social alienation that typically accompanies something very positive, the Laoist way of being in which one develops a satisfying relation to "the nourishing Mother*"—the hypostatized* quality of mind one cultivates, felt as a sustaining internal presence that substitutes for the lack of external social support.

This chapter shows well the Laoist feeling of alienation, in contrast to the much less alienated Confucians. This I believe is the primary reason why Laoists developed and stressed a relation to a world-transcending Tao/Mother. (Not, as some suppose, because unlike Confucians, Laoists were interested in cosmological/metaphysical speculation.)

1. Comm. 6,3.
2. Hawkes 1985.

14[23]

Speaking little is what is natural.   {1}

Yes: {2}
A whirlwind does not blow a whole morning
a downpour does not fall a whole day.
And who causes these things?—Heaven and Earth.
If even Heaven and Earth cannot make things last very long,
how much less can man.

Yes: {3}
One devoted to Tao:
Is a Tao man, merges with Tao
is a Te man, merges with Te
is a man left out, merges with What Is Left Out.

One who merges with Tao, Tao welcomes him
one who merges with Te, Te welcomes him
one who merges with What Is Left Out,
What Is Left Out welcomes him.

When sincerity does not suffice,   {4}
it was not sincerity.

Some try to be out there all the time, talking {1}, impressing {4}. But even nature cannot force a wind to blow forever {2}. People need to mentally drop out sometimes, drop into the space that by its nature can never look like anything important in the world. Pay attention, and there exists a presence that will welcome and sustain you there {3}.

Saying {1} is related to a group of sayings against excitement and agitation*—prolonged talking takes effort and wears one out (16[5]:3) and so, from a Laoist perspective, is not "natural*." Saying {2} is also related to sayings against mentally agitating* activity. It uses metaphorical* nature images as *negative* examples to make a common Laoist point—that intense human activity exhausts one's energy and is short lived (see also 69[30]:5, 29[52]:4, 22[50]:2). This contrasts with Laoist advice to conserve one's energy in order to "last* long." Saying {3} celebrates the wonderful benefits* of the internal quality cultivated by Laoists. We see here several uses of Tao*: (a) adjectival—one who cultivates (Laoist) Tao has a Tao quality to his being (*tao che*/"[is a] Tao-man");[1] (b) as an hypostatized*, entitylike quality with which one can "merge"; (c) as a supportive presence one feels inside, "welcoming" one (compare the "nourishing" Mother* in 13[20]:5, and the "supporting/completing" Tao in 44[41]:4). *Tao* and *Te* are equivalent names for the same presence, here called also the *shih*/"Left-Out [One]," because it generally goes unrecognized in the world (compare 13[20]:5, 35[39]:1–2). Saying {4} is related to sayings against impressive appearances*. Like 8[81]:1, it means to emphasize sincerity rather than eloquence in speech, correcting the tendency to think that sincerity alone will not suffice to convince an audience. Laoists are confident that *real* sincerity has a subtle power that will surely be felt.[2]

The composer's associations in this chapter are probably as follows: Whirlwinds and downpours {2} are metaphors for intense human activity, of which lengthy talking {1} to impress others {4} is an example. Such talking is also a form of very active participation in the ongoing life of the world. But, as in 13[20]:4–5 and 29[52]:3, Laoist self-cultivation is often accompanied by a sense of losing this normally vital social connection. Hence the connection with "merging with What Is Left Out" in {3}. (My new understanding of sincerity *in speech* as the reference in {4} has the advantage of relating {4} to {1}, framing* the chapter as a whole. Saying {4} also occurs in 54[17]:2, immediately followed by a saying praising reticence in speech.)

---

1. Karlgren's translation. Compare *mo che*/"Mo-man" (= a disciple of Mo Ti), *Mencius* 3A/5,1.

2. Compare *Mencius* 4A/12,3.

15[11]

Thirty spokes unite in one hollow hub— {1}
in this 'nothing' lies the wheel's usefulness.

Knead clay to make a jar—
in its 'nothing' lies the jar's usefulness.

Cut out doors and windows in making a house—
in their 'nothing' lies the house's usefulness.

Yes: {2}
'Being' makes for profit
'Nothing' makes for usefulness.

Social admiration gives certain qualities a feeling of solidity, and makes others feel like "nothing." But think of all the cases—wheel centers, pots, windows, and doors—in which some "nothing" makes the thing functionally worth something {1}. If you are not looking for social "profit," but for what is of genuine worth and brings real satisfaction {2}, pay attention to those parts of your being that seem like "nothing."

Stylistically {1} is related to sayings using metaphorical* nature images. In content, the images celebrate* the great "usefulness" of the Nothingness* Laoists cultivate. (Compare 16[5]:2 and the similar "useful Emptiness*" in 5[45]:1.) The Being/Nothing contrast in {2} is not philosophical but concrete, equivalent to the contrast solid/Empty*; that is, *Being* refers to those aspects of one's personal being that feel tangible (like the tangible sides of a jar) because they are socially admired (hence *li*/profitable, a negative term here, as it is in 78[19]:1. It is an especially negative term in the *Mencius,*[1] too. The term *li*/profit figures prominently in the utilitarian social thought of the Mohists*[2]). *Nothing,* like Emptiness, refers to those aspects that feel intangible because they make no impression on others.

In this interpretation, *Nothing* in this chapter is related to the *Emptiness* celebrated in the next chapter, 16[5], and to the social alienation implied in the previous two chapters—the socially "lost" person in 13[20], and the person cultivating "left-out" Tao/Te in 14[23]. Chapter 17[28], the last one in this Section 1, is a climax, advocating the cultivation of qualities that appear "disgraceful" and relating this theme to the central Laoist concept of the "Uncarved* Block." (See comments on climaxes at 39[25].)

---

1. 1A/1,1–6.
2. Graham 1989: 37–41.

16[5]

"Heaven and Earth are not Good   {1}
they treat the thousands of things like straw dogs.
The Wise Person is not Good
he treats the hundred clans like straw dogs."

The space between heaven and earth   {2}
isn't it like a bellows?
Empty, but not shrivelled up,
set it in motion and always more comes out.

Much talking, quickly exhausted.   {3}

It can't compare to watching over what is inside.   {4}

Why do we spend so much time talking {3}? Is it not because this gives us a tangible sense of our identity, confirmed by being part of social life? Sometimes this also is the motivation of the self-important person in authority, anxious to appear to her people as someone "Good" {1}. By contrast, if we are just looking into ourselves, by ourselves {4}, we easily lose a tangible sense of our own existence. Our being seems evanescent and empty. But this Emptiness is worth holding onto. Attended to and cultivated {5}, it is a potential source of endless energy {2}.

Saying {1} is a saying against Confucian* jen/Goodness as an ideal for the ruler.[1] It mocks the Confucian emphasis that the upper classes should have a strong sense of social responsibility, making fun of Confucian seriousness by posing an exaggerated image of the opposite attitude—having no concern whatsoever for the people—and appealing to nature's indifference in support of this. ("Straw dogs" is a reference to a religious ceremony described in the Chuang* Tzu,[2] in which dogs made of straw were first given a place of honor, then later discarded and trampled.) But this saying has no parallel elsewhere in the Tao Te Ching, and Laoists elsewhere advocate selfless devotion to the good of society (8[81]:2-4, 7[8]:1, 9[79]:2-4, 75[78]:4). So, although many commentators focus on {1} as central to Laoist teaching, I doubt that this is a Laoist saying. The composer of this chapter likes it because it mocks the sense of self-importance he thinks motivates the Confucian sense of "responsibility." But he contrasts "Goodness," not with indifference, but with the "Emptiness" of {2}. Saying {2} is a saying celebrating the wonderful benefits* of this "Emptiness*" Laoists cultivate—the fact that this Empty state of mind is a source of boundless energy. (It is thus related also to sayings against mentally agitating* excitement, which is "exhausting.") The metaphorical* nature image employed seems to envision the "empty" physical space around us as continuously and endlessly producing all the living things that fill it up. Saying {3} is a saying against stimulating and mentally agitating* activity (talking-as-exhausting suggests excited or prolonged talking). Saying {4} celebrates* the importance of self-cultivation (internally "watching* over" qualities one wants to develop.) The composer's probable associations are described in the paraphrase.

---

1. Compare Mencius 1A/7,1-24.
2. Watson, 1968: 159.

17[28]

Be familiar with Masculinity   {1}
but watch over Femininity—
and become the Valley of the World.
Being the Valley of the World,
invariant Te will not leave you.
Turn back to being an infant.

Be familiar with what is pure and white
but watch over what is dark and black—
and become the Pattern for the World.
Being the Pattern for the World,
your invariant Te will be constant.
Turn back to being limitless.

Be familiar with what is praiseworthy
but watch over what is disgraceful—
and become the Valley of the World.
Being the Valley of the World,
your invariant Te will be sufficient.
Turn back to being an Uncarved Block.

When the Uncarved Block is cut up   {2}
then it becomes a government tool.
When the Wise Person instead uses it
then it becomes head of the government.

Yes: {3}
A great carver does no cutting,
a great ruler makes no rules.

There is a conflict between what our being tends to be if left to itself and the direction of growth it takes under the influence of social competition. The desire to be "praiseworthy" causes an artificial emphasis on some particular qualities and the repression of others that we become ashamed of. This does not result in a genuinely better personality, but in a loss of wholeness, a lessening of being and true worth. In practice, recovery of our own full and unique being requires that we find and cultivate the goodness in those parts of ourselves the conventional world ignores or looks down on. Such a fully recovered being is the center of the world.

Saying {1} is related to sayings against admiring impressive appearances*. But it also celebrates the way that Laoist self-cultivation gives a person the spiritual status of cosmic* norm. (The capitalized special terms describing these results are explained in the Topical Glossary.) *Femininity** and *dark and black* both refer to qualities that would be looked down upon by contemporaries, as is evident from the parallel with "disgraceful." The negative connotations are important, as part of the thrust of this passage is to shock, and to emphasize the reversal of conventional values. In {3} I have used two lines where the text has one, to capture the play on words: The word translated "carver" also means "ruler." The basic implied image is the woodcarver, who brings out the beautiful form already inherent in a piece of wood, doing as little cutting as possible. This is a metaphor* for the ideal ruler, who imposes as few explicit rules as possible on his society, drawing out instead its intrinsic goodness. (See "Naming*" and "Strict*.") Here "the great ruler" probably refers to the ideal person generally.

In the composer's comments in {2}, the *Uncarved* Block* serves as an image of a personality before it is "carved up" into standardized, socially desirable qualities (compare 63[32]:1–3). Recovering an "uncarved" personality is described as "using*" the Uncarved Block, whose great status is described in political metaphors: *Tool* describes a minor official—an "instrument" used by his superiors—in contrast to the exalted status of "prime minister." Reading {1} as aphoristic*, *corrective* wisdom, one would say that for Laoists, what it takes to recover "wholeness" is not (as in later *yin*/yang* Taoism) *equal* attention to both Masculinity and Femininity. One should rather cultivate Femininity. (One could see the difference as more apparent than real, however; because the universal tendency of everything is to "embrace* *yang*" [36[42]:2], *yang* Masculinity takes care of itself.)

2

Stillness and Contentment

18[13]

"Favor and disgrace: this means being upset   {1}
high rank does great damage to your self."

What does it mean,   {2}
"favor and disgrace: this means being upset"?
Favor is degrading:
Gaining it you will be upset
losing it you will be upset.
This is what it means,
"favor and disgrace: this means being upset."

What does it mean,   {3}
"high rank does great damage to your self"?
What is the source of the great damage done me?
It is because I have a self.
If I had no self, what damage could be done me?
This is what it means,
"high rank does great damage to your self."

Yes: {4}
A valuing of one's self
    that regards the self the same as the world—
this means one can be entrusted with the world.
A loving of one's self
    that regards the self the same as the world—
this means one can be given the world.

Being in the public eye disturbs your peace of mind. You might feel fine during those times when you're well liked and successful. But as long as your identity is wrapped up in your success there will be some underlying anxiety {2}. The answer is not to withdraw from public life. It is rather to cease to identify yourself with your public image {3}. A person who doesn't insist on being treated as someone special, is after all the best kind of person to have in charge {4}.

The text of this chapter is difficult and translations vary widely. My understanding is new in many places and more than usually conjectural. (See "Additional Textual Notes.") I believe that {1} is a saying from a "hedonist" thinker like Yang* Chu. The original saying advises *shih** not to seek public office, because this disturbs one's peace of mind.[1] Saying {4} is related to sayings against self-promotion.* It celebrates* the supremely high status of spiritual "Emperor*" that a self-effacing person deserves (the meaning of "can be entrusted with the world.") In {4:3 and 7}, I take *i shen wei t'ien hsia*/"treat self as world" to mean: Attribute no special status to your self over against the rest of the world.

Sections {2–3} are "interpretations" of the Yangist saying by the Laoist composer. Section {2} captures fairly well the sense of the original: It is not only disgrace that is upsetting. Even if you are currently "in favor," you will be anxious about losing favor. (Compare the similarly worded 19[44]:1, which implies that "gaining" fame, not losing it, is the real cause of pain.) Section {3} however, turns the original meaning of the Yangist saying completely around. The saying advocates entirely avoiding high rank. But Laoists aspire to public office, and accordingly the composer's "interpretation" says that what is "damaging" (upsetting) is not occupying high office but "having a self"—that is, being concerned with one's public image or persona (see comments on this meaning of *shen*/self at 10[7]:2). The composer's thought in {2} and {3} is related to the sayings against desire* for status as something disturbing one's peace of mind. One who is not preoccupied with maintaining a public reputation can maintain peace of mind while in public office, and in fact this attitude will make one deserving of the highest leadership role {4}.

Three chapters are grouped here (18[13], 19[44], 20[46]) that speak of the way desire* for fame or wealth is mentally agitating* and so "damaging" to our being. (19[44] and 20[46] also share the theme of content/discontent.)

---

1. Compare *Mencius** 2A/2,1.

19[44]

Your fame or your self, which is closer to you?   {1}
Your self or your possessions, which counts for more?
Gaining or losing, which brings the pain?

Indeed: {2}
Very fond, much expended
much hoarding, heavy loss.

Be content and there will be no disgrace.   {3}
Know to stop and there will be no danger.   {4}

And you can last very long.   {5}

It might seem that, when you acquire more possessions or make a name for yourself, you are "adding" to what you are—all you need to worry about is losing these things. But the real problem lies in gaining, not in losing. In attaching so much importance to gaining these things, you are really just expending energy and wearing yourself out {2}, making your existence anxious and precarious by staking so much on what can easily be lost {1}. You should learn to stop this flow of your energy outward, and to rest content in your own being {3–4}. This is the ultimate security {5}.

Saying {1} counters the desire* for wealth and fame by calling to mind that loss of these things is painful only because one first became attached to gaining them. Saying {2} counters the same desire* by calling to mind the cost in energy and resources and by evoking the quasi-superstitious* feeling that the person who hoards wealth is setting himself up for a downfall. Sayings {3} and {4} (= 63[32]:3:4) use an oracle* formula. "Knowing to stop" in {4} refers to "stopping" the outward-directed mental activity of desiring fame and possessions mentioned in {1} and {2}, hence it has a meaning here similar to resting content* in yourself {3} and to the recurrent term *turning* back*. See further comments on the phrase *knowing to stop* in 63[32]:3.

The composer's comment in {5} evokes the Laoist idea that remaining content within oneself conserves one's energy and so allows one to "last* long."

20[46]

When the world has Tao,   {1}
    they have no use for saddle horses,
    using them to haul manure.
When the world has no Tao,
    they raise war horses on sacred ground.

Nothing is more crime producing than desirable things   {2}
nothing is a worse misfortune than not being content
nothing makes for more guilt than desire for gain.

Yes: {3}
Be content with enough, and there will always be enough.

"Desirable things"—everyone wants them, but what do they do? They ruin your peace of mind {2} and set you at greedy war with your neighbors {1:4–5}. Rather than paying attention to what everyone considers "desirable," think of what is of solid practical use {1:1–3}. Contentment is an attitude, and the main key to being content is finding contentment in what you already have {3}.

Saying {1} is a normative* description of a society imbued with the spirit of Tao*, countering the desire* of Warring States rulers for territorial expansion and high living standards. It poses contrasting images: On the one hand, the ruler whose greed for more territory causes him to raise war horses wherever he can, even (sacrilegiously) on sacred ground. On the other hand, an ideal state in which people live simply and place no special value on luxury items like saddle horses. ("Hauling manure" is an extremely practical, "useful" task, in contrast to the luxury of pleasure riding. Compare 76[80]. "Sacred ground" in {1:5} follows Waley's understanding of *chiao* as a reference to a sacred mound outside the capital city that figured in ancient Chinese ritual. Others translate *chiao* as "suburb.") Saying {2} also counters the desire* for wealth. As in 79[3]:1, its three lines are complementary: "Desirable things" stir up "desire for gain," causing discontent, leading to the misfortune of crime and guilt. Note the emphasis on the damaging *personal* effects of desires—crime and guilt are added "misfortunes" for the discontented greedy person. Saying {3} counters the desire* for more by suggesting that contentment is a matter of one's state of mind, not how much one has.

21[12]

The five colors make people's eyes go blind   {1}
the five tones make people's ears go deaf
the five flavors make people's mouths turn sour.
Galloping and racing, hunting and chasing,
    make people's minds go mad.
Goods hard to come by corrupt people's ways.

And so the Wise Person: {2}
Goes by the belly, not by the eye.

Yes: {3}
He leaves 'that' aside, and attends to 'this'.

In the midst of ordinariness, stimulating things seem very attractive, apparently promising to enrich our lives. But this is like foods that excite the eye then pain the belly {2}. If you're looking for real enjoyment of the world, the most important thing is to preserve a healthy state of mind {3}, capable of subtle pleasures and a deeply satisfying relation to things—and this is what constant stimulation destroys {1}.

Saying {1} counters the desire of the Warring States upper classes for an exciting and luxurious life: Colorful clothes and decorations, fine music and food, horse racing and hunting, collecting rare objects. (*Five* is merely a conventional categorization, without special significance here. The colors: red, blue, yellow, white, black. The tones [of the ancient Chinese scale] are C, D, E, G, A. The flavors are sweet, sour, bitter, acrid, salty.) Note that the negative images posed in {1:1–4} are not moralistic, but call to mind the way overindulgence agitates* and damages one's mind and senses, an obstacle to the deep enjoyment and satisfaction in things possible to a Still* mind and healthy senses. (Rare goods corrupt people by arousing criminal desires; see 20[46]:2 and 79[3]:1. The parallelism implies that this corruption too is seen as a kind of "damage" to one's mind.) "The belly" in {2} is probably a metaphor for what is truly satisfying, as opposed to what is eye-catching but also ultimately agitating*. I believe that *this* in {3} originally referred to internal self-cultivation as opposed to a concern for external effectiveness ("that"). (See discussion under "This*".) The composer of this chapter probably is stretching its meaning here to refer to concern for one's state of mind (maintaining healthy senses), in contrast to concern for eye-catching but agitating* things out there. This reading makes the contrast this/that very similar to the contrast belly/eye.

This chapter and the next, 22[50], are directed against the attraction to a luxurious and exciting life.

22[50]

"Setting out to live is entering into death."   {1}

"Thirteen are the life givers   {2}
thirteen are the death bringers."
The thirteen body parts are also death spots
*   in people's life and activity. Why?*
Because they live life so lavishly.

So we hear: {3}
One who Excels at fostering life
"travels on land without meeting rhinoceros or tiger
enters combat without armor or weapon."

The rhinoceros finds no place to jab its horn   {4}
the tiger finds no place to lay its claws
a weapon finds no place where its point can enter.
Why?
Because he has no death spot.

Sometimes the marvelous health of the body sustains a person and seems to make everything in life go right. Sometimes the body is what makes us vulnerable to every passing disease and danger. The difference? Some people protect and foster their life energy. Some people waste it in lavish living.

The wording of this chapter is difficult and has been variously translated. My understanding is new and conjectural. I think {1} was originally a pessimistic folk-saying to the effect that coming into the world at birth is also the first step toward death. The original point of {2:1-2} was that the same thirteen body parts that sustain our life also make us susceptible to death. ("The thirteen" are the four limbs and the nine apertures of the body mentioned in the *Nei* Yeh*.[1]) Lines {2:3-5} are an addition by the composer. They reinterpret *live* in {1}, so that "setting out into life" becomes "setting out to live it up" (to *sheng sheng chih hou*/"live life's thickness," compare the similar phrase in 51[75]:1). *This* ruins one's health and so is a first step toward death. The composer also reinterprets the saying in {2:1-2} so that the body parts are not *by nature* points of vulnerability ("death spots"), but become so because people "live it up." *Fostering life* {3} probably refers to a particular aspect of Laoist self-cultivation: Getting in touch with one's life-energy and fostering it, perhaps through some kind of meditation* (see further comments under "Life*" and "Yang* Chu"). Here this is contrasted with "living life lavishly." The marvelous benefits* ascribed to this in {3-4} indicate that Excel* has a strong meaning here, referring to highly developed self-cultivation. (Saying 33[55]:1 also pictures magical invulnerability as one result of self-cultivation.) The composer's thought here is related to Laoist criticism of mentally agitating* excitement as exhausting and the contrasting Laoist ideal of "lasting* long" by conserving one's health and energy.

The connection of the "state of mind" Laoists cultivated with *physical* health, evident here, is a point of connection between early Taoism and later Taoist groups who made physical self-cultivation much more central, through the use of diet, physical exercises, breathing techniques, herbs and drugs, and so on.[2]

---

1. Quoted in Waley, 1958:48.
2. See Welch 1957: 101–112; Maspero 1981: 445–554; Kohn 1989 passim.

23[26]

Heaviness is the root of lightness {1}
Stillness is the master of agitation.

And so the Wise Person: {2}
Travels all day, not departing from the heavy baggage wagon
although there are grand sights, he sits calmly aloof.
Why is this?
A 10,000-chariot lord,
mindful of his self, takes the world lightly.

Light, then lose the Root {3}
agitated, then lose the mastery.

A mind needing constant stimulation is a shallow mind, a light-weight mind. Stimulation is a shallow space. Deep Stillness is where one's true worth lies. Even though it seems a heavy space, rest there.

Saying {1} probably borrows a formula from the speculation concerning the "conquest* cycle," to celebrate the superiority of the heaviness/Stillness* that Laoists cultivate over their opposites, lightness and agitation*. The metaphorical* image in {2:2–3} is that of a gentleman of very high status, traveling in a caravan. Where one might expect him to be sightseeing with others along the way, he unexpectedly plods along with the baggage wagon—something one would expect of the servants. The image serves as a metaphor for the ideal Laoist attitude, resting in a Still/heavy state of mind, in contrast to a mind attracted to exciting things.

The composer plays on several meanings of *heavy* and *light*. *Chung*/heavy also means "dignified." The heavy wagon is associated with the lord's "heavy" dignity, which in turn is an image for the value/dignity of the *shen*/self cultivated for its own sake. (Compare the contrast between *shen*/self and fame/possessions in 19[44]:1, and further comments on *shen* at 10[7]:2.) One who gravitates toward exciting but agitating* things loses the Stillness that is for Laoists the Root of the self's true dignity and its high status as *chün*/master {3}. An excited person becomes a "light" person of little consequence, as opposed to the person who learns to value his self and take the exciting external world lightly.

This chapter links the theme of mental agitation*, the target of the preceding chapters in Section 2, to the special recurrent term *Stillness**. Achieving mental Stillness is one of the central goals of Laoist self-cultivation, the theme of Section 3 to follow. Stillness and contentment are especially central ideas in Chapters 28[16], 29[52], 30[56], and 31[4].

3

Self-Cultivation

24[33]

One who understands others is clever   {1}
one who understands himself has Clarity.
One who wins out over others has power
one who wins out over himself is strong.

One who is content is wealthy   {2}
one strong in his practice is self-possessed.

One who does not leave his place is lasting   {3}
one who dies and does not perish is truly long lived.

Occupying yourself with figuring out the others and beating them, you lose the centeredness in yourself {1}. Gaining self-possession and contentment in yourself {2}—this takes practice, but brings real security {3}. Make this your project.

All three sayings here refer directly to self-cultivation. Saying {1} advises *shih** to give priority to self-cultivation over political achievement. (Compare 53[72]:4. "Understanding others" probably refers to the political skill of being a good judge of others.) Based on the use of *li hsing*/"vigorous practice" in the *Doctrine of the Mean*[1] to describe self-cultivation, I believe *ch'iang hsing*/"strong practice" in {2} is a reference to persevering effort in self-cultivation, leading to self-possession (*yu chih*, lit. "possess mind"). This gives one the internal "wealth" of a contented* mind. (This new interpretation gives {2} a strong connection to {1}.) I take *not leave* [your] *place* in {3:1} to mean something like "stay centered in yourself," in contrast to "losing yourself" in external preoccupations (see remarks on "Dwelling*" and on "know to stop" at 63[32]:3). This conserves one's energy and leads to "lasting*" longer. Line {3:2} may be an indication that some Laoists extrapolated from the enhanced vitality and deep sense of inner security self-cultivation brought them to an expectation of surviving death. (This is not, of course, the same thing as saying Laoists undertook self-cultivation *for the primary purpose of* achieving immortality, as Maspero[2] suggests.)

The connections suggested here between *being content* {2}, *not leaving one's place,* and *lasting* {3} are similar to the train of associations in 19[44]. One might think from other passages that Laoists advocated "being natural*," in the sense of leaving one's own being alone, not consciously trying to be any particular way. But the state of mind they tried to achieve clearly was an extraordinary one, and the phrase *winning out over oneself* in {1} shows that the process of achieving Laoist "naturalness" involved also some inner struggle with oneself.

Section 3 on self-cultivation opens with three chapters (24[33], 25[48], 26[59]) that speak primarily of the importance of self-cultivation and the great benefits to be gained from it. After this follows four chapters (27[10], 28[16], 29[52], 30[56]) that contain more instruction in the practice of Laoist self-cultivation.

---

1. 20,10.
2. 1981: 416.

25[48]

"Doing Learning, one profits everyday."   {1}
Doing Tao, one suffers a loss everyday—
loses, and loses some more
and so arrives at not doing anything.

Doing nothing, nothing will remain not done.   {2}

Taking over the world: only by not working.   {3}

A person who sets to working,   {4}
doesn't have what it takes to take over the world.

Confucians say that doing Learning brings one some benefit every-day. One could say, cultivating Tao makes one suffer a loss—some-thing is subtracted from one's being—everyday. Subtract over and over, and you will come to live in a space where there is no trying, no doing. Rule from this space, and everything will take care of itself. Only the Non Worker shows herself fit to be in charge of the world.

I think {1:1} is a Confucian* saying in praise of Learning, quoted as a take-off* point for a tongue-in-cheek Laoist reply: Laoist practice con-sists partly in stripping away those qualities people develop to win social admiration. There is probably an intended play on "doing*": "Doing Learning...Doing Tao*...not doing [anything]"; the last phrase describes a state of mind that is the goal of Laoist practice. (*Yi/profit and *sun*/loss in {1} are usually translated by more neutral words like *add* and *subtract,* the meaning I give them in 36[42]:5. The composer's comments take advantage of this connotation of the words. But two passages in the Confucian *Analects*[1] use *yi/sun* in the more evaluative sense of "profit/loss," and this is the basis for my translation and interpretation here.) Sayings {2} {3} and {4} counter the tendency of rulers to want to "work* on" society; that is, to impose plans on it from without (see 62[29], 72[64]). Sayings {2} and {3} (a version of 77[57]:1:3) celebrate* the marvelous benefits* that come from ruling in a "not-doing*" spirit. The results of this are pic-tured in exaggerated utopian imagery: "Take over the world" suggests that this leadership style will attract the allegiance of all, and enable the "not-doing" ruler to become the new Emperor*, reuniting the Empire under his rule.

---

1. 16:4 and 15:30.

26[59]

"When it comes to governing the people and serving Heaven,   {1}
there's no one like a farmer."

Just being a farmer—   {2}
this means getting dressed early.
Getting dressed early means increasing one's store of Te
increasing one's store of Te, then nothing is impossible
nothing impossible, then no telling the limit
no telling the limit, then one can possess the state.

One who possesses the Mother of the state   {3}
can last a long time.

This means having deep roots and strong foundations,   {4}
the Way of 'lasting life, good eyesight into old age'.

Getting to that quality of mind is not a matter of just thinking about it. It is like farming—a lot of hard work and very slow results. But the results are solid; they put you in possession of the one thing necessary, the foundation of the world. With it you can manage anything.

I think {1} was originally a paradoxical saying to the effect that a (simple? hard-working?) peasant farmer would make the best ruler. ("Governing the people and serving Heaven*" is a conventional way of describing the ruler's task.) But in {2} the composer takes the "farmer" as an image of someone working hard at self-cultivation, "getting dressed early" to store up Te*/charisma:power. (Mencius* also speaks[1] of "rising at cockcrow" to practice virtue.) Saying {2} celebrates the marvelous benefits* of this accumulated Te, which translates into irresistible political power (here described in idealized and exaggerated terms. Further marvelous powers are ascribed to accumulated Te in 33[55]:1.) Saying {3} celebrates the marvelous *personal* benefits* ("lasting* long") gained by "possessing the Mother* of the State." I take *kuo chih mu*/"State's Mother" as equivalent to "Mother of the World" (29[52]:1): Both phrases refer to the ideal foundations of Chinese society and culture. Laoists felt that the quality of mind they were cultivating *was* this foundation. I take {4:2} to be a conventional description of a ripe and healthy old age, that is, lasting* long by conserving one's energy.

---

1. 7A/25,1.

27[10]

When 'carrying your soul,' embracing the One Thing,   {1}
can you be undivided?

When 'concentrating *ch'i*', bringing about Softness,
can you be like an infant?

When 'cleansing and purifying the mysterious mirror,'
can you be without blemish?

When 'loving the people and caring for the kingdom,'
can you be without knowledge?

When 'the Doors of Heaven open and shut,'
can you remain Feminine?

When 'Clarity and bareness penetrate everywhere,'
can you remain not doing?

Produce and nourish.   {2}
Produce but don't possess
work but don't rely on this
preside but don't rule.
This is mysterious Te.

About meditation: At first you are nervous, your mind at odds with your body energy. Give the energy all of your attention. Think of embracing it, "carrying" it with your mind. Slowly identify with it, becoming less divided in yourself. Things will feel softer, infantlike, womanlike, gentle. With softness gradually comes mental clarity, things press less insistently. With long practice the mind becomes fresh, a clear mirror for reality seen plainly and without trouble. Sometimes you will hear or see things, or travel in your mind—like passing through the gates of Heaven. What is important is to retain the femininity of your soft mind. With this you can manage all your responsibilities well and selflessly {2}.

Saying {1} is the most explicit and detailed instruction for meditation* in the *Tao Te Ching*. Many of the terms are common ones: *Embracing the One* *Thing, Softness*, Clarity*, Femininity*, not doing*, infancy* (for *without knowledge* see comments on "Understanding*"). Unfortunately, there also seem to be many esoteric phrases (placed in single quotation marks), whose concrete reference is now lost to us. Groups of people who meditate regularly often develop a highly differentiated awareness of inner states and movements and a special vocabulary to describe them, which outsiders always will have difficulty understanding. The paraphrase gives my best conjectures (based partly on attempts to practice what I think is being said). I think the primary reference of words like *p'o*/soul is to concrete internal self-perceptions, perhaps in this case to bodily energy concretely felt by someone in introspective meditation. (If this is so, ancient Chinese *theories* about the *p'o*/"bodily soul" and *hun*/"spiritual soul" are not important to the meaning in this context.) *Chuan-ch'i*/"concentrate ch'i*" may refer to some special meditation technique, but it may mean simply "[mentally] concentrate."[1] "Heaven's Gate" may reflect the theme of the "spirit journey," a feeling of being mentally transported through spiritual realms. This is common in shamanistic traditions, of which some survivals reflected in the contemporary *Chuang* *Tzu*[2] and the *Ch'u tz'u*[3] mention passing through heavenly gates. Saying {2} (a version of 42[2]:5, 52[77]:3, and 65[51]:4) counters the desire of rulers to capitalize on their achievements for self-promotion*. Laoist Te*/virtue expresses itself instead in a self-effacing spirit.

The stanza in {1} beginning "when 'loving the people'" is advice for the ruler, so I believe it was not an original part of the meditation instruction, but a connective* addition added by the same person who added {2}. The purpose of both additions is to emphasize that meditation is preparation for ruling (compare 26[59]:1–2, 37[14]:5).

---

1. See *Mencius** (6A/9,3) where *chuan-hsin*/"concentrate mind" describes the concentration of a chess player.

2. See Watson, 1968: 119, quoted on p. 234–35.

3. Quoted in Maspero 1981: 415.

28[16]

Push Emptiness to the limit,   {1}
watch over Stillness very firmly.

The thousands of things all around are active—   {2}
I give my attention to Turning Back.
Things growing wild as weeds
all turn back to the Root.

To turn back to The Root is called Stillness.   {3}
This is 'reporting in'
'reporting in' is becoming Steady.
Experiencing Steadiness is Clarity.

Not to experience Steadiness   {4}
is to be heedless in one's actions—bad luck.

Experiencing Steadiness, then one is all-embracing   {5}
all-embracing, then an impartial Prince
Prince, then King
King, then Heaven
Heaven, then Tao
Tao, then one lasts very long.

As to destroying the self,   {6}
there will be nothing to fear.

Everything wants to be active. The mind is active, things are active {2}. Caught up entirely in activity, they lose the Still center—Still, Empty, Steady, Clear {1, 3}. Turn back to this stillness and the world around will also become still {2}. In gaining it, you will feel like you are losing the self that is part of the active world {6}. But activity passes. This is the enduring root of everything worthwhile, the center of the world {5}.

Saying {1} is a brief instruction* in self-cultivation. Saying {2} is instruction in "turning* back," one description of what one does in Laoist meditation* (compare 34[40]:1). Based on a passage in the *Chuang* *Tzu*[1] I believe the saying pictures a shift* in the world as perceived, due to a shift in one's own mental state: To a racing, agitated* mind, the world seems full of nervous activity too. (*Tso*/active is the negative opposite of Stillness in 81[37]:3.) "Turning back" describes Stilling* one's active mind, so that one perceives the agitated multiplicity of the world as though it stems from a single Still origin (see "Origin*"). "Growing wild as weeds" [lit. "weedy weedy"] evokes a sense of disordered multiplicity. Saying {3:4} (= 33[55]:3:2) celebrates the way that Steadiness* is linked* to Clarity*. Saying {4} uses an oracle* formula to picture a life "out of control" because it lacks Steadiness*. Saying {5} celebrates the cosmic* importance of Steadiness: One who achieves it occupies the spiritual status of the Emperor*, and is one with the cosmic principles Heaven* and Tao*. Saying {6} also occurs in 29[52]:3 in close conjunction with a saying about "turning* back," suggesting that Laoists sometimes experienced the movement toward Stillness, away from external activity, as one threatening a loss of *shen*/self, a loss of a tangible identity as part of the world (compare 13[20]:4–5, 14[23]:1–3 and comments on *shen*/self at 10[7]:2). This saying (using an oracle* formula) is reassurance in the face of this frightening experience.

Line {3:1} is a connective* addition by the composer, connecting {2:4} to "Stillness" in {1:2}. In {3:2–3} "reporting in" translates *fu ming,* a phrase sometimes used of a soldier or emissary reporting back to his superior,[2] suggesting that the Still quality of mind is a "command post" to which one returns from "action in the field." Line {5:6} departs from the images of the rest of {5}, and so I think it is another connective* addition by the composer. "Lasting*" refers to the security one finds in Tao, in contrast to "losing oneself" {6} which might seem to threaten.

---

1. Watson 1968: 122, quoted p. 211.
2. See Legge 1891 ad loc. Compare *fan-ming* in *Mencius** 3A/2, 3.

29[52]

The world has a Source, the Mother of the World.   {1}

Once you get the Mother   {2}
then you understand the children.
Once you understand the children
turn back and watch over the Mother.

As to destroying the self,   {3}
there will be nothing to fear.

Close your eyes   {4}
shut your doors,
till the end of your life you will not get tired.
Open your eyes
carry on your business,
till the end of your life you will not be safe.

Keeping your eyes on the Small Thing is called Clarity   {5}
watching over Weakness is called strength.

Engage with the flashing things   {6}
turn back to Clarity
do not deliver yourself to disaster.

This is cultivating Steadiness.   {7}

Being constantly outgoing, living on the surface, wears you out. And you never truly understand the truth about things in the world. It is not safe. Withdraw sometimes, shut your door, go inside {4}. Find that space where the truth of everything resides {2}. In contrast to the active world, what is there will at first appear small and weak {5}, and you will feel like you are losing your self being there {3}. But there you will find a sustaining presence—strength, Clarity, and Steadiness {5,6}.

Saying {2:1–2} celebrates the benefits* of *te mu*/"getting [the] Mother*," one description of the goal of Laoist self-cultivation. This puts one in touch with the foundation of all meaning in the world, and thus gives one an intuitive true understanding* of all worldly situations (the Mother's "children." Compare 43[1]:5). Saying {3} reassures one against the fear of losing oneself one might experience in Laoist self-cultivation. (See comments on this saying at 28[16]:6.) Saying {4} is instruction in Laoist self-cultivation, which sometimes requires withdrawing from the world to Still* one's mind. It is closely related to sayings picturing excitement and agitation* as exhausting. Saying {5} celebrates the way that cultivating one quality of mind is linked* to the achievement of other ideal qualities as well. (The *hsiao*/"small thing" is the frail-feeling quality of mind cultivated. Compare the *hsiao*/small:insignificant:"of-no-account" Tao in 63[32]:1 and 64[34]:4.)

I think the origin* statement in {1} is the composer's lead into {2}. The composer's warning in {2:3–4} goes against the original celebratory point of the saying in {2:1–2}: Don't get too caught up in the "children" (worldly affairs) and forget to turn* back to the [internal] Mother. I think *huang*/"flashing [things]" in {6} refers to lively events in the world (compare the same word in 30[56]:3). Hence, this term parallels "children" in {2} (and "carrying on your business" in {3}). Correspondingly, "turning* back to [internal] Clarity" parallels "turning back to the Mother" in {2}.

30[56]

Those who understand are not talkers   {1}
talkers don't understand.

Close your eyes   {2}
shut your doors.

Dampen the passion   {3}
untie the tangles
make the flashing things harmonious
make the dust merge together.
This is called the mysterious Merging.

Yes: {4}
You cannot get close
you cannot stay away
you cannot help It
you cannot harm It
you cannot treasure It
you cannot look down on It.

Yes:
It is the Treasure of the World.   {5}

Excited, talking away, the mind in tangles, the world all heated up {1–2}. But there is something else, something always there whether you are attending to it or not {4}. This something will untangle the world. It is a place where everything merges together harmoniously {3}. It is the world's treasure {5}.

Saying {1} criticizes admiring only impressive appearances*, posing the contrasting images of impressive but empty speech, on the one hand, and silent wisdom, on the other. Saying {2} is a fragment of the saying in 29[52]:4, urging regular withdrawal from the world to Still* the mind. Saying {3:1–4} (= 31[4]:3) functions here as meditation* instruction. *Tangles, flashing things,* and *dust* describe the agitated and confused state of the world as it appears to an agitated* state of mind. If one can bring about a shift to a calmer state of mind, this causes a corresponding shift* in the character of the world as experienced. Saying {4} is also about meditation*, criticizing the dominating, "doing*" attitude a meditator might take, thinking of the quality of mind cultivated as something produced by one's own action. The saying reflects instead the Laoist feeling that this hypostatized* quality of mind (left unnamed here) has an autonomous existence, which one tries to find within and identify with, rather than "produce" (compare the criticism in 33[55]:4). In its genre this saying resembles 37[14]:3,4, 38[21]:2, 46[35]:3. Saying {5} (= 48[62]:7) celebrates the cosmic* importance of Tao.

As in 16[5]:3 and 14[23]:1–2, the composer probably takes "talking" in {1} as an example of excited* and exhausting activity (somewhat contrary to the original intention of the saying). Sayings {3} and {4} are important for showing the meaning of *t'ung*/Merging*, used as a special term here and in 43[1]:4–5. Line {3:4} uses *t'ung* as a verb, "*make* the dust *merge* together." The composer's connective* addition then describes the resultant state of mind as *hsüan t'ung*/"mysterious Merging," implying that when the "dust" of the world settles in our experience, the internal forces of our mind also are "merged together" rather than in conflict, because we withdrew from the world and quieted our strong feelings. But then, by his placement of {4}, the composer indicates (as in 43[1]:4–5) that he takes "The Merging" also to refer to the hypostatized* quality of mind Laoists cultivate, pictured in {4} as having an autonomous existence.

31[4]

Tao being Empty,   {1}
it seems one who uses it will lack solidity.

An abyss,   {2}
it seems something like the ancestor
    of the thousands of things.

It dampens the passion   {3}
it unties the tangles
it makes the flashing things harmonious
it makes the dust merge together.

Deep,   {4}
it is perhaps like an enduring something.

I don't know of anything whose offspring it might be—   {5}
it appears to precede God.

Some things are inspiring, stirring, exciting. They also heat up the world and make it feel more tangled. Tao feels different: subtle, hardly perceptible {1}, but deep and fundamental, more fundamental than God {2, 4, 5}. Its subtle presence does not make the world more exciting and disturbing, but more quiet and filled with harmony {3}.

Saying {1} gives a normative* description of the way of being of one who has Tao: Because Tao is very intangible ("Empty*"), such a one does not project a "solid*" presence in the world. (I follow Karlgren's construal of these lines, departing from most other translators; see "Additional Textual Notes." See also comments on 6[15]:4, a version of this same saying.) Saying {2} is about Tao as the origin* of the world. ("Ancestor" in China not only referred literally to earlier progenitors of a noble family, these symbolized its idealized foundational spirit. So the unified spirit behind Laoist sayings can be called in 45[70]:2 "the ancestor" of the words.) Saying {3} (= 30[56]:3) functions here as a celebration of the great benefits* of cultivating Tao. (The same Chinese verbs can function as either indicatives or imperatives, and this allows the same words to describe benefits here and function as directives in 30[56]:3.)

By following {1–2} with {3}, the composer indicates that internally cultivating the "Empty" (subtle and very intangible) Tao produces a shift* in the world as experienced, calming it down. He also emphasizes the association between Tao as something "deep," and the image of Tao as primordial origin, "preceding God." I believe these two ideas have the same basis in Laoist experience: What is experienced as "deeper" and foundational is expressed via the imagery of chronological priority (see further under "Origin*"). (Ti/God in {5} is a pre-Chou name for the supreme deity. Chou usage favored the name Heaven* instead, but ti continued to be used also, as here. In this period some kings began to claim Ti as a title for themselves.[1]) Note that the composer repeats words throughout this chapter that emphasize tentativeness: Huo/seems, ssu/perhaps, jo/"something like" "I don't know"). This is probably associated with the elusive character of the "Empty" Tao.

This chapter shares a saying, {3}, with the previous chapter, 30[56]. Instead of centering on instruction in self-cultivation like the previous four chapters in this section, its intent is primarily celebratory*, celebrating the cosmic* importance and wonderful benefits* that flow from the hypostatized* quality of mind cultivated. It shares this celebratory intent with the remaining chapters of this Section.

---

1. Bodde 1981: 105.

32[6]

"The Valley Spirit is undying."   {1}
This is mysterious Femininity.

The Abode of mysterious Femininity: {2}
This is the Root of Heaven and Earth.

It seems to endure on and on.   {3}

One who uses It never wears out.   {4}

There is a mental abode within that is like a valley: feminine, misty, low lying, empty space. It is the foundation of the world, and an inexhaustible source of energy for you.

Saying {2} celebrates the mental space ("abode") where Femininity* resides as a cosmic* foundation and origin*. ("Abode" translates *men,* more usually translated as "gate." See comments on "Dwell*," and on 43[1]:5 where *men*/abode also occurs. Because Femininity is an hypostatized* mental quality, there is no significant difference between Femininity and the mental "space" that feels Feminine.) Saying {4} celebrates one of the great benefits* of the mental quality Laoists cultivate—inexhaustible energy, enabling one to last* long. (Compare 16[5]:2. This theme is related to sayings against agitated*, "exhausting" excitement.)

I believe that {1} was originally a folk saying about the spirit of a certain valley (ancient Chinese believed in many such nature spirits). But among those devoted to self-cultivation,[1] *shen*/spirit was also used to refer to the mind or to a certain quality of mind. (See also the saying about spirits in 37[14]:1, applied there also to the quality of mind Laoists cultivate.) And "Valley*" is associated in 6[15]:2 and 17[28]:1 with the ideal Laoist state of mind (and see 44[41]:3). Hence the composer reinterprets the popular saying to refer to the "Valley Spirit" that Laoists cultivated internally, associating it with the quality "Femininity" {2}. The "immortality" mentioned in the saying is reinterpreted in {3–4} as reflecting the Laoist theme that the mental quality they cultivate is a lasting*, inexhaustible source of energy.

---

1. For example, in the *Nei* Yeh* (Rickett 1965: 158 A); see Graham 1989: 101.

33[55]

One who has an abundance of Te   {1}
is like a newborn child:
Poisonous bugs will not bite it
fierce beasts will not snatch it
birds of prey will not attack it.

Its bones are Soft, its sinews Weak,   {2}
but its grip is firm.
It has not known the union of man and woman,
but its organs get aroused:
Vital energy at its height.
It will scream all day without getting hoarse:
Harmony at its height.

To experience Harmony is called being Steady   {3}
to experience Steadiness is called Clarity.

'Increasing life': ominous   {4}
'the mind controlling the *ch'i*': forcing.

Things are vigorous, then grow old: {5}
A case of 'not-Tao'.
Not-Tao, soon gone.

How do you increase vitality? Not by forcing yourself to be up; this will quickly fade {4–5}. Find the softness in which strength lives, the energy that is self-generating. Learn steady smoothness in intense activity {2}. This makes you an innocent in the world—harmless, attracting no harm {1}.

Saying {1} celebrates the marvelous benefits* attributed to the Te*/virtue Laoists cultivate. Laoist Te can be described partly as a kind of fresh innocence that radiates peace, conveyed here in the image of the innocent child safe from dangerous insects and wild animals (compare 22[50]:3). Saying {2} uses the infant* image as an extended metaphor*, illustrating several aspects of the quality of mind Laoists cultivate: Softness*/Weakness, Harmony*, and vital energy. The arousal of sexual organs without sexual contact is probably an image of *ching*/"vital energy" generated completely from within rather than through external stimulation. (*Ching*/"vital energy" occurs in 38[21]:2, and is also a focus of self-cultivation in the *Nei* *Yeh*[1]). "Screaming all day without getting hoarse" is an important corrective for the tendency to take Laoist mental Stillness* literally, as though it signifies the simple absence of any vigorous activity. Here we have the ideal of a very vigorous action that is yet smooth and Harmonious* (not "agitated*"), because it arises out of a different (unstimulated, basically "Still") state of mind. (Compare 6[15]:3, which describes first stilling the mind and then slowly returning to being active.) Saying {3} celebrates the link* between various qualities of mind Laoists culti-vate ({3:2} = 28[16]:3:4). In {4}, I take "increasing *sheng*/life" and "the mind controlling the *ch'i**" as descriptions of the self-cultivation prac-tices of others, who attempt to increase their internal energy (*ch'i*) directly, by will power. (Such practices also are criticized in the *Men-cius**,[2] as attempts to artificially "force*" things.) "Fostering *sheng*/life" describes a Laoist goal, too (see "Life*"). But this must be the indirect result of cultivating internal Softness and Stillness. Saying {5} (= 69[30]:5) takes the seasonal flourishing and dying of plants as a nega-tive metaphorical* image of what happens in human life when things are done in a *pu-Tao**/"un-Tao-[like]" spirit: One gets a short-lived flash in the pan rather than a "slow burn," the lasting* inexhaustible energy associated with Tao (see 16[5]:2). (Saying {5} follows a criticism of "forcing*" in 69[30] as well. In content it is related to sayings criti-cal of exhausting agitation* and excitement.) The composer's point here is that a forcing* approach to self-cultivation will not produce the kind of internal Softness/vital-energy/Harmony Laoists aim at.

---

1. Rickett 1965: 158 A.
2. 2A/2, 9–10 and 16.

34[40]

Turning Back is Tao movement   {1}
being Weak is Tao practice.

"The thousands of things in the world are born of Being"   {2}
Being is born of Nothing.

What is the essential practice? Reverse the striving for strength, for tangible Being. Turn back to what feels weak, Nothing. This space is the essential source.

Saying {1} gives a normative* description of Laoist self-cultivation. I think "Tao*" has an "adjectival" meaning here, referring to specifically Laoist practice and goals. Read this way, "Tao* practice" (*tao chih yung*, lit. "Tao's use*") is a description of Laoist self-cultivation—here, the cultivation of Weakness*. (Compare the connection of "using Tao" with being Empty* in 31[4]:1.) The parallel phrase "Tao's movement" would then refer to the internal movement characteristic of one engaged in Laoist practice. Because "Being" plays no positive role elsewhere, but is contrasted with "Nothing*" in 42[2]:2 and 15[11]:2, I think that the first line of {2} is a bit of non-Laoist speculation, placed here only as a take-off* point for a Laoist line using origin* imagery to celebrate the "priority" (the more foundational importance) of the "Nothingness*" they cultivate, pictured as a cosmic* force. I believe my understanding of both sections here is new.

If *wu*/Nothing in {2} is understood experientially, to refer to scarcely tangible internal qualities, it is close in meaning to "Weakness" in {1}. (*Wu yu*/"No Being" is connected with Weakness also in 47[43]:1.).

This chapter and the two to follow (35[39], 36[42]) celebrate the cosmic importance of the quality of mind Laoists cultivate by picturing it as the origin* of the world.

35[39]

Those that of old got The One Thing: {1}
The sky got The One Thing,
    and by this became clear.
The earth got The One Thing,
    and by this became steady.
The spirits got The One Thing,
    and by this obtained their powers.
The rivers got The One Thing,
    and by this became full.
The thousands of things got The One Thing,
    and by this came to life.
The princes and kings got The One Thing,
    and by this became the Standard for the World.
This is how things came about.

The sky, without what makes it clear,
    is likely to crack.
The earth, without what makes it steady,
    is likely to quake.
The spirits, without what gives them powers,
    are likely to vanish.
The rivers, without what makes them full
    are likely to dry up.
The thousands of things, without what gives them life,
    are likely to perish.
The princes and kings,
    without what makes them *eminent and noble*,
    are likely to fall.

Yes, the eminent takes the common and ignored as a root   {2}
the noble takes the lowly as a foundation.
And so the princes and kings call themselves
'the orphan...,' 'the poor...,' 'the destitute...'
Is this not using the common and ignored as a root?
Is it not so?

Yes, enumerate the carriage parts—still not a carriage.   {3}

He doesn't wish to glitter and glitter like jade   {4}
he falls like a stone, falling into oblivion.

The one thing necessary is something that does not glitter in the world. Cultivating it means being willing to go unrecognized, take the low place. But this nothing is the foundation of the order of the world.

Saying {1} is an origin* saying, picturing the present world order as the result of everything at the beginning having "gotten the One* Thing." (It is an order-from-chaos cosmogony, different from most other Laoist origin sayings, which picture how things first came into existence.) *Te i*/"get* [the] One [Thing]" is primarily a description of the goal of Laoist self-cultivation (compare *te mu*/"get [the] Mother" in 29[52]:2). Saying {1} celebrates the cosmic* importance of this project, picturing it as what gave rise to and sustains the order of the cosmos. (Note that here the earthly rulers of China take their place as fundamental elements of the cosmic order, an important part of Chou dynasty Emperor* ideology.) Saying {2:1–2} speaks against impressive* appearances, posing the counterimage of the ruler who gains true nobility and respect by his deferential and self-effacing manner (see "Low*"). Lines {2:3–4} give a stock Laoist example of this idea, commented on at 36[42]:4. Saying {4} criticizes self-promotion*. The last line reads literally "fall fall like stone." But *lo*/fall means also "die," which I take metaphorically as the opposite of "glittering," that is, falling out of sight so far as the conventional world is concerned. (This is connected also with "low" in {2}). The translation of {3} (lit. "count carriage not carriage") is very conjectural. I think that the point is this: What makes a carriage one unified thing is not identical with the collection of tangible carriage parts, but is something single yet intangible—"the One Thing" of {1}. (Compare 45[70]:2, which implies that a single but difficult to grasp principle constitutes the unity behind the multiplicity of Laoist sayings. The parts of a horse are the basis for a similar image in the *Chuang* Tzu*.[1] And see the very similar use of the chariot image in the early Buddhist *Questions of King Melinda*.[2])

In the final lines of {1}, "eminent and noble" interrupt the parallelism with the first stanza and provide a connection with {2}. These words are a connective* alteration by the composer, suggesting an equation between adopting a "lowly" stance in society, on the one hand, and "gaining the One Thing," on the other. These are two aspects of the quality of mind and way of being Laoists cultivate.

------

1. Watson 1968: 290.
2. Stryk 1969: 90–93.

36[42]

Tao produced The One   {1}
The One produced Two
Two produced Three
Three produced the thousands of things.

The thousands of things: {2}
Turn their backs on the quiet and dark
and embrace the aggressive and bright.

An Empty ch'i brings Harmony.   {3}

What people look down upon: {4}
to be orphaned, poor, destitute.
But the kings and princes
     make these names into titles.

Yes, things: {5}
Sometimes you reduce them, and they are enlarged
sometimes you enlarge them, and they are reduced.

What another has taught, I also teach: {6}
"A violent man will not reach his natural end."
I will make of this the father of my teaching.

Man runs to escape what he has forgotten.[1] All want to enlarge themselves—to become strong, to win, to make a name. People flee from what appears soft, weak, empty in themselves. But this is the foundation, the source of everything important. Turn back to it.

Saying {1} is an origin* saying, celebrating Tao as the single foundation of meaning in the world of distracting variety and multiplicity. (Many commentators try to identify what "Two" and "Three" stand for, but no contemporary source I know of gives any solid clue about this.) Saying {2} describes the tendency of "things*" (people) to embrace* the *yang*/aggressive:bright, socially desirable qualities, and to shun the *yin*/quiet:dark ones—an unfortunate tendency in Laoist eyes. (*Yin* and *yang*, which became central to later Taoism are mentioned only here in the *Tao Te Ching*.) Saying {3} links* two qualities: Cultivating an internal Empty* *ch'i*/energy also brings mental Harmony*. Saying {5} counters the desire of rulers to project an impressive* presence, posing contrasting images of the person whose deferential (self-"reducing") manner enhances ("enlarges") people's respect for him, and the person whose attempts to impress diminish this respect. Section {4} refers to what was apparently a custom among some Chinese nobility whereby a King Wu, for example, would refer to himself self-deprecatingly as "the poor Wu." The composer here (and in 35[39]:2) refers to this custom as an example of how a self-deprecating manner gains one true respect. Saying {6:2} is introduced as a non-Laoist saying, probably of popular origin (compare, "He who lives by the sword will die by the sword.")

The composer gives no direct hint of the connection he sees between these various sayings, and so my reconstruction is more than usually conjectural here. I think {2} is the pivotal saying that unites the piece: The tendencies toward self-glorification and violence criticized in {4–6} count as "embracing* *yang*," the masculine aggressiveness implicitly deplored in {2}. Violence, as the extreme of *yang*, here represents *yang* qualities in general. This is why the composer can claim that the popular saying against violence is the main principle behind (the "father" of) all Laoist teaching*. All this contrasts with the *yin* Feminine Emptiness Laoists cultivate {3}. To reverse the general gravitation toward *yang*, turning back to *yin*, is also to identify with the most fundamental cosmic reality, Tao as the source of all true meaning in the world {1}. This turning back to the *yin* Tao is a reversal, on a psychological level, of the original cosmogonic process described in {1}. (According to Girardot,[2] just such a reversal played a part in meditation practices in later esoteric Taoism.)

---

1. I owe this line to a student whose name I have forgotten.
2. 1983: 282–292.

37[14]

"Look for It, you won't see It: It is called 'fleeting'.   {1}
Listen for It, you won't hear It: It is called 'thin'.
Grasp at It, you can't get It: It is called 'subtle'."

These three lines   {2}
        are about something that evades scrutiny.
Yes, in it everything blends and becomes one.

Its top is not bright   {3}
Its underside is not dim.
Always unnameable, It turns back to nothingness.
This is the shape of something shapeless
the form of a nothing
this is elusive and evasive.

Encountering It, you won't see the front   {4}
following It, you won't see Its back.

Keep to the Tao of the ancients   {5}
and so manage things happening today.

The ability to know the ancient sources,   {6}
this is the main thread of Tao.

When you're sitting, trying to get in touch with the Softness, the One important thing, it evades your grasp—like a spirit that appears here, then there, then is gone {1}. You think you see it, then it recedes into nothing. This is the only way to describe the presence that is formless {3}. But in this practice we achieve a oneness {2}. And we come in contact with the deep sources of all things {4}, the ancient sources that enable us to handle whatever comes to us today {5}.

Saying {1} is a version of a saying about spirits, quoted also in the *Doctrine of the Mean*.[1] (Compare a similar use of a saying about a spirit in 32[6]:1.) Sayings {3 and 4} describe the experience of trying to grasp an elusive mental quality one is cultivating in Laoist meditation* (compare 38[21]:2, 46[35]:3, 30[56]:4). Saying {5} describes a benefit* of cultivating Laoist Tao, here pictured as the true Tao taught in the ancient*, idealized Golden Age. This will enable *shih** to handle any contemporary problems they encounter as government administrator-advisers. Saying {6} is a normative* description of what Laoist self-cultivation entails. As in 11[38]:6, *Tao* here probably is short for "cultivating Tao." I take "know the ancient source(s)" of things to mean gaining an intuitive understanding* of the deep truth about affairs. (As often, "ancient" serves to express what we more commonly express by images of "depth." See further under "Origin*." Note that here *Tao* is not the name of the ancient source that one knows, but of the practice by which one comes to know it.) Section {2} reads more literally: "these three, cannot be scrutinized, yes blend and become one." It seems very unlikely that "these three" refers to three different *things* mentioned in {1}, which "become one." It makes more sense to suppose that "these three" refers to the three-line *saying* in {1}, which is *about* a presence or mental quality incapable of being grasped through close mental scrutiny. In this mental space everything is Merged*, "blends and becomes one." This observation is a partial basis for my solution to the puzzle about the meaning of 43[1]:4:1, reading literally "these two, merged." That is, it refers to the previous two-line *saying* in 43[1]:3, which is (partly) *about* the state of "not desiring," which 43[1]:4 identifies with a mentally Still* state called *t'ung*/"the Merging*." Mencius[2] shows a similar use of "these two." Compare also "these two" and "these three" in 80[65]:4 and 78[19]:2.

---

1. 16,2.
2. 4A/7,1.

38[21]

The impression made by magnificent Te   {1}
comes only from Tao.

Tao is a something   {2}
but elusive, but evasive.
Evasive, elusive,
inside it lies the mind's true form.
Elusive, evasive,
inside it lies something substantial.
Shadowy, dim.
Inside lies vital energy.
This energy is very strong
inside it lies true genuineness.

From ancient times until today   {3}
Its name has not been forgotten
allowing us to see the beginnings of everything.

How do I recognize the form   {4}
    of the beginnings of everything?
By this.

Sitting, trying to grasp it, it eludes your mind. But this elusive something is also the most substantial and real thing there is. In it lies the key to recovering the mind's true nature, vital energy at its best, human genuineness in its perfection {2}. If you want to radiate goodness, this is where to be {1}. Being there gives insight into the nature of whatever you meet {3}. What's the secret? Polish the mirror of your pure mind, and look {4}.

Saying {1} celebrates a benefit* of Tao: One who has it radiates a subtle but powerful presence (Te*). Saying {2:3–10} describes the experience of one at meditation*, trying to grasp an internal presence one feels as elusive yet containing "inside" it the highest qualities. Ching/"vital energy" is an object of internal cultivation in the Nei* Yeh[1] and Laoist cultivation in 33[55]:2, illustrated there by the image of the self-generating sexual energy of an infant. I translate hsiang/form as "the mind's true form" on the basis of the Nei* Yeh's use[2] of a similar term, hsing/form, to mean something like "the mind in its prime condition." Saying {3} celebrates a benefit* of cultivating Tao: Tao's "name" (= its power) enables the mind to see the "beginnings" of things; that is, to understand them "in depth," to understand the foundations of their true meaning (compare 37[14]:6, and further comments on origin*-sayings.[3] In {4}, I think "How do I know...? By this" is a stock Laoist reply to demands to back up their opinions with arguments: "By this" refers to the powers of one's own mind, developed through self-cultivation. (See further under "This*." The formula occurs also in 61[54]:4 and 77[57]:2.)

I mark {2:1–2} as a connective* alteration by the composer mainly because of the repetition of wu/thing:substance in {2:1} and {2:6} ("a something" and "something substantial," respectively). This addition identifies the evasive something described in {2} as "Tao" and thus connects {2} to {1}. The juxtaposition of {3} and {4} implies that intuitions springing from the right state of mind (gained at meditation {2}) are the same as intuitions springing from the power given by Tao.

This chapter and the previous one (37[14]) picture Tao as a hypostatized* internal presence that eludes the grasp of one who tries to grasp it introspectively. Both chapters end with the suggestion that cultivating this elusive presence enables one to understand* the truth about reality, seeing everything in relation to its source/foundation.

---

1. Rickett 1965: 158 A.

2. For example, ibid.: 161 E, 167 N. See also the Chuang* Tzu passage quoted under Meditation*.

3. See pp. 210–211.

39[25]

There was a chaotic something, yet lacking nothing   {1}
born before Heaven and Earth.
Alone.
Still.
Standing alone, unchanging.
Revolving, endlessly.
It can be thought of as Mother of the World.

I do not know its name,   {2}
one can call it 'Tao.'
The name of its powerful presence:
One can call it 'The Great One.'

Great means going forth   {3}
going forth means going far away
going far away means turning back.

Yes: {4}
Tao is great
Heaven is great
Earth is great
(the king is also great
In the universe there are four great ones
and the king takes his place as one of them).

Earth gives the rule for people
Heaven gives the rule for Earth
Tao gives the rule for Heaven
the rule for Tao: things as they are.

Sitting still, she saw something. Everything mixed together, but perfect. Nothing else existed. It circled around, forever. A vision of Tao, the Mother of the World {1–2}. Its greatness overflowed, and the world came to be. The present world has gone far from it, but everything secretly wants to return to Tao {3}, the ultimate cosmic norm. Where do we find this norm? By looking at concrete things in their naturalness {4}.

Saying {1} reads best as a description of a vision someone saw at meditation* (perhaps in a "spirit journey" like that evoked in 27[10]:1). If this is so, the cosmogonic, nonvisual comments ("born before Heaven and Earth...the Mother of the World") are probably additions to the original vision-description. "Chaotic" probably is associated with idea of the "Uncarved* Block." Saying {3} seems to encapsulate a basic aspect of the Laoist vision of reality: Tao is the origin* and foundation of everything (everything has "gone out" from its greatness). But the social atmosphere in which we now live represents an alienation ("going far") from that source, due to the development of superficial social conventions. The true inner desire of everything is to "turn* back" to Tao (the object of Laoist self-cultivation). Sayings {4:2–4 and 8–10} celebrates the status of Tao as supreme cosmic* norm, above the principles of Heaven* and Earth conventionally thought to be supreme.

The lines about the *wang*/Emperor:king in {4:5–7} seem to stray from the main point of the saying in {4}, going out of the way to reaffirm the traditional Chinese belief that the Emperor is one of the pillars of the cosmic order (see 35[39]:1). These lines may have been added to please a royal patron who claimed the title of Emperor*,[1] or perhaps to correct genuinely "anarchistic" tendencies within the Laoist school itself. The final line of {4} seems anticlimactic, and I suspect it was added by the composer of this chapter to make a point similar to that of 38[21]:4. After the mystical flight in {1}, he wants to emphasize the very concrete, everyday character of Tao as it appears in our experience: *Tao* is just the name for a quality we perceive in things when they (and we) are in an ideal *tzu-jan*/natural state of Stillness.

Placing this chapter last in this section reflects my view that cosmic images are best understood as "climaxes" following on the "build-up" provided by the more mundane and practical aspects of Laoist wisdom. This stands in contrast to traditional interpretations of the *Tao Te Ching* that treat cosmic ideas first, as the "foundation" of Laoist thought and an essential basis for understanding the practical "conclusions" deduced from this foundation.

---

1. See Bodde 1981: 105.

4

Knowledge, Learning, and Teaching

40[71]

"Aware but not aware of it: a high thing."   {1}
Not aware but aware of it: sick of this.
Simply sick of the sickness—and so no longer sick.

The Wise Person's lack of this sickness: {2}
He became sick of being sick, and so he's no longer sick.

Some say to have true awareness but to be unselfconsciously unaware of this is a high achievement. One could also say: It is a great thing if a person lacking true awareness is painfully aware of her lack. Is not the pain at not having it, a sign that she actually does have it?

Lines {1:1–2} read literally: "Know not know high / not know know sick." I believe the puzzle as to their meaning is best solved if we regard the first line as a saying quoted here only as a take-off* point for the second line, which plays with the same words to make a completely different point. Line {1:1} is a saying in praise of the modest person who has great understanding but is unpretentious about this—he makes nothing of this and ignores it. Line {1:2} is about the person who has come to realize that he lacks true understanding* and is distressed by ("sick of") the lack. This line then leads in to a Laoist saying in {1:3}, repeated in {2}. This saying suggests a cure for the "sickness" (lack of true understanding) that afflicts us all: Recognition that one's conventional views are defective, and distress at this, can only spring from something in oneself that has in germ a different, better way of seeing things. If this intuitive wisdom becomes strong enough, it creates enough revulsion at defective views to throw them off and replace them.

The first four chapters of Section 4 (40[71], 41[47], 42[2], 43[1]) deal with Laoist views about how one gains a true understanding* of the world, and what such an understanding consists in.

41[47]

Understanding the world   {1}
    without going out the door.
Understanding Heaven's Way
    without looking out the window.

Traveling very widely, understanding very little.   {2}

And so the Wise Person: {3}
Knows without any going
names without any looking
accomplishes without any doing.

How is it that some people can travel the world and end up understanding nothing of life {2}? They develop no depth of understanding; they do not engage deeply with things they meet. A person who develops this depth can understand the true nature of things while hardly stepping out of her door {1, 3}.

Sayings {1} and {2} counter the assumption that to be a knowledgeable *shih** one must travel widely and learn about many different things. Saying {2} poses the negative image of the person whose wide travels have left him with a superficial understanding of things. Saying {1} evokes the exaggerated image of the person who develops the ability to intuitively understand* things in depth without ever leaving home; that is, by devoting himself to mental self-cultivation. For an example of the view these sayings oppose, see the opening passage of the *Hsün Tzu*.

The composer's images in {3} are even more exaggerated. For example, "naming*" things here probably means understanding the truth about issues and events, which for Laoists is the same thing as seeing them from the right perspective, in the right state of mind (43[1]:1:2 also seems to use *names* to mean the real nature of things). So "names without looking" is hyperbole, expressing this ideal by exaggerated contrast with the person who thinks that close inspection of details will give him true understanding. In the final line— "accomplishes [knowledge] without any doing [close examining]"— the composer stretches the meaning of *not doing* to apply to this area of life as well (see comments on 51[75]:2).

42[2]

When everyone in the world	{1}

When everyone in the world {1}
    recognizes the elegant as elegant...
then ugliness has just appeared.
When all recognize goodness as good...
then the not-good has just appeared.

Yes: {2}
'Being' and 'nothing' give birth one to the other
'the difficult' and 'the easy'
    give full shape to one another
'what excels' and 'what falls short' form one another
'the noble' and 'the lowly' give content to one another
the music and the voice harmonize with one another
the back and the front follow one another.
Always.

And so the Wise Person: {3}
Settles into his job of Not Doing
carries on his teaching done without talking.

The thousands of things arise and are active— {4}
and he rejects none of them.

He is a doer but does not rely on this {5}
he achieves successes but does not dwell in them.
He just does not dwell in them,
and so they cannot be taken away.

"If only we could teach everyone to label *elegant* only what is truly elegant," they say. But what would really happen? A person would learn to mark certain things off as outstandingly elegant—and suddenly her world also would be filled with many more ugly things standing out by contrast {1}. Some things appear to "excel" only if the world gets cut up into a few eye-catching things that "excel" and many rejects that appear to "fall short." Really, what "excels" stands on the shoulders of what is rejected as "falling short" {2}. Some things then are unnecessarily rejected {4}; and the world loses its fullness, becoming less than it was. People come to dwell in these half-realities, taking pride in their "noble" activities and their "excelling" status {5}. The person who understands this teaches without using names like *elegant* and *noble* {3}. She aims for success but does not depend on appearing "successful." She never rests on her laurels, and that is why no one can take them away {3} and {5}.

Sayings {1} and {2} are probably directed against "rectifying names*," the attempt to establish and enforce one correct way of using judgmental names like *good* and *bad*. I believe that {1} twists a common slogan favoring that program, which originally described a positive result. The Laoist twist describes a negative result instead: Conscious and pronounced evaluative labeling produces a negative shift* in the way people experience the world. Both {1} and {2} have as their background the Laoist idea of the Uncarved* Block: The ideal state of mind is a state in which one experiences reality directly—not overlain with conscious conventional judgmental concepts, not "cutting up" the world and pigeonholing things (see 63[32]:1–3). In this state one will see conventional good-bad opposites as parts of a whole, complementing each other like voice and musical accompaniment. Like the flexible Tao in 64[34]:2, one will not then "reject" those things one finds annoying {4}. (*Tso*/arise:act is a negative term in 28[16]:2 and 81[37]:2:3, so I believe {4} evokes an experience of things in which they assert themselves annoyingly.) Saying {3} (a version of 47[43]:2) emphasizes the "wordless" character of Laoist teaching* in contrast to the "naming" criticized in {1} and {2}. Saying {5} (a version of 27[10]:2, 52[77]:3, 65[51]:4) counters the tendency toward self-promotion*: The person who does not "dwell* in" (build his identity on) his external successes is the one who truly deserves the merit. One who relates to reality without accentuating conscious value judgments also will not focus on the public impression made by his work.

43[1]

The Tao that can be told is not the invariant Tao   {1}
the names that can be named are not the invariant Names.

Nameless, it is the source of the thousands of things   {2}
(named, it is 'Mother' of the thousands of things).

Yes: {3}
Always: being desireless,
    one sees the hidden essentials.
Always: having desires,
    one sees only what is sought.

These two lines are about The Merging—   {4}
it is when things develop and emerge from this
that the different names appear.

The Merging is something mysterious—   {5}
mysterious, and more mysterious,
the abode of all the hidden essences.

There is a place in the mind that is Still, desireless, where there are no concepts, no separate perceptions, just engagement with reality as a whole. There resides Tao, the source and norm of the world {1–2}. Residing here, one sees things the way they are {1, 5}. But something about the mind desires clear and separate things to see, labeled by clear and definite concepts {1, 3}—the beginning of life on the surface. People who live on the surface of their minds live on the surface of the world. Out of touch with the depths of their mind, the depth of things and events is hidden from them.

Saying {1} is directed against rectifying names*. Any Way that can be spelled out in concepts is not the true (Laoist) Tao. Situations in the world have a true nature ("name*"), but this needs to be understood in direct experience rather than grasped through concepts ("names"). Saying {2:1} pictures the nameless Tao as the origin* of the world. The interpretation of the rest of this chapter is very controversial and the following interpretation is new. Saying {3} celebrates a benefit* of the ideal "desireless*" state Laoists cultivate. Being in this Still* state causes a shift* in the way one experiences the world, allowing one to understand* the true inner meaning (*miao*/"hidden essentials") of events and situations. One whose mind becomes active, stirred up by desires and conceptual thinking, perceives only in categories that satisfy the seeking mind but cover up the real truth.

"Different names appear" in {4} refers back to the attempt in {1} to name things correctly and give a conceptual definition of Tao. Hence {4} is essentially an account of the unfortunate process by which conceptual naming arises out of a superior mental state described as *t'ung*/"[the] Merging" (compare 30[56]:3), which the composer identifies with the state of "not desiring" mentioned in {3}. (On the phrase "these two *lines*," see comments in 37[14]:2.) This is a Still*, desireless and conceptless, mental space (*men*/dwelling*) in which one knows Tao, the foundational "source" of the world, which is the same as knowing the true natures of things (see 38[21]:3)— knowing their *heng*/invariant Names {1} (see "Steady*"), which is the same as knowing their *miao*/"hidden essences" {3, 5}. (On *miao*, see 49[27]:5; and compare 63[32]:3, which describes a similar unfortunate process of "names" coming to be when one "cuts up" Tao as norm, an originally "nameless" "Uncarved* Block.") The contrast between named and nameless Tao in {2:2}, which many make much of, plays no part elsewhere. I believe {2:2} makes the relatively simple point that Tao also has some "names," such as the name *Mother*.

44[41]

"When the best *shih* hears Tao,   {1}
    he puts out great effort to practice it.
When the average *shih* hears Tao,
    he will keep it sometimes, and sometimes forget about it.
When the poorest *shih* hears Tao, he just has a big laugh."
If he does not laugh, it must not quite be Tao.

Yes, the 'Well-Founded Sayings' has it: {2}
The bright Tao seems dark
the Tao going forward seems to be going backward
the smooth Tao seems rough.

The loftiest Te seems like a valley   {3}
great purity seems sullied
abundant Te seems insufficient

Well-founded Te seems flimsy
what is pure and natural seems faded
the best square has no corners

A great bronze takes long to finish
great music has a delicate sound
the Great Image has no shape.

Tao is something concealed, nameless.   {4}
It is just Tao,
    good at sustaining a person and completing him.

The Tao and Te taught in our school don't look like very much at first. Our Tao is a backward, dark, and rough road {2}. It's like natural beauty that looks to some only crude and faded, like subtle music that appeals only to a delicate ear, like a square whose corners are suggested rather than drawn in, like a great ceremonial bronze whose beauty comes about so slowly {3}. Many who come think it's laughable {1}. But to one who makes the effort to cultivate it, this Tao is a sustaining presence, fulfilling her best potential {4}.

---

*Shih** in {1} refers to men aspiring to careers as government officials or advisors, who traveled to study with respected teachers in *shih* schools. Saying {1:1–5} is about the varying aptitudes of students in such schools for appreciating moral and spiritual teaching. Other schools also referred to their teaching as *Tao**, so there is nothing specifically Laoist about the saying before the final line. I think this is added by the Laoist composer to make a point very different from the original: It is in the nature of true (Laoist) Tao that it will appear ridiculous to a conventional mind. Saying {2} describes the paradoxical character of Laoist self-cultivation, playing on the meaning of Tao as "road." (It apparently quotes from a now-lost sayings collection.) Saying {3} is related to the sayings against impressive appearances*. In the background here is the idea that attempts to achieve strikingly positive appearances always result in something rather artificial. Genuine, "natural" goodness typically will not be striking in its appearance, but subtle, even appearing negative at times. Lines {3:6–8} use various metaphorical* images illustrating this idea, described in the paraphrase. Because {3:9} is difficult to make sense of as a metaphor, I think it is a connective* alteration written by the composer: As in 46[35]:1, "The Great Image" is Tao (called *shapeless* in 37[14]:3), and so this line leads into {4}.

The composer's comment in {4} pictures Tao as an hypostatized* inner presence, felt as elusive and "nameless*," beyond one's mental grasp, yet supportive of the one who cultivates it (see 14[23]:3, 13[20]:5). The chapter as a whole, then, is about the character of the Tao/Te taught in the Laoist *shih* school—not a doctrine but a subtle way of being animated by an intangible but sustaining inner presence.

45[70]

My words are very easy to understand,   {1}
    very easy to practice.
No one in the world can understand,
No one can practice them.

The words have an ancestor   {2}
the practice has a master.
They just do not understand
and so they do not understand me.
(So few understand me—a rare treasure indeed.)

And so the Wise Person: {3}
Dressed in shabby clothes, jade under his shirt.

The Tao that we teach: It's nothing strikingly unusual. It is found in the middle of ordinariness—in some ways the easiest thing to grasp, in some ways the hardest {1}. All our sayings and ways of doing things are expressions of only one thing, but this one thing cannot be put into words {2}. A student has to sense it—but most do not. A good teacher is like the Tao she teaches: precious jade under grubby clothes {3}.

Sayings {1} and {2:1-2} reflect on the nature of Laoist teaching*—the relation between the words used to teach and the spirit taught, which can't be directly captured in words. Lines {2:3-5} and saying {3} reflect on what it is like to be a teacher teaching the Laoist way (compare 3[67]:1).

The preceding chapter (44[41]) and the following four (46[35], 47[43], 48[62], 49[27]) center on the teaching and learning that takes place in the Laoist *shih** school, including especially reflections on what it is like to be a Laoist teacher* and the special style of teaching that matches the character of the Tao being taught.

46[35]

Grasp the Great Image and the world will come   {1}
it will come and not be harmed—
a great peace and evenness.

For music and cakes, passing strangers stop   {2}
Tao flowing from the lips—
flat. No taste to it.

Look for it: you will not be satisfied looking   {3}
listen for it: you will not be satisfied listening
put it into practice: you will not be satisfied stopping.

Music and pastry at a fair will catch people's attention. When someone is teaching Tao it will appear as though nothing is going on {2}. And yet, given time, it attracts everyone {1}. Practiced over time, it is like a nourishing but unspiced meal—it leaves you like you are, only much better {1}. You will not want to stop {4}.

"Grasp the Great Image [= Tao]" in {1} describes an ideal ruler who mentally keeps hold of Tao and lets it inform his leadership style. The saying celebrates the benefits* of this. "The world will come" refers to the desire of each feudal prince in Warring States China to establish a great social order that would attract people from all over China wanting to be part of it.[1] "Not harmed" is brought up because of an implied contrast with the "impressive*" ruler: Striking and inspiring ideals stir people up but also "hurt*" them; that is, cause them to feel bad and guilty about the contrast between the ideal and their present state. (Compare 55[66]:3, 81[37]:2:6–7.) But when one rules by the spirit of Tao, one exercises a subtle rather than striking and "inspiring" influence. This spirit brings out the natural goodness already present, rather than confronting people with something they are not. Saying {2} reflects on what it is like to be a Laoist teacher, teaching* a subtle "tasteless" Tao. Saying {3:1–2} is a version of 37[14]:1, describing what it is like to try to grasp Tao at meditation*.

The composer probably intends {1} here as a description not of a ruler but of the Laoist teacher, whose Tao attracts students from all over.[2] "You will not be satisfied stopping" is a new and conjectural understanding of {3:3}. I think this is probably a composer's twist added to {3:1–2}, celebrating one of the benefits* of cultivating (*yung*/using) Tao, subtle but deep satisfaction.

---

1. Compare *Mencius** 1A/7,18.
2. Compare *Mencius** 7A/20,4.

47[43]

The Softest thing in the world   {1}
rides right over the Hardest things in the world.
What-has-No-Being enters what-leaves-no-opening.
This makes me realize the advantage of Not Doing.

Teaching done by not talking   {2}
the advantage gained by Not Doing—
few things in the world can match this.

Sometimes a student is very set in her ways, a hard nut to crack. Closed up tight, words bounce off of her. What will get through is only the teaching that is not really in the words, but exists between the lines. Don't act as though teaching is a big project that needs a lot of "doing." Appear as a nondoer. Present to her the subtle Nothing that will get through.

Saying {1} uses a metaphorical* nature image (water eroding rocks, or perhaps penetrating and cracking them as ice) to celebrate the power and benefits* of Softness* and Nothing*, mental qualities Laoists cultivate. ("Rides over" refers to riding down hunting prey, and evokes the idea of *sheng*/overcoming, a recurrent formula in the *Tao Te Ching* borrowed from speculation about the "conquest*" cycle. Compare 75[78]:1–2.)

I think that teaching* {2:1} is the main subject here for the composer: Laoist teaching is "Soft*" (nonconfrontational), and it feels like "Nothing*"; that is, it has little definite *surface* content that can be presented directly in words or "names*" (see 42[2]:3, 43[1]:1, 45[70]:1, 46[35]:2). This is why it can penetrate the "hard" surface of the resistant student (compare 49[27] on the magical and irresistible effectiveness of imperceptible, "trackless" Laoist teaching). Note the equivalence implied here between *Softness*, No-Being, no words,* and *not doing*. All these have an equivalent experiential reference, describing the subtle presence of the Laoist teacher as felt by others. This passage is important in showing that "no-being" is not intended literally or philosophically, but experientially, as hyperbole referring to something experienced as relatively intangible.

48[62]

Tao is the honored center for the thousands of things. {1}

The treasure of the good {2}
what protects the not good.

Elegant words can buy and sell {3}
fine conduct gets people promoted.

People who are not good, {4}
why are they rejected?

Yes: {5}
When they are enthroning the Son of Heaven
or installing the Three Ministers—
although they are presenting in tribute
    jade medallions out in front of four-horse teams,
this cannot compare to sitting and setting forth this Tao.

What was the reason that the ancients treasured this Tao? {6}
Is it not said:
"By it the seeker obtains
by it the guilty escapes."

Yes: {7}
It is the Treasure of the World.

It's a difficult world. People ashamed of their lives, looking for something, wanting to become what they should be (and rejected by some teachers, who offer only elegant words that profit themselves {3–4}). Tao is this world's secret desire, the thing that will get for the seeker what she wants, that will turn around the life of the person gone wrong {2, 6}. One can do nothing in the world that is better than teaching people this Tao {5}.

Sayings {1} and {7} (= 30[56]:5) celebrate the cosmic* importance of Tao, as that which all things instinctively cherish above all. (Ao/"honored center" refers to the religious shrine in a house for the household gods; the central place of honor in the house.) Sayings {2} and {6} celebrate Tao's great benefits*, its power to "save" by mere contact those shih* who come to the Laoist school looking for something better than their wayward or mediocre life. Saying {5} celebrates the greatness of teaching* Tao, by comparing the Tao taught to the expensive gifts offered in tribute at grand court ceremonies. ("Son of Heaven" is a title of the Emperor*.) On the basis of similar wording in 49[27]:3 and 4, I believe that {4} is directed against the practice of some shih* teachers who refused to accept as students those they judged unfit. (Pu-shan/"not good" may mean not immoral but inexperienced in self-cultivation, as in 49[27]:4. To judge from 49[27], the connection here is that Laoist Tao is so effective that it can penetrate even the poorest student, hence rejection would be groundless. Mencius* also is said[1] not to have rejected even criminally inclined shih who wanted to study with him.) Saying {3} counters the admiration of fine appearances* by picturing eloquence and refined manners as serving only the selfish and commercial interests of their possessors. (I am guessing the composer intends a contrast between eloquence and teaching "tasteless" Tao [see 46[35]:2]. But this saying may have crept in here by mistake. My understanding of it is new.)

This chapter is the one with the most "religious" flavor, assuming that there are "guilty" people who need to be "saved" by Tao. I take this as a measure of Laoist alienation: One cannot find meaning by participating in conventional social life, but finds it instead in the Laoist shih school. The Tao that is the focus of community life there takes the place of the Emperor* and the ceremonial surrounding him, the traditional cultural center of meaning, now replaced by teaching and learning self-cultivation which takes place in the Laoist school.

---

1. 7B/30,2

49[27]

Excellent traveling: no tracks or traces   {1}
Excellent speaking: no blemish or blame.

Excellent counting does not use counting slips.   {2}
Excellent locking: no bolt or bar,
    but the door cannot be opened.
Excellent tying: no cord or rope,
    but the knots cannot be undone.

And so the Wise Person: {3}
Always Excels at rescuing people
    and so does not turn anyone away.
Always Excels at resolving things
    and so does not turn away from anything.
This is called 'being clothed in Clarity.'

The Excellent person   {4}
    is the teacher of the person who is not Excellent.
The person who is not Excellent
    is material for the Excellent person.

Not to treasure one's teacher   {5}
not to love one's material,
though 'smart,' is a great mistake.
This is an important secret.

Some teachers have something very definite and forceful to teach. Some students accept it, but many resist—the teachers can do nothing with them. The Tao we teach is different. It gets into people subtly, without them knowing it—like a good hunter who can walk leaving no tracks, like a magician who can tie up people using no ropes, or fasten a door using no lock {1–2}. This is a Tao for all occasions— the one who teaches it needs to turn down no person and no problem {3}. Teaching it requires an atmosphere in which students look up to teachers who embody Tao, and teachers love the students whom they mold {4–5}.

Saying {3} celebrates the great powers and benefits* of teaching* done by an accomplished Laoist teacher, enabling him to cope with any student or problem. (Compare 48[62]:4. I take *wu*/things* in {3:4} to mean "affairs, problems," hence I translate *chiu*/rescue as "resolve" in this line.) The images of {1–2} here serve as analogies to the quasi-magical influence, imperceptible but irresistible, of his style of teaching (compare 47[43].) Saying {4} is about the respective roles of teachers* and students in the Laoist school. *Shan*/Excellent* throughout this chapter has a strong meaning, referring to people who are "experts" in what they do, including especially {3–4} expert teachers well advanced in Laoist self-cultivation ("clothed in Clarity*" {3:6}). Hence I translate *pu shan* as "not Excellent"—that is, a relative beginner—although the phrase also could mean "not good" (see 48[62]:4).

Sections {4–5} give the most direct indication in the *Tao Te Ching* of sharply defined roles of teachers and students in the Laoist school. Section {5} seems intended to correct some bad tendencies the composer sees among both students and teachers within the school. It seems unlikely that the composer would direct general criticism at teachers unless there was more than one, hence I take {5:2} as indirect evidence that in fact there was more than one. "Secret" in {5:4} is *miao,* translated "hidden essences/essentials" in 43[1]:3 and 5. The use of *miao* here shows that advice such as that given in {4–5} is the kind of thing Laoists mean by "understanding the hidden essence" of situations.

5

Majesty That Is Not Awesome

50[53]

If I had the least bit of understanding	{1}
I would walk on the great Way.	

Only display will be dangerous. {2}

The great Way is very smooth {3}
but people love bypaths.

The court is very well kept {4}
the fields are very weedy
the granaries very empty.

"Their clothes are fine and colorful {5}
on their belts are sharp swords,
they are filled with food and drink"
a superabundance of expensive goods.

This is robbers boasting, {6}
certainly not the Way.

People admire the parties of the rich: the fine clothes, the abundance of great food {5}. But what are they doing? They take great care of the court (for themselves), but neglect their responsibilities: they ignore weedy fields, and fail to see that grain is stored against famine {4}. What are their parties really like? A gang of thieves showing off booty stolen from the people {6}.

Sayings {1} and {3} contrast the obvious importance of the "easy" Tao*/Way with its neglect by the unthinking majority. Saying {2} speaks against self-promotion*, using an oracle* formula. Saying {3} criticizes contemporary rulers who give their attention to the elegance of court life at the expense of their public responsibilities, like managing agriculture and storing grain against famine (compare 52[77]:1). Because lines {5:1–3} seem so glowing, I suspect they are a quotation. Line {5:4} expresses the composer's disapproval of the banquet scene described.

The saying criticizing "display" in {2} is connected with the criticism of conspicuous consumption in {5} and "boasting" in {6}. It is placed near the beginning to frame* some of the material, giving this composition more unity. Section {6} further unifies the composition: "Robbers boasting" characterizes the court's conspicuous consumption in {4–5}, and "the Way" refers back to {1} and {2}.

In {2} most translators emend *shih*/display to *yi*/"go astray," yielding "[I would] only fear going astray," which might seem to make much better sense in the immediate context of talk about the "Great Way" and the "bypaths" (see Duyvendak). But (a) the catchy *wei shih shih wei*/"only display will be dangerous" makes sense as an independent saying using an oracle* formula, and (b) the location of this saying at the beginning follows a unifying "framing*" technique visible elsewhere. This is a good example of the way form and redaction criticism[1] sometimes can provide solutions to textual puzzles without resort to emendations.

This Section 5 begins with three chapters (50[53], 51[75], 52[77]) expressing Laoist protest against the unjust distribution of wealth and the luxury the upper classes enjoy at the expense of the peasantry.

---

1. See pp. 196–199.

51[75]

'The people are starving.'   {1}
It is because those high up eat too much tax grain,
this is why they are starving.

'The people are hard to govern.'
It is because there is Working among those high up,
this is why they are hard to govern.

'The people take death lightly.'
It is because they pursue a lavish life,
this is why they take death lightly.

Simply: {2}
Those who do not Work at 'living'—
these are better men than those who 'love life.'

People in office are always complaining, "the people are hard to govern"; "the people are uncontrollable"; "the people are starving." Can't they see that they themselves are the cause? If they tax the people so heavily, of course the people will starve. If they themselves are reckless in pursuit of pleasure, do they think the people are not going to be {1}? The poor farmers who do not waste all their efforts trying to live it up are better than the all those officials who "love life" {2}.

I think the first lines of the first three stanzas here are quotations of common complaints by rulers (compare 66[74]:1). The criticism of wealth derived from burdensome taxation in {1:1–3} is similar to that in 50[53]:4, 52[77]:1, and 53[72]:2. As to {1:7–9}: 76[80] mentions, as part of its description of an ideal society, that the people in this society "take death seriously and do not travel far distances." Hence the opposite here "taking death lightly" probably means that the people are reckless, or perhaps that they can't be controlled by fear of capital punishment. (The criticism of capital punishment in 66[74]:1 mentions people's lack of "fear of death.") Hence the overall meaning here is that rulers are responsible for the people's recklessness because their own reckless quest for high living sets a bad tone for the society.

"Work" in {1:4–6} doesn't go well with the criticism of luxury in the other two stanzas. I take it to be the composer's addition. As in 8[81]:4, *work* is an elliptical reference, spelled out in {2}: People are hard to govern because those high up set a bad tone by "working *at living*"; that is, at living luxuriously, which they claim manifests their "love of life." (Compare the similar criticism of lavish living in 22[50]:2, where *sheng sheng chih hou*/"live life's lavishness" matches *chou sheng chih hou*/"pursue life's lavishness" here.) The composer here seems to be stretching the more usual meaning of the key Laoist term *working**, to cover "working" at luxurious living (see also 41[47]:3). I'm guessing that "those who don't work at living it up" are peasant-farmers, objects of the complaints in {1}.

52[77]

Heaven's Way is like the stringing of a bow: {1}
It pulls down what is high
it lifts up what is low
it takes away from what has an abundance
to give to what has not enough.

Heaven's Way:
Take away from what has an abundance
help along what has not enough.
People's way is not like this:
Take away from what has not enough
to offer it to what has an abundance.

Who can have an abundance to offer the world?   {2}
Only the one who has Tao.

And so the Wise Person: {3}
Works but does not rely on this
achieves successes but does not dwell in them
has no desire to show off his worth.

Look at nature's leveling: High river banks get pulled down, low-lying ravines get filled in. What do people do? Those who are on top get lifted higher. Rulers demand that the lowest people in need feed the coffers of those who already have more than enough {1}. The abundance they receive is a source of pride for them. But what is real "abundance"? What is the "abundance" that will benefit the people? It is the Tao that one has inside, the spirit that enables a leader to make a real contribution {2} without puffing herself up over it {3}.

Saying {1} uses a metaphorical* nature image, described in the paraphrase. In its criticism of wealth as imbalance, it is similar to 50[53]:4–6, 51[75]:1, and 53[72]:2. Underlying these sayings is a feeling for the social whole that Laoist *shih** wanted to promote among contemporary leaders. When "the rich get richer," this is bad because it means that resources are diverted from those who need it most to those who need it least, and that resources are spent on luxuries rather than on what is most useful to the society (50[53]:4). Saying {2} celebrates the benefits* one who has Tao* can confer on his society. Saying {3} criticizes the tendency toward self-promotion*, by posing the image of the ideal *shih** who is very competent and successful in his managerial tasks, but does not rely on them for his sense of self-worth, and so is not possessive of them and does not "dwell* in" (identify himself with) them. (Versions of this saying occur also at 42[2]:5, 65[51]:4, and 27[10]:2.)

In the second half of this chapter, the composer shifts the focus away from wealth as imbalance, to a contrast between the implied "false abundance" of wealth {1} and the more real spiritual "abundance" of the *shih* who possesses the spirit of Tao {2}, spreading this spirit by the self-effacing style of his leadership {3} (see comments in 7[8]:1).

53[72]

When the people are not in awe of your majesty   {1}
then great majesty has been achieved.

Do not restrict where they can live   {2}
do not tire them out by taxing what they live on.
Simply do not tire them
and they will not tire of you.

And so, the Wise Person: {3}
Knows himself
does not make a show of himself.
Loves himself
does not exalt himself.

Yes, he leaves 'that' aside, and attends to 'this.'   {4}

Some rulers need to make their importance felt {1} by constant assertion of their privileges: Staking out "royal lands" where the people
aren't allowed to live, taxing heavily the farm produce the people live
on {2:1–2}. The people know this does not represent true "majesty."
They'll soon tire of such a person, and that will be the end of his rule
{2:3–4}. Rulers indeed ought to know and love themselves better, paying more attention to developing their own character {3–4}. Then
they could be easier on the people. Then *true* "majesty" will have
arrived {1}.

Saying {1} counters the desire of Warring States rulers to awe their
subjects with an impressive* and commanding presence. The image
of the nonawesome ruler it presents, evokes the Laoist idea that the
internal spirit he cultivates {3–4} fits a ruler for true greatness—and
this spirit is not something that makes a striking external impression.
(Compare 54[17]:1. The translation of {1} here is new, based a passage
in the *Mencius**[1] using the same words for *awe* and *majesty* in the
sense I give them here.) Saying {2:3–4} counters the tendency of these
rulers to impose burdens on their people, picturing not burdening
the people as the best way to keep their allegiance (a constant worry
of Warring States rulers). Saying {3} urges introspective concern for
the quality of one's own being, in contrast to self-promotion*. I think
that "this" in {4} refers also to concern for one's own being, as
opposed to concern for the external impression one makes on others
("that"). (See discussion under "This*." This saying also occurs in
11[38]:8 and 21[12]:3.)

The "burdensome" restrictions and taxation referred to in {2:1–2}
have not only a practical purpose, but are a means of imposing recognition of the ruler's special status and "majesty" {1}. (Compare the
criticisms of similar practices in *Mencius**.[2]) The composer redirects
the ruler's attention to introspective care for and development of his
own being {3–4} in contrast to a preoccupation with gaining public
recognition (compare 24[33]:1). His own inner spirit thus cultivated
will win more subtly, but more effectively, the respect and allegiance
of the people.

This chapter shares the social criticism of the previous three
chapters, but relates this also to the main theme of the following four
(54[17], 55[66], 56[61], 57[68]): Laoist opposition to the "impressive*"
ruler.

---

1. 1B/3,3.
2. For example, 1A/5,3, 1B/2, 1B/5,3.

54[17]

The greatest ruler: those under him only know he exists   {1}
the next best kind: they love and praise him
the next: they are in awe of him
the next: they despise him.

When sincerity does not suffice   {2}
it was not sincerity.
("Reticent—he is sparing with words.")

He achieves successes   {3}
he accomplishes his tasks
and the hundred clans all say: We are just being natural.

Why do rulers want so much to impress their people? First the people give them love and respect, but this is only one step removed from awe—and awe is only one step removed from resentment and hatred. The ruler who stands out is a burden {1}. Why give impressive speeches? Real sincerity will always be sufficient, even when it's not impressive {2}. The best turn of events: You work hard, but your work is invisible—people think things are just going well naturally {3}.

Sayings {1} and {3} counter the ruler's desire to be impressive*—to gain the love and respect of his people, and to have them credit him with the society's order and prosperity. The idea behind the progression in {1} is that when the ruler is so exalted in the people's mind this "hurts*" them (55[66]:3) and causes them to feel inferior (81[37]:2:6), which eventually leads to resentment. The contrasting image is the ideal Laoist ruler whose greatness consists in the intangible and unimpressive spirit he cultivates, which expresses itself by keeping an extremely low profile. Thus he actually works hard and competently at social organization {3:1-2}, but calls so little attention to himself that the people think social harmony came about spontaneously {3:3}. Saying {2:1-2} (= 14[23]:4) counters the feeling that speech will be effective only when it is eloquent, sincerity will not suffice to convince. I think {2:3} probably is a quotation about some great "man of few words." (Its presence here is one reason that I think {2:1-2} is about sincere *speech*. See further comments at 14[23]:4.) For Laoists, sincere speech counts as something relatively unimpressive in contrast to eloquence (see 7[8]:2:4, 8[81]:1), hence the connection of this saying with the idealization of the unimpressive ruler in {1} and {3}.

55[66]

The Yang-tze and the ocean: {1}
How are they able to be Kings of the hundred streams?
Because they excel at being low—
this is how they are able to be Kings
    of the hundred streams.

And so: {2}
Wishing to be high above the people,
    you must by your speech put yourself at the bottom.
Wishing to be out in front of the people,
    you must put your self in the last place.

And so, the Wise Person: {3}
Stands above, but the people are not weighed down
stands out in front, but the people are not harmed
and so the world delights in praising him,
    and does not tire.

Because of his not contending   {4}
no one in the world can contend with him.

With some leaders, every word they speak, every action they take, says, "I am someone of great importance. You are my lowly subjects." Such a person is an oppressive weight on the people, hurting them by casting them always in a bad light, as "inferior." People will not accept this. Weighed down, they weary of her. The people wearied, she loses their support {3}. She becomes just one more individual, joining in society's quarrelsome competition for honor and status. (And she wonders why people become so contentious and quarrelsome with her {4}.) Look at the ocean and the Yang-tze, greatest of rivers. Did they become great because of their talent for being impressive? No, their uniqueness among rivers lies in their surpassing lowness, occupying the place toward which all the water naturally flows {1}. This is an image of the weightless authority of the one who occupies the Central place, but also the lowly place.

Sayings {1}, {2}, and {3:2–3} criticize the ideal of the impressive* ruler. The metaphorical* nature image in {1} represents the idea that the quality Laoists cultivate gives a ruler true claim to Emperor* status and will attract the spontaneous allegiance of all the people, but this quality expresses itself partly in a deferential manner, a willingness (as in {2}) to adopt the stance characteristic of someone of low* social standing in dealing with others. (See 35[39]:2. *Mencius**[1] also uses water's gravity flow as an image of the people's "natural" allegiance for a true ruler, but without the emphasis on lowness. Not just any kind of "being low" is involved here: The ideal ruler has a greatness *all the more* attractive because it expresses itself in a deferential manner in dealing with his people.) Saying {3:2–3} reflects the Laoist ideal for the ruler, setting a high tone for the society, yet doing so in such a way that his presence is not felt as overbearing or in any way hurtful* or accusatory (see also 81[37]]:2:6.) Line {3:2} plays on *chung*/heavy, which also means "dignified": The ideal ruler is one whose great weight/dignity does not "weigh on" the people (compare 53[72]:1, 54[17]:1). Saying {4} (= 4[22]:6) criticizes the tendency to *cheng*/contend*:quarrel with others for high social standing. ("Lowness" and "not contending" are connected also in 7[8]:1 and 57[68]:1–2.) The noncontentious person "has no competition" in the contest for *real* worth.

Line {3:4} interrupts the parallelism of the previous two lines, it is introduced by the standard introduction *shih yi*/"and so," and its point seems equivalent to the universal attractiveness theme of {1}— this is why I think it is a connective* addition by the composer.

---

1. 4A/9,2.

56[61]

The great state is a low and easy   {1}
woman for the world
the one the whole world unites with.

Femininity always overcomes Masculinity, by Stillness,   {2}
in Stillness it takes the low place.

Yes: {3}
A great state,
    by putting itself lower than the smaller state,
    will win out over the smaller state.
A small state,
    by putting itself lower than the great state,
    will win out over the great state.

Yes: {4}
One puts itself lower so it will win out,
if the other gets lower, then it will win.

(A great state has no further desire   {5}
than to embrace and protect other states.
A small state has no further desire
than to enter and serve other states.
So both get what they want.)

The greatest should be the lowest.   {6}

Some hope to make their state great by forming grand plans and gaining a reputation for high ideals, thinking that in this way they will attract people from all over. But what state will really attract the world? The one that imitates the prostitute: Feminine, Still, low, loose, and easy. In dealing with other states, diplomacy that plays the lower part wins out in the long run over arrogance.

Several individual states were competing with each other in this period, each wanting to restore unity to the Chinese empire under *its* leadership. More powerful states regularly swallowed up their weaker neighbors. A favorite strategy was for one ruler to try to attract the allegiance of a rival state's people. Saying {1} criticizes the ideal of the strict* ruler, one who hopes to attract people and make his state great by upholding the highest moral standards. The saying means to shock by proposing the extreme opposite ideal: Attract the people's allegiance by being like a prostitute who has no moral standards. (Seeing a prostitute image underlying this passage is new. See "Additional Textual Notes.") A positive Laoist ideal underlies the negative prostitute metaphor*: The ideal ruler rules by a spirit that is just the spirit of an ideal organic harmony already potentially present in the society, needing just to be brought out (see 60[49]:1). This is why it will be attractive to the people, but will not be experienced by them as a moral norm imposed from without. Saying {2:1} borrows a formula from thought about the "conquest* cycle," to celebrate the superiority of the Femininity*/Stillness* Laoists cultivate over the Masculine spirit. (I take {2:2} to be the composer's connective* addition, linking {2:1} to the theme of lowness, the leitmotif for this chapter.) Saying {3} celebrates the power and benefits* of Laoist lowness*, which here expresses itself in a deferential manner when conducting interstate diplomacy (a common task of Warring States *shih**). Saying {6} also advises deference, as especially suited to those (people or states) with great power and status (compare our principle of noblesse oblige).

Section {5} seems to be in conflict with {1–4}. Sayings {1–4} suggest that even small states can win out in struggles with larger states if their rulers cultivate Laoist Femininity/Stillness/lowness. Section {5} only appears to uphold this idea, by a contorted interpretation of "winning out": A small state now "wins out" by "getting what it wants," and this turns out to be annexation by its larger neighbors! Note also the way that the meaning of *ta*/great changes. In {1} it means "great in stature," in {3–6} it means "large in size." Perhaps {5} was added as propaganda defending the ambitions of some large state to take over its smaller neighbors.

57[68]

The best soldier is not warlike   {1}
the best fighter shows no anger
the one best at defeating the enemy does not engage him
the one best at managing people puts himself below them.

This is the Te of not contending   {2}
this is the power to manage people.
This is being the Counterpart of Heaven
equalling the very best of the ancients.

Managers should take a lesson from the soldier: The good soldier puts aside his personal stake in the fighting, doesn't get angry or go looking for a fight. She does only what she has to do {1}. The best supervisor has no stake in being boss, but treats her people as though she is there to serve them. The workers feel it {2}.

Saying {1:1-3} counters excessively aggressive tendencies among solders, posing the opposite image of one who is more effective because his judgment and actions are not distorted by anger, and he is willing to use indirect tactics (the point of the exaggerated image in {1:3}; compare 58[73]:1, 68[69]:1-2).

The composer uses the saying about soldiering to present a model for being a good *supervisor,* the ambition of many *shih**. The association is aided by the connotations of *cheng*/contend*:quarrel, which can refer to both physical fighting and the social struggle for status. The ideal supervisor is not "contentious" in his desire to establish himself as the boss {2:1}, but is able to treat those under him as though he were their social inferior {1:4}, someone "lower*" than they. "Te*" here has the meaning of subtle influence and power, emanating from the supervisor's "noncontentious" spirit. Such a one, even if he is only a minor administrator, achieves the *spiritual* status of the idealized ancient* Emperors*, the "Counterparts of Heaven*" in ruling the world {2:3-4}.

58[73]

"One who shows bravery by being daring will get killed   {1}
one who shows bravery by not being daring will survive."

But in both these cases: {2}
"Sometimes it helps, sometimes it harms."

"What Heaven picks to hate—who knows the reason?"   {3}

And so the Wise Person: {4}
Treats things as difficult.

Heaven's Way: {5}
Not contending, but excels at overcoming
not speaking, but excels in getting answers
not summoning, but people come of themselves
lax, but excels at organization.

Heaven's net is very wide—   {6}
loosely woven,
but it lets nothing slip by.

Some rulers are at the people all the time, watching every move, summoning them, demanding answers—as though at war with the people {5}. But this isn't the way the world works. Consider fate. It appears unpredictable—now taking a life, now sparing a life {1-3}; but in the end, justice prevails. The best ruler is like that, appearing easy, planning and managing things quietly, so order is maintained but she never has to play the policeman {5-6}.

Saying {1} speaks against aggressive soldiering, posing the opposite image of a brave but smarter soldier. Sayings {2:2} and {3} look like common proverbs about our inability to predict what brings good or bad fortune. (Saying {3} invokes an idea common in ancient China that bad fortune is a sign of Heaven's* hatred toward someone.) Saying {4} is a fragment of the saying found in 71[63]:7, advising caution rather than carelessly making light of things. Saying {5:2-4} counters the ideal of the strict* and aggressive ruler, posing exaggerated images of the opposing ideal: The low-key ruler who elicits cooperation and overcomes opposition by indirect means and the subtle power of his Te*.

The composer takes {1} not as an aphorism*, but a literal prediction of who will survive and who will die. He uses this as a take-off* point for criticism of confidence in predictability, expressed in the sayings about uncertainty in {2} and {3} (compare 59[58]:2, 62[29]:3, and comments on "Understanding*"). Saying {4} counters confidence in simplistic predictive laws, advising that one treat the course of events as difficult to understand*. Saying {6} and the composer's addition in {5:5} interpret the unpredictability of "Heaven" {1-3} as apparent laxity in enforcing justice, a laxity that is *only* apparent, however: In the long run no one gets away with anything. (I mark {5:5} a connective* addition because it interrupts the parallelism of the previous lines and leads into the image of {6}.) The chapter thus outlines a "Way of Heaven" that is a model for the ideal ruler, who will often *appear* easy and "lax," rather than a strict policeman. But this is because of his subtle *style* of ruling, flowing from the state of mind and attitude he cultivates, a style that ultimately has the effect of enforcing justice. This chapter makes it clear that the policy of being "low and easy" advocated in 56[61], and the "nonintervention" some other chapters might appear to recommend, are not to be taken literally as a description of the ultimate *goal and effect* of the ideal Laoist ruling style, which still aims at enforcing justice.

59[58]

When the ruler is dull and incompetent,   {1}
the people are pure and simple.
When the ruler is sharp and alert,
the people are a bad lot.

"Bad luck: good luck depends on it   {2}
good luck: bad luck hides in it."
Who knows where this ends?
There is no norm.
What accords with the norm turns around and becomes weird
what is excellent turns around and becomes ominous.

"People's blindness—   {3}
it has been going on so long now."

And so the Wise Person: {4}
Is square and honest but does not cut
is pointed and exact but does not hurt
is straight and direct but not tactless
shines but does not dazzle.

Some rulers think they know exactly what's right and what's wrong, which plans will succeed and which will come to ruin {2}. They keep a sharp and constant watch {1}, judging everyone and everything by their sure knowledge. They try to dazzle their people {4} with the inspiring high standards of their government, but their self-assurance makes them abrasive {4}. This is a very old kind of blindness {3}. Better is the ruler who remains always aware of uncertainty and who emphasizes tact, managing to uphold high standards without hurting anyone's feelings {4}. She accepts the risk of appearing dull and incompetent {1}—this is so much better than a "dazzling" ruler who constantly makes the people feel lacking.

Sayings {1} and {4:2–4} counter the ideal of the strict* ruler. The image of the "dull and incompetent" ruler in {1} (Karlgren's translation) is an exaggerated self-caricature emphasizing the opposite Laoist ideal—a ruler who actually stands for high standards, but who is not dramatic and confrontational about this and so sometimes appears not to know what is going on. The "sharp" ruler provokes a rebellious attitude in his people, whereas the "dull" Laoist ruler fosters organic* social harmony. Saying {4:2–4} poses the image of the person whose interactions manage to combine honesty and uprightness with tact, so as not to hurt* anyone. (It uses metaphors taken from measurements in carpentry: The word for "square" also means "honest," the word for "right-angled" also means "scrupulous, exacting," etc.) Saying {2:1–2} looks like a folk proverb emphasizing uncertainty, countering the human tendency to construe one piece of apparent good or bad luck as a "trend" (see comments on "Understanding*"). The saying that follows in {3} deplores this tendency as a manifestation of all-to-common ignorance (compare 13[20]:3:2).

The composer adds {2:3–6} emphasizing our inability to know easily and name* correctly what is lucky or unlucky, good or bad. Such knowledge would give a person in authority a good basis for taking an uncompromising moral stance toward his subjects, hence the connection to the criticism in {1} and {3}. (Compare similar implied associations in 58[73] and 62[29].) *Dazzle* in the final line refers to the striking moral impressiveness* some rulers strive for, contrasted with the subtle shining of the tactful Laoist.

This chapter belongs to a group of three chapters (58[73], 59[58], 60[49]) criticizing the ideal of the strict* ruler.

60[49]

The Wise Person is always a man without a mind— {1}
he takes the mind of the hundred clans as his mind.

Those who are good, I am good to them {2}
those who are not good, I am also good to them—
Te is good.

Those who are honest, I am honest with them
those who are not honest, I am also honest with them—
Te is honest.

The Wise Person {3}
lives in the world all drawn in
for the world's sake he keeps his mind muddled.

The hundred clans {4}
all strain their eyes and ears toward him.
The Wise Person treats them all as his children.

Some officials have a very set mind regarding good and bad {1}. They find it easy to recognize which people they meet are insincere and no good—and they know that such people should be dealt with in kind {2}. This attitude is hurtful. The best official is like someone who has no mind of her own. She takes the mind of the people as a guide to policy {1}. In her respect for the people she shows unwavering goodness to all, good and bad alike {2}, like a loving parent {4}. She does not inhabit the world like something with bristles all extended, constantly waiting to puncture those doing wrong in her eyes. Rather she appears drawn in, "muddle minded" some might say—all so she will not hurt the people {3}.

Saying {1} counters the ideal of the strict* ruler who thinks it is *his* role to represent high mindedness in contrast to the people who are lacking in this. It poses instead an exaggerated counterimage of a man with no mind of his own at all. The ideal he holds up for the society does not *confront* them as something coming from outside. It is nothing but an idealized version of the organic* goodness already inherent in the society ("the hundred clans"). Saying {2} counters the tendency to respond to others in kind, giving a normative* description of the way one acts who has Te*. Laoist Te expresses itself in a selfless generosity to all, regardless of their deserts. (A similar quality is ascribed to Te in 9[79] and 71[63]:3).

"Keeps his mind muddled" in {3} is an exaggerated image of the ruler who keeps his mind free of sharply defined moral standards to impose on his people. (This would "hurt*" them [see 81[37]:2:6], hence the statement that he does this "for the world's [society's] sake.") He also presents the appearance of someone "drawn in," rather than aggressive (compare 6[15]:2). ("Muddled" and "drawn in" follow Karlgren's understanding of the Chinese words involved.) In {4} I take "strain their eyes...toward him" to mean that people look to him for moral guidance, and "treats them all as children" to signify a protective attitude. The Chinese phrase could mean instead that he "acts like a child."

61[54]

Excellently founded: it will not be uprooted   {1}
Excellently embraced and cared for: it will not slip away
so sons and grandsons
    will never cease to offer the sacrifices.

Cultivate It in your person, its Te will be pure   {2}
cultivate It in the clan, its Te will be abundant
cultivate It in the village, its Te will be lasting
cultivate It in the state, its Te will be ample
cultivate It in the empire, its Te will be all-embracing.

Yes: {3}
Judge a person taking that person as the measure
judge a clan taking that clan as the measure
judge a village taking that village as the measure
judge a state taking that state as the measure
judge the world taking the world as the measure.

How do I know the nature of the world?   {4}
By this.

Like individuals, groups and societies also have a spirit that needs cultivation {2}. Some great families last and last because they are founded on a solid spirit {1}. How do you know what to cultivate? Pay attention to that inner something which is this group at its best—it differs from group to group, and it cannot be known by any grand plan {3}. How do you come to know it? Cultivate the right state of mind, and look {4}.

Large family clans were an important element in ancient Chinese society, and {1} is about building up and maintaining the greatness of the clan to which one belongs.[1] The enduring greatness of a clan is made manifest here in the fact that clan descendants continue to offer sacrifices to clan ancestors for generation after generation. If this is a Laoist saying, *shan*/Excellently* refers to cultivating clan greatness according to Laoist ideals, and the saying celebrates the wonderful benefits* of this. Saying {2} also celebrates the benefits* of cultivating this spirit (here called simply *It*) at all levels of society. (Te* here probably refers to the character of the social unit as it makes itself felt in its reputation.[2]) Saying {3} reads, literally, "By person examine person, by clan examine clan, etc." My conjecture is that the target of the saying is the tendency to judge smaller social units in the light of larger ones, all according to some normative scheme. Against this, the saying advocates understanding* and judging each individual unit on its own, and furthermore viewing each in its uniqueness ("measured by itself"), rather than according to some single norm applied to all. This understanding makes it easy to connect this saying with {4}, which employs a recurrent Laoist formula found also in 38[21]:4 and 77[57]:2. I think it is a stock answer to questions by opponents about the source of Laoist views, by appealing to immediate experiential intuition ("this*"), in the proper state of mind. The connection then would be that {3} also recommends evaluating a person just by one's direct experience of that person, without reference to other, external criteria. The ultimate point is similar to that in 60[49]:1, that norms should be derived from characteristics already in some sense inherent in social units, rather than from some scheme external to them.

This chapter belongs to a group of six (58[73], 59[58], 60[49], 61[54], 62[29], 63[32]) sharing a common opposition to the ruler who wants to base his policies on sure conceptual knowledge of norms and general laws governing social life.

---

1. Compare *Mencius** 1B/14,3.
2. As in ibid. 2B/2,9.

62[29]

When someone wants to take over the world	{1}
and do some work on it,	
I can see he won't be able.	
The world is a spirit-thing, it can't be 'worked' on.	

One who works ruins   {2}
one who grasps loses.

Yes, things: {3}
Sometimes they will go ahead, sometimes follow after
sometimes they will be snorting wildly
       sometimes breathing easily
sometimes they will be strong, sometimes weak
sometimes they will break, sometimes destroy.

And so the Wise Person: {4}
Avoids excess, avoids extravagance, avoids being grandiose.

Some people have grand plans for reforming the world. They possess the key to how the world really works, and they think "If only I were completely in charge." But the social world is always beyond our grasp and control, a sacred thing {1} with an unpredictable mind of its own {3}. People with the ambition to "work it over" stand out as grossly superfluous on the face of the world {4}. Wherever they go they ruin the irreplaceable goodness of the given {2}.

Saying {1} counters the ambition of some Warring States thinkers and rulers to get control of the entire Chinese Empire ("the world") and make it over according to some grand design. The term *shen-ch'i*/"spirit thing" probably means to evoke not only awe for something sacred, but the common ancient Chinese fear of spirits—the "superstitious*" feeling that offending them could easily bring retaliation or bad luck. (*Shen-ch'i* could also mean "spirit vessel," a sacred vessel used in religious ceremony.) The phrase conveys a Laoist feeling for the world that underlies their polemic against "working*": The "worker" typically thinks his own plans and efforts are all important, considering what he is working on as mere raw material. By contrast, Laoists emphasize reverence and respect for the givenness of things. Saying {2} (= 72[64]:4) criticizes the attitude of those who want to control things by their own efforts, suggesting that what is most valuable about things cannot be possessed by direct grasping and typically is ruined by attempts to work* on or "improve*" on them. Saying {3} counters the confidence in our ability to predict and control things in the world, posing as a counterimage the unpredictable behavior of barnyard animals (indicated by "snorting," etc.) Saying {4} is probably related to those criticizing self-promotion* as "excessive" (see 1[24] and 2[9]).

As in 58[73] and 59[58], the composer here associates emphasis on uncertainty {3} with criticism of ruling with a strong hand {1-2}. That is, this attitude on the part of a ruler typically results from self-assurance that he understands* things perfectly—a "grandiose" attitude. The emphasis on the unpredictability of events in the world is part of the Laoist insistence that the world always eludes our conceptual ("naming*") grasp. One who realizes this will not be so confident that implementing his reforming plans will actually be successful and beneficial.

63[32]

Tao will always be nameless, an Uncarved Block   {1}
although it is a thing of no account,
no one in the world can make it his subject.

If the princes and kings could watch over It,   {2}
the thousands of things
    would on their own be as deferential as guests.
Heaven and Earth would join together to send sweet dew.
The people on their own would share equally
    without anyone giving orders.

When you begin making decisions and cutting it up,   {3}
rules and names appear.
And once names appear, you should know to stop.
Knowing to stop, you can be without fear.

A comparison: {4}
Tao's presence in the world
    is like the relation of small river valleys
    to the Yang-tze and the ocean.

What is the Center of the World—the supreme thing which everything naturally wants to obey, the thing toward which all things naturally flow {4}, the thing that brings spontaneous peace to the world {2}? It is something that by its nature will always appear small, of no account in the world {1}. If those at the top could only cultivate and maintain it in themselves, what a world this could be. But what do they do instead? They feel it is too intangible. The Norm needs to be named. They chop up this simple and natural thing into a thousand pieces, relying on a thousand laws to keep people in line {3}. They've lost it.

Saying {1} celebrates* the Tao* Laoists cultivate, something of great power and importance although it appears insignificant in the conventional world. Saying {2} celebrates the marvelous benefits* brought to a society by a ruler who "watches* over" Tao and lets it animate his government. Saying {3:4} uses an oracle* formula to advocate "knowing to stop." This phrase occurs in a similar context in the *Nei* Yeh,*[1] "Life then thought, thought then knowledge, knowledge then stop." On the basis of this, and the occurrence of this saying in 19[44]:4, I believe this phrase has a meaning similar to "turn* back." It is based on the image of an "original" Still* state of mind that can become stirred up into various kinds of outward-looking mental "activity," like conceptual ("naming*") thought or desire for fame or possessions (as in 19[44]:1–2). When one becomes aware of such negative mental "activity," one should "know to stop" it. Saying {4} uses the same metaphorical* image as 55[66]:1 to represent the natural gravitation of everyone toward the "low*" Tao.

"Cutting up" in {3:1–2} refers to the Uncarved* Block of {1} and is directed against other contemporary *shih** schools that advocated explicit formulation of moral and legal norms (see "Naming*"). *Chi*/"cut up" also means "govern": Explicit legal naming and "decisions" deprive the ruler of real authority by making destructive "incisions" in the real Norm of the World, the Tao as Uncarved Block. When instead the ruler governs by the spirit of the insignificant/ low/uncarved Tao, it exerts a subtle but powerful influence that attracts the allegiance of all {4} and produces social harmony and prosperity {2}. See 17[28]:2, where the Uncarved Block refers to one's person as a whole, before it is "cut up" into good and bad qualities. (These are the same: For Laoists, Tao functions as a Norm through its existence in the person of the ideal ruler.)

---

1. Rickett 1965: 160–161 D. My (more literal) translation.

64[34]

Great Tao drifts—it can go right or go left.   {1}

The thousands of things depend on it for life,   {2}
it rejects nothing.

It achieves successes,   {3}
        but does not hold tight to the fame.
It clothes and feeds the thousands of things
but does not act the ruler.

Always: {4}
Desiring nothing, it can be called 'of no account.'
The thousands of things turn back to it
        but it does not act the ruler—
it can be called 'Great.'

Because in the end   {5}
it does not insist on its own greatness,
yes, it is able to achieve its full greatness.

The spirit that rules the world is like the spirit that animates the best ruler: All-accepting, infinitely flexible {1–2}. Everything depends on its loving care, everything obeys—yet it acts like the lowest person, daring to desire nothing for itself or impose its will {3–4}. Is this not its greatness {5}?

Saying {1} counters the ideal of the strict* ruler with a normative* description of the flexible Tao* that informs the actions of the ideal ruler, adhering to no fixed rules (see 56[61]:1, 60[49]:1), but able to bring out the best in every new and different circumstance, "rejecting nothing" {2}. Sayings {3:1} and {5} (= 71[63]:5) speak against self-promotion*.

The composer's additions in {2}, {3:3–4}, and {4} take the ideals expressed in these sayings, originally ideals for the human ruler, and project them onto Tao as cosmic ruler—which in turn is a model for the earthly ruler. As in 65[51], the net effect is to express the ultimate, "cosmic*" character of Tao as the norm for a government. These additions are a pastiche of motifs and phrases found elsewhere in Laoist sayings. (For "rejecting nothing" in {2} see 42[2]:4; for hsiao/"small:of no account" in {4} see 63[32]:1; for "not acting the ruler" in {3} and {4} see 27[10]:2; for "not desiring*" in {4} see 72[64]:7, 77[57]:5; for "turning* back" to Tao in {4} see 28[16]:2.) Note the association of "not desiring" with hsiao/"of no account" in {4}. Hsiao means "small," but also refers to a socially "insignificant" person. The underlying (conventional) assumption here seems to be then that "great" people can legitimately impose their desires on the society—Tao's lack of such desires is a sign of its smallness/insignificance.

This and the next chapter share the theme of Tao as cosmic ruler. Chapter 63[32] is related to this, picturing the cosmic importance of the Tao that is an hypostatization* of the spirit animating the government of an ideal human ruler. As in the case of the final chapters of Sections 1 and 3, placing these "cosmic" chapters last in this section reflects my view that they are "climaxes" of Laoist thought on this topic, rather than "foundations" (see comments on 39[25]).

65[51]

Tao produces them   {1}
Te rears them
events shape them
talents complete their development.

And so: {2}
Among the thousands of things
      there are none that do not honor Tao and treasure Te.
This honoring Tao and treasuring Te—
no one commands it, it always happens naturally.

Tao produces them,   {3}
Te rears them
makes them grow, nurses them,
settles them, heals them,
sustains them, protects them.

Produces but does not possess   {4}
works but does not rely on this
presides but doesn't rule.
This is mysterious Te.

The ruler who cultivates Tao and Te participates in the force that rules the universe. It is a generating, sustaining, selflessly giving force—which also animates her government. It is the secret spontaneous desire and treasure of all the world.

Sayings {1} and {3} are origin* sayings, celebrating the foundational importance of Tao* and Te* by picturing them as the cosmic source and ideal cosmic ruler. The qualities of Te as a cosmic ruler in {3} are a projection of paternalistic Chinese notions about the role of the ruler as loving parent. Saying {4} (= 27[10]:2) speaks against self-promotion*, picturing the way Laoist Te expresses itself in a self-effacing attitude toward one's political accomplishments. Saying {2:2} celebrates the cosmic* importance of Tao as that which everything spontaneously treasures (compare 48[62]:7).

Several Laoist feelings and assumptions are merged here. Tao is that good toward which everything "naturally*" gravitates {2}. Hence, on the Chinese assumption that people "naturally" give their allegiance to someone who truly merits being ruler, Tao is something easily imagined as the "ruler" of the world. But Tao is also the name of the spirit that animates the ideal human ruler, who is caring {3} and self-effacing {4}, and who does not try to force allegiance {2}. Tao/Te as world ruler, "setting the tone" for the world as perceived by Laoists, must have this same character.

6

The Soft Way

66[74]

"The people are always lacking in the fear of death."   {1}
Then why frighten them with death?

Supposing the people always had the fear of death,   {2}
and we could catch law breakers and kill them—
who would dare?
There is always The Executioner—he does the killing.
Doing the killing in The Executioner's place,
this is like
"doing the cutting in the master carpenter's place."
One who cuts in the master carpenter's place—
seldom it is he does not cut his hand.

Some rulers complain, "My people are reckless, not even afraid of death. I can do nothing with them." And what solution do they reach for? Executions, to scare these fearless people into line by threatening them with death! {1} They don't realize the death of a person is very serious. Taking it on oneself to kill is assuming a position above anyone's reach. It will come back on the person who does it {2}.

I believe {1:1} quotes a common complaint on the part of rulers (quoted also in 51[75]:1, see comments there), used as a take-off* point for comments by the composer. "The Executioner" {2:4} is probably either a personification of Death or a reference to the deity Heaven*. This chapter reflects the quasi-superstitious* side of Laoist thought, the sense that the ruler who becomes self-important and high-handed enough to presume to take lives is showing hubris, and this will somehow come back on him. He is letting his position as ruler go to his head and not showing enough respect for the givenness of the social world in his charge, a "spirit thing" (62[29]:1) he must stand in awe of. This quasi-superstitious feeling is especially evident in Laoist thought about violence.

Section 6 begins with four chapters (66[74], 67[31], 68[69], 69[30]) expressing Laoist views on capital punishment and war. Their negative view of violent confrontation is related to their positive ideal of the "Soft," delicate, and nonconfrontational style they think ought to guide all a ruler's actions and policies. This positive ideal is the subject of the remainder of the chapters in this section, after these first four.

67[31]

'Fine weapons' are ill-omened instruments. {1}

Things seem to detest them {2}
so the ambitious man does not dwell here.

"The gentleman at home favors the left {3}
when at war he favors the right."

Weapons are ill-omened instruments {4}
not instruments for the gentleman
he uses them when he has no choice.

What is calm and quiet is highest. {5}

When victorious, he does not think this a fine thing {6}
because to think it fine is to delight in slaughtering people.
One who delights in slaughtering people
    cannot achieve his purposes in the world.

"In fortunate times, prefer the left {7}
in *mourning,* prefer the right."
The lower officer takes his stand on the left
the higher officer takes his stand on the right.
This says: He takes his stand as at a mourning ceremony.

At the slaughter of such masses of men, {8}
    he weeps for them, mourning and lamenting.
When victorious in the battle—
he takes his stand as at a mourning ceremony.

Some glory in their fine weapons {1} and look for the day when they can show their strength in glorious battle. But what is this? It is delight in slaughtering people {6}. There sometimes comes a day when battle cannot be avoided, but the superior person looks on this as the most unfortunate of days {1,3,4}. In the attack, tradition assigns the right flank of the army to the superior officer. Why? Because this is also the place assigned when one is in mourning {7–8}.

Saying {1} counters the admiration of "fine weapons" by casting them as "unlucky." Saying {2} (= 1[24]:4) is a quasi-superstitious* Laoist saying that can apply to many ways in which people put themselves at odds with reality ("things*"). Saying {6} counters the admiration of war, again on a quasi-superstitious* basis. I think {3} and {7:1–2} are common sayings reflecting customs as to how gentlemen of the nobility should place themselves differently at gatherings during peacetime and wartime, normal times and mourning times.

The composer's main point is given in {7:5}: He reinterprets the traditional custom of placing the highest officer on the right in battle ({7:4}), to mean that the superior man should look upon battle, even victory in battle, in an attitude of mourning (compare 68[69]:4). He makes this point by conflating and reinterpreting three different customs, related to differences in peacetime and wartime etiquette {3}, to battlefield positions {7:3–4}, and to mourning {7:2, 8:4}. (He is probably reading new meanings into old customs here. Saying 75[78]:4 also reads a new "hidden" meaning into ancient custom, and this practice is reflected in the Confucian *Doctrine of the Mean*[1] as well.)

The arrangement of the sayings here leads many commentators to suspect textual corruption of some kind. I think it shows many techniques used by the composers elsewhere: The composer here frames* his material, by placing {3} at the beginning and picking it up again in {7}. (Compare the placing of 50[53]:2, picked up in 50[53]:6). He also makes use of many catchwords to connect the different sayings: Section {4} repeats {1} and *gentleman* from {3}, thus connecting {1} and {3}. The contrast in {7:1–2} probably was originally "good fortune/ill fortune"—the composer has changed "ill fortune" to "mourning," as a connective* alteration linking this saying to {7:5} and {8} (see "Additional Textual Notes"). Section {8} picks up *slaughter* and *victorious* from {6}. I think the repetitions in this chapter express a sense of pathos.

*Shih** sometimes served as soldiers or military officers. This chapter and the following two seem partly addressed to *shih* considering this possibility.

---

1. 19/6.

68[69]

Military men have a saying: {1}
"I do not presume to act as master, I act as guest
I do not presume to advance an inch, I retreat a foot."

This is like   {2}
"going forward without going forward
rolling up the sleeves but baring no arm
attacking without showing hostility
drawing with no sword."

Nothing brings greater disaster than the motto: {3}
"The enemy is nothing."
Thinking, "the enemy is nothing":
close to losing my Treasure.

Yes, when they cross weapons and attack each other   {4}
the one in mourning will win.

Some soldiers take every occasion to show off how strong and fearless they are, charging the enemy recklessly at the drop of a hat. But there is a better way: Playing the submissive one {1}. Advancing in such a way that they will think you are retreating. Attacking them in such a way they will not even know they have an opponent {2}. The "fearless" soldier likes to attack with the attitude, "The enemy is a nothing!" With such bloated self-importance one loses the essential thing one should never lose {3}. The best soldier is not the one who treats the enemy as nothing, but who respects life and goes into battle reluctantly and with great sadness {4}.

Saying {4} counters the attitude of glorying in war, posing the contrasting ideal of the one whose great respect for human life makes him approach battle in mourning (compare 67[31]:7–8).

I think {1} and {2} are sayings borrowed from contemporary military strategists, which recommend very indirect and deceptive tactics as the way to succeed. I take it that the images in these sayings describe how one's actions appear to the opponent; for example, "drawing with no sword" describes in concrete and highly exaggerated terms the deceptive and confusing appearance of the general strategy involved. "Motto" in {3:1} is not in the text. I add it because I take *wu ti*/"there is no enemy" in {3} as a motto, meant to convey complete lack of fear of the enemy. (Compare Mencius's description[1] of the bravado of the *shih** Po-kung Yu.) The interest of the composer is not so much in military success through deceptive strategy as in the connection between fighting style and *attitude:* Some soldiers take fighting as a chance to prove their own personal superiority. (They want to act the "master" rather than the deferential "guest.") This kind of soldier will prefer direct and dramatic confrontations, allowing him to show off his strength and courage. He will also take the attitude expressed in the motto "[For me] the enemy is nothing." Taking this attitude means that the person has lost what Laoists consider to be the essential "Treasure" {3:4}: the respect for others and the *non*-self-assertive spirit they cultivate. (Compare the three non-assertive virtues praised in 3[67]:2, which are also called there *my three treasures.*) The person who maintains this spirit will also be one who approaches war in the attitude of mourning {4}.

---

1. 2A/2,4.

69[30]

One who assists the people's rulers with Tao   {1}
does not use weapons to force changes in the world.

"Such action usually backfires."   {2}

Where troops camp, thorns and brambles grow.   {3}

Excellence consists in: {4}
Being resolute, that is all
    not venturing to take control by force
being resolute, but not boastful
being resolute, but not overbearing
being resolute, but not arrogant
being resolute, when you have no choice
being resolute, but not forcing.

Things are vigorous, then grow old and weak: {5}
A case of 'not-Tao.'
Not-Tao, soon gone.

Some high counselors urge rulers to take over the world by force of arms—and they themselves lead troops into battle {1}. But violent armies are a blot on the face of the world: Brambles grow where they camp {3}. Forced success is always short lived {5}, and violence always comes back to visit the violent {2}. This is not the right Way. The excellent counselor must put aside masculine pride and boasting, and simply stand steadfast, doing battle when circumstances leave no choice {4}.

Saying {1} is a normative* description of what one does who has Tao. It counters the readiness of some *shih**-advisers ("assisting rulers with Tao") to advocate war or lead armies themselves, as a means of gaining political objectives. (Mencius[1] also criticizes such *shih*.) *Ch'iang*/forcing* is often a negative term in the Laoist vocabulary. It is one of the words elsewhere translated as "hard," the opposite of Laoist *jou-jo*/Softness*-Weakness. Saying {2} looks like a common saying that might apply to many things. Saying {3} probably has a quasi-superstitious* basis: Brambles growing where troops camp is an image of the "unlucky" character of war. Saying {4} is related to sayings against boastful self-promotion*, countering the boasting/forcing* attitude of those who glory in war as an occasion for proving personal prowess, posing instead the ideal attitude of the soldier who is just resolute, fighting only when he must. In {5} the seasonal flourishing and dying of vegetation serves as a negative metaphorical* image of the short-lived nature of human actions that are "forced*." (Originally this saying was probably related more to sayings against "exhausting" excitement and agitation*. But it occurs following a criticism of forcing also in 33[55]:5.)

The composer's point lies in the association between (a) "boastful" self-assertion {4}, (b) a "forcing*" attitude expressed in the readiness to resort to violence {1}, and (c) the idea that such forcing can have no lasting* good results {2-3, 5}. On the connection between (a) and (b), compare the associations linking 71[63]:5 with the rest of 71[63]. Underlying (c) is an insistence that human action should be integrated into reality as given. Violence is the extreme case of something extraneous imposed on given reality from without. (Because {4:3} interrupts the parallelism and duplicates {4:8}, I believe it is a connective* addition. The catchword *forcing* connects {4} to {1}.)

---

1. 7B/4,1.

70[60]

Governing a large state is like cooking a small fish. {1}

Rule the world by Tao {2}
then ghosts will not take to haunting.

It is not that the ghosts will not haunt {3}
their haunting will cause no hurt to humankind.
(It's not only that their haunting will not hurt humankind,
the Wise Person also does not cause hurt to them.
These two do not hurt each other.)

Yes, Te unifies and restores. {4}

Some rulers think that a large state can endure rough handling. But no matter how large, a society is a delicate thing, requiring a soft touch {1}. Heavy-handed intrusion can throw everything out of balance, stirring up even the ghosts of the dead to roam around doing mischief {2–3}. To avoid hurt of any kind, what is needed is rule by subtle Tao, and by the gentle Te that unites and restores everything in the world to its natural harmony {4}.

Saying {1} counters the tendency of rulers toward heavy-handed intrusion, calling to mind instead the delicacy needed to cook a small fish as the appropriate attitude (compare 71[63]). Saying {2} celebrates the benefits* of ruling by Tao. It has a quasi-superstitious* basis: Ancient Chinese believed in ghosts of the dead who if provoked might use their supernatural power to hurt people. There was also a belief, apparently shared by Laoists, that the ruler has a powerful but invisible effect on the structure and dynamics of all parts of the world: If he rules wrongly, it can throw everything out of kilter—society, nature, and ghosts. Ruling by the subtle spirit of Tao, the ruler blends in with the organic harmony of society and causes no disturbance in the order of things. Saying {3} celebrates the powers and benefits* of Te*.

Section {3} is difficult to make sense of. I tentatively take {3:4–5} to mean that the ruler does not "hurt" the ghosts by his bad rule, and so they don't hurt him either (personally? by hurting his people?). Note the composer's implied equivalence between (a) ruling delicately {1}, (b) ruling by Tao {2}, and (c) ruling by Te {3}.

For the effect of the ruler's conduct on the world in general, see the mention of "phantom women coming out after dark" in the quotation cited under "Superstitious*," and also the *Chuang Tzu*'s description of a good king's reign, "gods and ghosts did no harm, the four seasons were perfectly proportioned...all that lived escaped an untimely death."[1] The king's effect on nature is also vividly dramatized in the *Yüeh Ling* section of the *Li Chi*,[2] which prescribes that, on the day beginning each season, the king should enter a certain palace with specially arranged rooms. He should ritually enter the proper room, wear certain clothes, and eat certain foods appropriate to the season just beginning. Doing the wrong thing will throw the seasons out of kilter; for example, if he eats "winter food" in summer, he might cause summer snowstorms.

This chapter begins a series of four chapters (70[60], 71[63], 72[64], 73[36]) dealing with the Soft*—delicate, careful, subtle, non-confrontational—style of ruling that Laoists advocate.

1. Quoted in Graham 1989: 305.
2. Legge 1885: 249–310.

71[63]

Be a Non Doer   {1}
work at Not Working
acquire a taste for that which has no taste.

Treat small things as though they were great   {2}
treat few things as though they were many.

"Reward what is injurious, with kind Te."   {3}

Plan difficult things focusing on the easy parts   {4}
do great things focusing on the small details.
Difficult tasks in the world always begin from what is easy
great tasks in the world always begin from what is small.

And so the Wise Person: {5}
Does not 'do great things'
and so is able to fulfill his greatness.

Yes: {6}
Light agreement is never very trustworthy
considering everything easy makes everything difficult.

And so the Wise Person: {7}
Treats things as difficult,
and in the end has no difficulty.

People full of themselves are always anxious to "do great things" {5}. They think only the great and difficult result is worthy of them; they are too important to be bothered with the "easy" details. What difficulties they will have {6}! The smart person is not full of herself, as a great "doer" {1}. She submits herself to the task, developing a subtle appreciation for the importance of what seems barely noticeable to others {1}. She begins with the most insignificant details and approaches these with the care one gives to what is most difficult {2, 4}. She treats everything as almost beyond her and in the end brings everything under control {7}.

Saying {1} is instruction* in Laoist self-cultivation. Note the connection between "not doing*" and developing an extremely subtle sensitivity—opposite the "doer," who is typically preoccupied with putting his stamp on reality, rather than sensitive to the subtle particularities of always-new situations. Sayings {2}, {6}, and {7} speak against underestimating the difficulty of tasks, and hence being careless. "Treat things as difficult" means dealing with them carefully (see also 58[73]:4). Saying {4:1–2} counters the tendency to focus attention on the great results one hopes to attain, neglecting attention to the small tasks necessary to get there (compare 72[64]:3). Saying {3} is a common saying, quoted also in the Confucian *Analects*.[1] (See the similar association with Te* in 9[79] and 60[49]:2.) In {5} I take *wei ta*/"do great things" to suggest a person attracted to impressive projects as a means of self-promotion*. The saying poses instead the ideal of a self-completion associated with a self-effacing attitude. (Saying {5} is a version of 64[34]:5.)

By placing {5} with the other sayings here, the composer suggests that the person who wants to focus only on "great" things, neglecting small beginnings, does so because of his own sense of self-importance. Like 72[64], this chapter is important in showing the particular, nonliteral meaning of *not doing*. *Doing* here means doing something obviously *significant*, something that stands out as great over against the ordinary routine of things, allowing the doer also to stand out. Conversely, *not doing* describes the attitude and style of one who can take his eyes off of the outstanding results that will bring him personal glory and submit himself entirely to the practical demands of the task, including especially subtle sensitivity {1} and painstaking attention to its most insignificant details. (Compare the idealization of the person willing to take on his state's "dirty work" in 75[78]:4.)

---

1. 14/36.

72[64]

When sitting still, they are easy to hold down   {1}
no omens yet, it is easy to plan
when fragile, they are easy to break
when small, they are easy to scatter.

Work on it when it isn't yet   {2}
put it in order when it is not yet disordered.

A tree you can barely get your arms around,   {3}
    grows from a tiny shoot
a nine-story tower begins as a heap of earth
a thousand-mile journey begins under your feet.

Working ruins, grasping loses.   {4}

And so the Wise Person: {5}
Does not work, so does not ruin
does not grasp, so does not lose.

"When the people are engaged in some task,   {6}
they are always on the point of finishing when they ruin it."
Careful at the end just as at the beginning
then there will be no ruining of the work.

And so the Wise Person: {7}
Desires to be desireless
does not prize goods hard to come by
learns to be un-Learned
turns back to the place all others have gone on from.

So as to help along the naturalness   {8}
    of the thousands of things
without presuming to be a Worker.

A natural state of society is not achieved easily. People start being disruptive, things start going in the wrong direction, and soon the organic harmony of the world is gone. Something must be done. And yet "working ruins"—the solution can be as disruptive as the problem {4–5}. The answer is this: Pay careful attention all the time, as though you were always at the beginning of something {6}. Catch problems in their smallest beginnings. Head off the difficulty before anything seems really to have gone wrong {1–3}. Then you will never have to be disruptive yourself. Acting in this way requires a certain state of mind: A constant returning to that deep state before desires have arisen, before the mind has become "Learned"—the place everyone else has long since run away from {7}.

Note that (like 73[36]:1) {1} and {2} assume it sometimes is necessary to take strongly intrusive measures against movements in the society that the ruler judges to be harmful. Saying {3} (like 71[63]:4) counters the tendency to focus on great goals, neglecting the necessary small beginnings. Saying {6} looks like a common complaint among managers about the way workers become careless toward the end of a job. Saying {4} is the same as 62[29]:2. Saying {5} celebrates the benefits* of operating with a "not working*" attitude. Saying {7} gives instruction* in Laoist self-cultivation. The "place all others have gone on from" is the Still* state of mind before it has been stirred up by desires* and become active in conceptual Learning* (see also comments on "Dwelling*").

"Working" in this chapter describes the *attitude* of one who sees things in terms of "my important work" versus inert things to be worked on. Having no respect for things to be worked on, such a person will tend to be inattentive to the subtleties of the issues he is dealing with. "Not working" by contrast, describes not literal nonintervention, but the attitude of one strenuously attentive to the smallest details, able to nip things in the bud and so avoid the kind of *overt and dramatically disruptive intervention* necessary when things have gotten very out of hand. This kind of intervention will ruin the *tzujan*/naturalness* {8} of the social world, the organic* harmony deeply rooted in the given state of affairs. This "natural" organic harmony is an *ideal* state of things brought about by the extremely careful work of a "not working" ruler. Saying {7} implies that this acute sensitivity and subtle style of intervention is possible only to one who has "turned* back" to a deeper state which the conventional mind tries always to get away from.

73[36]

When you want to shrink something   {1}
    you must always enlarge it.
When you want to weaken something
    you must always strengthen it.
When you want to neglect something
    you must always involve yourself with it.
When you want to deprive something
    you must always give to it.
This is called 'Subtle Clarity.'

Softness and Weakness overcome what is hard and strong.   {2}

"The fish must not leave the depths   {3}
the state's 'sharp weapons' must not be shown to others."

Confrontation is not the way. When something goes wrong, do not oppose it directly. Build it up, let it overreach itself and come to its own ruin {1}. This is the Soft Way {2} of the Clear-sighted {1:9}. (It only works if they do not know you are doing it, {3}).

Saying {1} corrects the tendency to react to opposition by using the most obvious and direct methods of attack. It relies on the strategy expressed in our proverb, "Give them enough rope and they'll hang themselves." Saying {2} celebrates the superiority of Softness*/Weakness over its opposite, using a formula borrowed from speculation about the "conquest* cycle." (Ch'iang/hard also means "forcing*," the opposite of the "Soft" tactics advocated in {1}.) Because of the context here, I take "sharp weapons" in {3} to be a metaphorical reference to clever stratagems devised by a ruler or his counselors, such as that described in {1}, which the saying says must be kept secret. (The same phrase occurs in 77[57]:3.)

For the composer, the indirect strategy of {1} is an example of how a Laoist ruler's Soft/Weak quality of mind expresses itself in dealing with opposition. "Soft/Weak" describes an indirect and nonconfrontational *style* of acting, which might also be very intrusive however and even "destructive" in the results aimed at. (Compare Japanese "judo," derived from the Chinese *jou-Tao*/"Soft Tao.") I take "subtle Clarity*" in {1:9} to refer to the intuitive insight the composer sees manifest in {1} and {2}. (Compare 49[27]:4.)

74[76]

People begin life Soft and Weak   {1}
when they are dead they are hard and firm.
Among the thousands of things:
Grass and trees begin life Soft and tender
when they are dead they are withered and brittle.

Yes, strength and hardness accompany death   {2}
Softness and Weakness accompany life.

And so: {3}
With a battle axe too hardened, you cannot win
when a tree becomes hard, then comes the axe.

The strong and the great stand lowest   {4}
the Soft and Weak stand highest.

"A great man is a strong man and a hard man. An unyielding man who makes clear decisions and carries them out with an absolutely firm will. A man who lets nothing get in his way."

Or so some think. But consider infants, with fresh life in their young bodies: They're Soft and Weak. The most "unyielding" kind of body is the stiff corpse. Likewise with plants—the young shoot most full of life is also the most flexible and tender. Dead branches are "hard" and "strong" {1}. The "hardest" tree is the one that has died and is ready for the axe. And axes—the "hardest" axes just chip and shatter when you try to use them {3}. To become really Alive, it's necessary also to cultivate what seems Soft and Weak in yourself {2}. Hard men are dead inside.

Saying {1} uses some metaphorical* images to celebrate the felt character of Softness* as an internal energy: Like fresh *sheng*/life* newly begun. Saying {2} makes the same point as {1} only more briefly. Saying {3} uses two metaphorical* images to picture the negative character of a "hard" state of mind: Brittle and short lived. (It reads literally: "Axe hard then not win, tree hard then axe." Because of "win" in the first line I think *ping*/axe:weapon there refers to a metal weapon—it has been tempered incorrectly and so is too brittle and breaks in battle. My understanding of both lines is new. For the short-lived character of what is *ch'iang*/hard:forced* see 69[30]:4–5.) Saying {4} celebrates the superiority of Softness over hardness. The connection between "strong" and "great" in this saying provides a good suggestion as to the kind of person Laoists have in mind when they criticize being "hard and strong."

This chapter and the next (75[78]) celebrate directly the greatness of the hypostatized* Softness/Weakness Laoists cultivate internally. The four chapters immediately preceding them (70[60], 71[63], 72[64], 73[36]) give examples of how this internally cultivated Soft/not-working state of mind expresses itself in the governing style of the ideal ruler.

75[78]

Nothing in the world   {1}
is Softer or Weaker than water.
But when it attacks what is hard and strong
none of them can win out,
because they have no way of affecting it.

Softness overcomes what is hard   {2}
Weakness overcomes what is unyielding.

Everyone in the world understands it   {3}
no one can practice it.

And so the Wise Person says: {4}
Taking on a state's dirt makes one lord of its earth altars
taking on a state's misfortunes makes one King of the world.

Right words seem the opposite.   {5}

Some present a rigid and unyielding front. But a stiff front is most easily chipped at. The smart person is firm underneath, but completely Soft and flexible on the surface. Being flexible means having no fixed shape that others can hammer at {1}. Inside, everyone already knows that this "Weak" way is the most effective way—but carrying it out is another matter {3}.

What does it mean to cultivate this Weakness? It means also learning to be the Weak one in the government, the one who has to take on the difficult and unglamorous jobs others do not want to dirty their hands with. But while others are enjoying themselves, this one is doing the job that fits her to be true ruler of the world {4}.

Like 47[43]:1, {1} uses water as a metaphorical* image to celebrate the powers and benefits* of Softness*/Weakness. The "Weakness" of water here seems to refer to its infinite flexibility: Because it identifies itself with no fixed shape, neither can it be negatively affected (yi, lit. "changed") by piercing, breaking, bending, and so on. I take the "hard and strong" things that water wins out over to be rocks on the riverbank (compare 47[43]:1). Saying {2} celebrates the superiority of Softness/Weakness over their opposites (using a formula borrowed from speculation about the "conquest* cycle"). Both {3} and {5} are sayings about the paradoxical character of Laoist teaching*. (Saying {3} is a version of 45[70]:1.) In the background of {4} is a Chinese investiture ceremony at which the Emperor symbolically entrusted a particular territory to a local feudal lord by giving him a clod of earth from a special mound.[1] "Receiving this dirt" made the recipient official master of the Earth altars set up to the god of the soil of that particular territory. But kou/dirt also means "garbage, filth," and this allows the person who coined this saying to reinterpret the entire ceremony: What makes one a true ruler is to take on oneself the "garbage" of the state; that is, its most "unlucky" happenings, its most difficult problems. (Compare the importance ascribed to hard work at governmental tasks in 71[63] and 72[64].) This gives one the spiritual status not only of feudal lord, but of Emperor*, King of the world. (Compare the reinterpretation of traditional customs in 67[31].)

Both {1–2} and {4} are examples of paradoxical wisdom {5}. Jou/Soft and especially jo/Weak have negative connotations (greatness is conventionally connected with overt strength, see 74[76]:4). This may also be involved in the composer's association between being "Soft/Weak" and lowering oneself to do a state's dirty work.

---

1. See E. Chavannes 1910: 452–453.

7

Against Disquieting "Improvements"

76[80]

Oh for a small country with few people!   {1}

Supposing there were men   {2}
    with the talents of dozens and hundreds,
    but no one employed them.
Supposing the people took death seriously,
    and did not travel far distances.

Although there exist boats and carriages,   {3}
    they have no occasion to ride in them.
Although there exist armor and weapons,
    they have no occasion to show them off.

Supposing people returned to knotting cords,   {4}
    and using this as writing.

They find their food savory   {5}
they find their clothes elegant
they are content with their homes
they are fond of their folkways.

Neighboring states are in sight of one another   {6}
so they hear the sounds of each others' dogs and roosters—
but people reach old age and die
with no comings and goings between them.

The dream of some rulers is a large territory with a huge population; the latest in carriages and boats and military gear; talented men arriving by the hundreds from all over, wanting to serve in the government; the whole state abuzz and ambitious for progress. But if you want to dream, why not dream peace: A small country with a few contented people {1}. They might have talents and contrivances to spare, but they like simplicity so much that they find little use for them. Everything they want is in their backyard—what need is there to invent new things or travel to new places {2–6}?

This chapter counters the desire* of Warring States rulers to encourage "progressive" improvements*. Saying {1} is intended paradoxically: In place of the usual ambition to reign over large territories and population,[1] it suggests the ambition of ruling over "a small country, few people." Saying {3} criticizes the desire for better equipment for travel and war (the sign of an "advanced" state), posing the counterimage of a society which has such things in abundance but ignores them (compare 20[46]:1:1–3). Saying {2:1–3} counters the desire to attract skilled people from all over,[2] posing the same kind of counterimage as in {3}. "Traveling far distances" in {2:5} describes a restless and ambitious, mobile population, contrasted with the exaggerated image in {6} of people so content they never even visit the next village nearby. "Take death seriously" in {2:4} probably describes a sober rather than reckless people (see comments at 51[75]:1). According to legend, "knotting cords" {4} was a primitive recording device prior to writing, hence {4} poses an exaggerated counterimage of a people deliberately becoming more "backward." Although there were some literal "primitivists" in ancient China,[3] I doubt if this chapter describes a literal program advocated by Laoists. For example, why would there be modern contrivances in abundance in a primitive society? This "unrealistic" touch shows that the whole is an aphoristic*, exaggerated corrective image, not a literal description.

This chapter, presenting an idealized and exaggerated contrast to "improvement" programs others advocated, is followed by four others (77[57], 78[19], 79[3], 80[65]) criticizing specific programs Laoists are opposed to, and proposing an ideal governing style that runs directly counter to these programs.

---

1. See *Mencius** 7A/21,1.
2. See ibid. 1A/7,18.
3. See ibid. 3A/4, Graham 1989: 64–74.

77[57]

"Rule the kingdom by the norm   {1}
wage war by the unexpected."
Take over the world by Not Working.

How do I know it is so?   {2}
By this.

In the world: The more rules and restrictions there are   {3}
    the poorer the people will be.
The people: The more 'sharp weapons' they have,
    the more disordered the state and the clans will be.
Men: The more clever and skillful they are,
    the more weird things will start to happen.

The more you publicize rules and laws,   {4}
the more robbers and thieves you will have.

Yes, the Wise Person says: {5}
I Do Nothing,
    and the people transform themselves.
I love Stillness,
    and the people bring themselves to correctness.
I do No Work,
    and the people enrich themselves.
I have no desires,
    and the people by themselves become Simple.

Rulers are becoming more ambitious and clever. They have schemes for making better laws. Schemes for improving job skills among the people by education and encouragement {3}. They think such programs will eventually make them King of the world {1}.

But all this 'doing' is interference in the natural harmony of the world. People are restrained, on the one side, making them poor. People are encouraged, on the other side, making them overambitious and unruly. Hemming them in with rules just makes them resentful and rebellious {3–4}. What the society really needs is a nondoing ruler who is most Still and content in herself, and who spreads her Still spirit to all the people. Then the people's natural goodness and energy will come out, and this will be fully sufficient to transform the society and enrich the state {5}.

I believe {1:1–2} is a common proverb contrasting tactics appropriate for peacetime governance, with tactics best suited to war. This is used as a take-off* point to introduce a Laoist motto about not doing* in {1:3} (= 25[48]:3). Saying {2} is a stock reply of Laoists to the demand for reasons for their views—"by this" means by intuitive insight (see comments under "This*"). Sayings {3:1–2} and {4} protest attempts to improve* the social order by publicizing written laws (see further under "Naming*"). On *li ch'i*/"sharp weapons," see 73[36]:3. The prediction of "weird" things resulting from raising people's skill levels {3:5–6} reflects a quasi-superstitious* sentiment: Attempts to introduce fundamental changes will disrupt the established ("natural*") order of things and cause weird things to happen (ghostly apparitions, deformed animals, and so forth, see 70[60].) Saying {5} celebrates the great benefits* that occur when the ruler sets the proper tone for the society by ruling it in the right spirit—"not doing*," "not-desiring*," "Still*." (*P'u*/Simplicity in the last line is elsewhere translated "Uncarved* Block." Because *wu shih*/"not working" in {5:6} duplicates *wu wei*/"not doing" in {5:2} and repeats the *wu shih* in {1:3}, I think it is a connective* addition by the composer of this chapter.)

As in 79[3] and 62[29], the composer here characterizes various social improvement programs {3–4} as a negative "doing" {1, 5}. As in 71[63] and 72[64], one can see that here *doing* means doing something significant that stands out against the ordinary routine—here, doing something that introduces new "improvements" in the society—in contrast to a "not doing" style of administration that actively strives to preserve the "natural" organic* harmony of the given (see 72[64]:8).

78[19]

Discard "Wisdom," throw away "Knowledge"—   {1}
the people will benefit a hundredfold.
Discard "Goodness," throw away "Morality"—
the people will turn back to respect and caring.
Discard "Skill," throw away "Profit"—
robbers and thieves will disappear.

Taking these three lines as your text—   {2}
    this is not sufficient.
Give them something to fasten on to:
Pay attention to the Raw, embrace the Uncarved
discount your personal interests, make your desires few.

Everyone urges new government mottoes: "Be a Wise Person!" "Goodness and Morality!" "Calculate what is Profitable!" "Encourage Skill!" But what does this do? Children and parents cultivate artificial Goodness—and lose the respect and caring that comes naturally to them. You begin looking for profit and encouraging skill—and the people also look for profit and become skillful thieves. Dropping all these programs is the best thing you can do for your state {1}. But this is not really enough. Give the people something concrete to hold on to: Cultivate the subtle spirit that comes from getting rid of your desires and ambitions. Put "civilizing" projects out of your mind and show how much you care for things in their raw state. Embrace the Uncarved Block {2}.

Saying {1} criticizes several movements Laoists lump together as attempts to improve* the world according to some ideal plan. The capitalized words designate mottoes that summarize programs advocated by others. *Knowledge, Goodness,* and *Morality* are keywords for Mencius*,[1] but Laoists lump these with *li*/profit, a key word in Mohist utilitarian thinking,[2] which Mencius also viewed negatively.[3] *Sheng*/wisdom normally describes the Laoist ideal *sheng jen*/"Wise Person" (an "inconsistency" in Laoist word use, see "Naming*."). Note also that *respect and caring* represent artificial Confucian virtues in 12[18], but here represent "natural" goodness.) Saying {2:4–5} is instruction* in Laoist self-cultivation. The composer's introduction in {2:1–3} is probably intended somewhat ironically and humorously: Following it, one expects a description of a very tangible basis for social order that the people can hold on to. Instead we get something *less* tangible, the subtle internal spirit of the ruler who sets a tone for society by cultivating the mental state called *not-desiring** and *Uncarved** Block. (*Wen*/text in {2:1} also means "culture," allowing for the alternate reading, "not sufficient to take as refined culture.")

Section {2} raises the question: Did Laoists expect rulers to engage in self-cultivation? My conjecture about this is based on a passage[4] which pictures Mencius as an indispensable guide[5] for a king who wants to practice *jen*/Good government, because Mencius has made a project of cultivating Goodness, and the king has not. Mencius must instruct the king on *policies*[6] that express an ideal Goodness that the king himself has only incipiently. If the analogy holds, Laoists did not expect kings to practice self-cultivation, but advised them to implement policies expressive of the state of mind which Laoist *shih* cultivated.

1. See for example *Mencius** 6A/6,7, 7A/21,4.
2. Graham 1989: 41.
3. 1A/1,1-6, 6B/4,5.
4. 1A/7.
5. 1A/7,19-20.
6. 1A/7,22-24.

79[3]

Not promoting the wise and worthy   {1}
    brings it about that the people are not contentious.
Not prizing goods hard to come by
    brings it about that the people do not become thieves.
Not paying attention to the desirable
    brings it about that the people's minds
    do not become disordered.

And so, the government of the Wise Person: {2}
Empty their minds, fill their bellies
weaken their ambitions, strengthen their bones.

Always bring it about that the people   {3}
    are without knowledge and without desires.
Bring it about that the clever ones
    do not presume to set about doing.

Do Not Doing   {4}
and nothing will be left un-*governed.*

"The way to build a great society is to provide incentives," they say. Promote the learned and outstanding and you will encourage people to excel in learning. They do not realize what they are doing. "Providing incentives" will turn people into social climbers, and quarrels will start where once there was peace. They are stirring up the destructive forces, neglecting the society's organic unity and harmony for the sake of the grand plans of some thinkers {1 and 3}. The ruler must have a Still, not-doing, not-desiring mind—a mind not active and ambitious for change. She and those she appoints must be the Still spirit of the contented society, and spread not ambition but Stillness and contentment, by everything they do {3–4}.

Saying {1} opposes the tone set for society by a ruler who accords special recognition to what appears especially "desirable" {1:5–6}—especially desirable goods (1:3–4), or especially desirable administrative staff {1:1–2}. This promotes social disharmony by stirring up disorderly desires in the people, causing both thievery and a *cheng*/quarrelsome:contentious* spirit among those competing for government appointments. *Shang hsien*/"promote wise and worthy [*shih**]" is a policy advocated by many contemporary *shih*.[1] It is unlikely that Laoists, who aspire to public office, are entirely opposed to promotion on the basis of merit. Line {1:1–2} is an aphoristic* corrective warning, rather than a rejection of the entire policy. (Mencius explicitly advocates promoting *hsien*, but he also[2] warns against the same negative side-effect mentioned here. Laoists may have regarded *hsien* as a description of *shih* they disliked—*hsien*/worth is used negatively in 52[77]:3.) Saying {2} is directed against contemporary "improvement*" programs encouraging an ambitious peasantry. It evokes the exaggerated counterimage of a program fostering a healthy peasantry whose contentment is not disturbed by such programs (see 76[80]). Saying {4} is a version of 25[48]:2. (*Chih*/governed is a connective* alteration, a link to *chih*/government in {2:1}, which in turn is an alteration of the standard introduction "And so the Wise Person...."). The composer's lines in {3} link previous themes: "No knowledge...no desires*" corresponds to "empty their minds...weaken their ambitions" in {2}. The "clever" ones are the *hsien*/"wise and worthy" of {1:1–2}, whom one should not put in positions where they can "do" anything, a connection to "not doing*" in {4}. As in 77[57], the last lines here link criticism of social improvement* programs to the recurrent theme of "not doing*."

---

1. See *Mencius* 2A/5,1 and *Mo Tzu* Sections 8–9 (Watson 1963: 18–33).
2. 1B/7,3.

80[65]

Those Excellent at doing Tao in ancient times—   {1}
it was not to enlighten the people, but to keep them stupid.

The difficulty in governing the people—   {2}
because of their knowledge.

Yes: {3}
By "Knowledge!" govern the state—
    a crime against the state.
By "Ignorance!" govern the state—
    a boon to the state.

Always: To understand these two lines,   {4}
    is also to understand the Ideal Pattern.
Always: To understand the Ideal Pattern,
    is to have mysterious Te.

Mysterious Te is deep, far-reaching,   {5}
in opposition to things—
only afterward comes the Great Harmony.

Some say, "Stop letting society run along the same old ruts. Take control. Learn how to think and plan, to steer the society along new and better paths. Teach your people to think and plan, to analyze everything in terms of ends and means. Make 'New Thinking' the motto of your government" {1-3}.

But thinkers are full of themselves and their plans, caring nothing for the goodness already present in the actual and present society. "Thinking" rulers ruin the society in their care. "Thinking" people upset the order of things. One should say rather, make "Not Thinking" the motto of your government {3}. Cultivate a not-thinking mind and try to infuse society with this not-thinking spirit. Yes, this will bring you into opposition with some strong tendencies taking root in society nowadays, but eventually you will restore the Great Harmony {5}.

Sayings {1}, {2}, and {3} are probably directed against programs such as that of the Mohists*,[1] who saw utilitarian rationality as a central instrument of progressive improvement*. Saying {1} is a normative* description of the policy of one who has Tao*. It poses a deliberately shocking and exaggerated image in which idealized ancient* rulers, far from encouraging the spread of rationality, had the policy of "keeping the people stupid." Saying {2} suggests that a rationalizing spirit will make people begin calculating their own self-interest and so make them uncooperative with their leaders. I think "Knowledge" in {3} is a motto describing a governing philosophy centered on utilitarian rationality, advocating both that governing officials calculate rational utility in deciding public policy and that the people be taught to think about their lives and tasks in the same fashion. For Laoists, rational calculation is the enemy of the *organic* social harmony they prize so highly (compare 79[3]:3, and comments on "Understanding*" and "Naming*"). Hence "Ignorance" is suggested as an exaggerated countermotto. Saying {5:1} celebrates the greatness of Laoist Te*.

The composer's comment in {4} presents {3} as an expression of the fundamental principle behind Laoist political wisdom. (This should not be pressed. Something similar is said of 36[42]:6:2.) To understand this principle—to see everything from this perspective—is to have (Laoist) Te. I take *yü wu fan*/"opposition to things" in {5:2-3} to refer to the way this Te, as the spirit guiding the ideal ruler, runs counter to the tendencies of people to develop in certain directions Laoists consider negative—here, the development toward increased rationality (compare 36[42]:2). "Only afterward" is it able to restore ideal Harmony. (*Shun*/harmony also means "submission." In paternalistic Chinese political thought, shared by Laoists, part of "natural*" social harmony is the submission of all to proper norms and authorities.[2])

1. See Graham 1989: 37-41.
2. See ibid.: 302-303.

81[37]

Tao invariably Does Nothing, and nothing remains not done.   {1}

If the princes and kings can watch over it   {2}
the thousands of things will change by themselves.
If they change, and become desirous and active,
I will restrain them with the Nameless One's Simplicity.
Restraining them with the Nameless One's Simplicity
     will cause them no disgrace.
Not being disgraced, they will be Still.

The world will order itself.   {3}

When self-assertion disrupts social contentment, something must be done. But strict law enforcement and strong repression makes people feel disgraced. Disgraced people are not at peace. The ideal ruler has cultivated in her own spirit the Simple Uncarved Block, which remains without names, without worded prescriptions. Such a person alone can restrain disruption gently and without making anyone feel humiliated. This brings about a real atmosphere of Stillness in the society {1–2}. Under the care of this person's Not-Doing spirit, the world will put itself in order {3}.

Sayings {1} and {2:1–2} celebrate the benefits* of ruling by Tao. Saying {1} pictures the Tao that animates the ideal government as identical with the spirit of "Not Doing*," and celebrates its wonderful effectiveness in ensuring social order. (It is based on the saying in 25[48]:2.) As in 77[57]:5, *hua*/change in {2:2} describes the utopian "conversion" of the society that results from ruling by Tao. Saying {3} counters the "doing*" attitude of self-important rulers, posing instead the image of a society whose order arises organically from within (when the ruler sets the proper tone).

The composer's comment in {2:3–7} uses {2:1–2} as a take-off* point. He reads *hua*/change now as something negative, leading to discordant "desire*" and "activity," which need to be restrained. (*Tso*/activity is a negative opposite to "Stillness" in 28[16]:2 too.) Such desire/activity poses a dilemma for Laoists: On the one hand, they are against ruling with a strong hand. On the other hand, they have a definite ideal of an organically harmonious society that the ruler ought to foster. This must mean sometimes taking firm action against disquieting movements in the society. The answer given here draws on the state of mind that is the focus of Laoist self-cultivation, here called *The Nameless One's Simplicity*. (*P'u*/Simplicity elsewhere is translated "Uncarved* Block.") Having cultivated this Simplicity, the ruler can act in a tactful and nonconfrontational way that restrains disruptive people without making them feel put down, which would stir resentment leading to further social disorder. (See further under "Hurt*.") His tactful treatment leads instead to a genuine Stillness* pervading the society. Like 72[64], this chapter helps to define what it means to engage in "Not Doing" government, under whose subtle influence the world will seem to order itself {3}.

This last chapter is a good climax to the earlier chapters in Section 7 (see comments concerning "climaxes" in 39[25]). In the traditional order, Chapter 37 is also the final chapter of the "first book" of the *Tao Te Ching* and the final chapter of the entire book in the newly found Ma-wang-tui version.

Additional Textual Notes

Included here are notes concerning (a) my choice of variants from the various Chinese manuscripts of the *Tao Te Ching* and (b) ways of construing the Chinese text that might be especially controversial.

Abbreviations and special terms used in these notes:

HSK = The Chinese text of the *Tao Te Ching* used in the commentary of Ho Shang Kung (as printed in Ho Shih-chi's *Ku pen tao te ching hsiao k'an*).

Lectio dificilior = "The more difficult reading." A principle of textual criticism I often have used in preferring MWT to WP, according to which the textual variant that is more difficult to make sense of, but still intelligible, is the one to be preferred. The rationale is that, over time, manuscript copyists are prone to introduce changes in the text to make it read more smoothly, thus the more difficult readings often are likely to be more original. This principle is especially appropriate to the *Tao Te Ching*, which frequently uses very colorful language, paradoxes, deliberately shocking images, and so forth.

MWT = The Chinese text of the *Tao Te Ching* as printed in two manuscripts from the second century B.C., recently discovered in a cave at Ma-wang-tui in China. I rely on the edition of this text printed in Henricks (1989). These are by far the oldest extant manuscripts, but they also clearly are corrupt in many places—many more than the Wang Pi text, I believe—and this counts against their replacing Wang Pi as the standard text.

WP = The Chinese text of the *Tao Te Ching* used in the commentary of Wang Pi, until recently accepted by all as the standard text. My translation is based on WP (as printed in Ho Shih-chi's *Ku pen tao te ching hsiao k'an*) except when there seems some positive reason for accepting the readings of MWT or HSK, in which case I always mention explicitly in these notes that I am doing so.

1[24]. "Ambitious" (lit. "has desires") is MWT both in {3} here and in 67[31]:2. This is the *lectio dificilior,* and it is doubtful that a mere copyist's error would be repeated twice. WP avoids the (seemingly un-Laoist) positive use of "desire" by changing to "has Tao."

2[9]. "Win the fame" in {2} is the *lectio dificilior* of HSK, omitted in WP and MWT.

3[67]. MWT's "I am great" in {1} is the *lectio dificilior*. WP avoids the seeming arrogance with "My Tao is great."

4[22]. "Shepherd of the World" in {4} is MWT. WP has "Pattern of the World."

18[13]. In {1:2} I borrow from Waley the understanding of *jo* as "your" rather than "like." My understanding of the line before this is new: I take *ch'ung-ju*/favor-disgrace as a phrase referring to the ups and downs of politics, being now in favor, now in disgrace (formally similar to phrases like *p'in-fu*/poor-rich, referring to financial circumstances generally). And (with Waley) I take *ching*/startle in a more general sense referring to a state of mental disturbance: "being upset" due to ups and downs of political fortune. I take *jo* in {1:1} as a quasi-copula, "is equivalent to," though perhaps it also could be taken to mean "your" (lit. "favor and disgrace [are] your upsetness"). My understanding of *ch'ung wei hsia* in {2} as "favor is degrading" also is new. I think it is meant to be a "shocking" opposite to the commonsense view that "favor raises one up" (*ch'ung wei shang*). A version of {4} is found in the *Chuang Tzu* (Watson 1968: 116), where however it is given a "Yangist" meaning opposite the one I suppose here (attribute no special importance to the world, take care of your self instead). In the *Chuang Tzu* there is a slight difference in the wording—a *yü* following *shen* that does not occur in WP: *i shen yü wei t'ien hsia*. The omission of *yü* in WP {4} produces the familiar construction *i X wei Y* "treat X as Y," which allows for my understanding of *i shen wei t'ien hsia* "treat yourself as [no more important than] the [rest of the] world." This interpretation makes the point of {4} accord with the point of {3}.

20[46]. {2:1} is a *lectio dificilior* found in HSK and MWT, omitted entirely in WP.

27[10]. *Wei tz'u*/"remain Feminine" in {1:10} is MWT. WP has *wu tz'u*/"not Feminine."

31[4]. Most translators punctuate {1} differently, yielding something like "Tao is empty but useful. It never [needs to be] filled." I follow Karlgren's basic understanding of this line, in which *yung chih/*"use it" is equivalent to *yung chih che/*"one who uses it," and *yung* refers to "using*" (practicing/internalizing) Tao, as in 46[35]:3.

36[42]. Most translators take *ch'ung ch'i* in {3} to mean "*blending* the *ch'i's*"; that is, blending the *yin ch'i/*energy and the *yang ch'i/*energy. But (a) although the character for *ch'ung* here also can stand for a word meaning "blend," *ch'ung* always means "Empty" elsewhere in the *Tao Te Ching*. And (b) the idea of *balancing yin* and *yang,* central to later Taoism, is not found anywhere else in this book, which always advocates cultivating *yin* qualities as opposed to *yang* ones.

42[2]. I take *ch'eng/*complete in {2:4} to mean that the idea "difficult" is given its full content only by contrast with the idea "easy." I take the MWT reading *ying/*fill in {5} and interpret it similarly: The content of the idea "noble" is fully "filled out" only when one sees it in contrast with the idea "lowly." The concluding particle *heng/*always at the end of {2} is the MWT reading. With MWT I omit "produces but doesn't possess," which WP places at the beginning of {5}.

43[1]. "Source *of the thousands of things*" in {2:1} is MWT, which has this same phrase in both lines of this saying. WP has "source *of Heaven and Earth*" in {2:1}. I think MWT rightly makes the *name Mother* the entire point of the contrast between the two lines. I also adopt the MWT reading of {3}, and Henricks's basic understanding of it. I believe that "what is sought" here is conceptual clarity. WP makes a very similar point with different words: Where MWT has the phrase *so chiao/* "what is sought," WP has the single word *chiao,* meaning here probably "boundary," "outer edge"—that is, the "outer surface" of things as opposed to their "hidden essences." Line {4:1} reads literally "these two, merged." I take "these two" as a reference to the partial *subject* of the preceding two-line *saying,* "not desiring." See the further explanation in 37[14]:2.

55[66]. I translate *chiang/*river as "Yang-Tze" because *chiang* is the name associated with the great southern river, the *Yang-tze chiang.* The great river in the north, the *Huang Ho* or "Yellow

River," is not called *chiang* but *ho*. This is one piece of evidence Erkes (1935) cites for the southern origin of the *Tao Te Ching*.

56[61]. Most translators take the phrase *hsia liu* (lit. "low flowing") in {1} as a river image, translating it "flows downward," or "low-lying river," and so on. But *liu* is used in the *Mencius* (7B/37,11) to refer to conduct following "*current* customs" in a negative sense (as opposed to the principled conduct of the superior man). Hence the advice in the *Doctrine of the Mean* (10:5) to be "*ho*/harmonious but not *liu*" must mean something like "agreeable, but not wishy-washy." The phrase *hsia liu* itself occurs twice in the *Analects* (17:24:1 and 19:20), where it clearly describes someone of very low social status. The term clearly has negative connotations, either of weakness ("floating" or "drifting") or excessively "common" ("current"), as opposed to aristocratic/principled moral conduct. In MWT (adopted here) the line about *hsia liu* is followed immediately by the phrase "woman for the world." It seems that anyone familiar with these resonances of *hsia liu* would naturally see here the image of a prostitute, which probably is why the WP text makes "woman of the world" the third line of this saying rather than the second. But *chiao* "unite with" in the remaining line of the saying is regularly used in the *Analects* of friendship and intimacy. Thus this word, too, helps reinforce the prostitute image.

60[49]. WP transposes MWT's *heng wu hsin*/"constantly no mind" to *wu heng hsin*/"no constant mind." I accept MWT as the more "shocking" *lectio dificilior*. Some think that Te in {2} makes no sense in its usual meaning and want to take the character as standing for another word *te*, "to get, obtain." This is unnecessary: As in 27[10]:2, this saying describes how the Te* cultivated by Laoists typically expresses itself in conduct. Line {4:1–2} is omitted in WP, but contained in MWT and many other texts.

65[51]. "Talents" in {1} is MWT, WP has "abilities." *Events* translates *wu*/things—I think *wu* has a very general meaning in the *Tao Te Ching* and "*events* form them" makes most sense here. See further under "Things*," p. 247.

67[31]. "Mourning" in {7} is the MWT reading, WP has "ill fortune." WP may retain the original wording of the oral saying, MWT's "mourning" being a change by the composer to connect this saying to {7:5} and {8}.

68[69]. "There is no enemy" (*wu ti*) in {3} is the MWT reading. WP has a phrase similar in meaning, *ching ti*, "make light of the enemy." MWT here has the *lectio dificilior*, which still makes sense if one regards it as a motto.

69[30]. WP adds another line to {3}, not found in MWT: "In the aftermath of a great war, surely there will be a bad year." I omit this because it sounds like a rationalizing explanation of the more "superstitious*" sounding thorns-and-brambles saying.

70[60]. My tentative understanding of 3:4–5 depends on taking the MWT reading, "the Wise person does not hurt *them* [i.e., the ghosts]." WP has "not hurt *jen*/people."

76[80]. I follow Karlgren's understanding of the somewhat difficult construction in {2:1–2}. Others take it to mean "[Enough] weapons for dozens and hundreds of men." (*Ch'i*/talent also can mean "utensil, weapon.")

80[65]. In {3} WP has "not by knowledge." I take here the MWT reading "by not-knowing" (translated here as "Ignorance!") because this fits better with the idea of "Knowledge/Ignorance" as mottos, applying both to the ruler and his subjects. WP also has a different *chih* in {2} and {3} that could be translated as (negative) "cleverness." This seems an attempt to tone down deliberately "shocking" language that is part of Laoist style. In {4} the first *heng*/always and the second *chih*/understand are in MWT, not in WP. In {5} "in opposition to things" follows Karlgren's understanding, which seems to me the most natural reading of *yü wu fan*. Others avoid this seemingly un-Taoist notion by translating, "It *fan*/returns *yü*/together-with *wu*/things."

81[37]. In {3} WP has "not desiring" instead of MWT's "not disgraced." I think the latter is the *lectio dificilior* here. The idea is connected to the theme of "not hurting" the people (see further under "Hurting*" p. 229. In {5} "order" translates MWT's *cheng*/norm:make-correct. WP has *ting*/settle: arrange.

Hermeneutics

A Reasoned Approach to Interpreting the
Tao Te Ching

In interpreting "scriptural" writings, we must make a choice: (a) We can use "meaningful for us" as the main criterion for deciding on the true meaning of the text. In this case, historical scholarship and critical hermeneutics[1] have nothing essential to offer. Arriving at interpretations "most meaningful for us" is something that might happen equally as well when an unscholarly person of great personal wisdom free associates on separate lines of the text. (b) We can try as best we can to reconstruct what the text meant to its initial authors and audience. In this case historical scholarship and hermeneutic reflection is essential. But also, in this case, we must abandon the traditional claim of scriptural interpretation to be discovering authoritative truth valid for all time. Trying to derive authoritative norms for ourselves directly from interpretation itself is always a distorting influence on any attempt to really uncover original meanings. The best that can be said for such scholarly interpretation is this: One who uses "meaningful for us" as a criterion looks in a mirror—the text is a stimulus for arriving at insights he or she already was on the verge of having. By contrast, trying to recover the original meaning most often means entering into a thought world very foreign to us— which is for that very reason a thought world liable to be a greater challenge to our current way of thinking. We are still left with the responsibility of deciding how best to respond to this challenge. Scriptural interpretation is no short cut to truth.

This book takes the reconstruction of historical meaning as its main focus. I believe that the *Tao Te Ching* also has some important relevance for today. (Briefly, the "civilizing" trends it protests against have reached their apogee today, and further civilizing is often destructive. We need to "turn back" to recover important things lost in the progress of civilization, the things conservative Laoists were trying to protect.) I do not deal directly with this issue here, partly to limit the scope of this book. Partly also this reflects my conviction that historical-interpretive skill as such, my academic specialty, gives one no privileged insight into issues concerning contemporary relevance. These issues are better dealt with in dialogue, in which nonspecialists in the general public participate as equal partners.

The interested reader will find further detailed discussions and argumentation for the interpretive method applied here, in a longer version of this book published in the same series.[2] This essay will summarize the results of this longer discussion, which constitute the essential underlying principles guiding the interpretation presented here. These results fall into three main areas:

1. *Social Background.* An attempt to reconstruct the nature of the social group out of which the *Tao Te Ching* arose is essential to understanding how the thoughts in this book relate to concrete life.

2. *Composition of the Book.* My thesis is that it consists of sayings from the oral tradition of a small "Laoist" community, which are artfully arranged into brief collages of sayings, the eighty-one "chapters" of the *Tao Te Ching.*

3. *How Sayings Mean.* Sayings in the *Tao Te Ching* cannot be taken literally, but this does not mean that they are vague or ambiguous and might mean almost anything. They have quite definite meanings that can be spelled out if we are careful and subtle enough in our analysis of their form.

Social Background

A central theme of the philosopher Ludwig Wittgenstein[3] is that the meaning of thoughts and words is not independent of the role these thoughts and words play in the concrete human life of the speaker. The first question we must ask about any writing, therefore, is not, What doctrines does it teach? but, How did these words and thoughts insert themselves into the concrete lives of the persons in whose lives they first arose? This above all is why it is necessary to form some opinions, to make some educated guesses,[4] about the concrete origins of the *Tao Te Ching.* If it seems most likely to have been written by a speculative thinker to teach us some doctrines, we must interpret it accordingly. If it seems to have grown out of some other human project (some other Wittgenstinian "form of life") then we must see its meaning in relation to that project instead. What follows here presents the conjectures on this matter that underlie the present interpretation of the *Tao Te Ching.* The conjectures are based primarily on an examination of internal evidence in the work itself, matched with the analysis of ancient Chinese society by the social historian Cho-yun Hsu[5] and a picture gathered from a study of some writings roughly contemporary with the *Tao Te Ching,* primarily[6] a book called the *Mencius* (see p. 235). Although the *content* of Mencius's teaching is in many respects opposed to that of the *Tao Te Ching,* I believe there are many illuminating formal sociological parallels, as well as many similarities in details such as vocabulary and imagery. Interpreting the *Tao Te Ching* against the particular setting I propose, so far as I know, is relatively new. Most commentators either ignore entirely the question of concrete setting or treat the *Tao Te Ching* as the work of a rather isolated philosopher or mystic.

Most critical scholars now place the *Tao Te Ching*'s origins sometime late in the Warring States period (463–222 B.C.) of Chinese history. Contemporary Chinese believed strongly in a hierarchical, "pyramid" theory of social organization. There was a Chinese Empire, presided over at the very top by a single Emperor, "The One Man," representing in his person the symbolic Norm of the World. Next came a larger class of nobility who presided in feudal[7] fashion over the smaller territories or "states" into which the Empire was divided. The base of the pyramid was made up largely of peasant farmers.

In previous times, social rank was relatively fixed by birth, but during the Warring States period there was much more mobility both up and down the social scale.[8] Social status and power increasingly came to depend not on birth but on personal ambition and competitive struggle. The Emperor had lost effective control, and the heads of the various states engaged in large-scale warfare with each other, each wanting to reunite the now fragmented Empire under his own leadership. Noble families engaged in what Hsu terms "class suicide" by constant internecine struggles.[9]

Out of this disorder arose a relatively new class of men called *shih,*[10] drawn from downwardly mobile, dispossessed nobility, and upwardly mobile, ambitious peasantry. Traditionally, *shih* had served in relatively minor roles as soldiers and as scribes, bookkeepers, minor administrators, and foremen for state governments and feudal manors. As states grew larger and more complex in this period and as rulers were less and less able to rely on fellow nobility for support, those in power increasingly came to rely on *shih* as a cadre of men with the specialized expertise necessary to foster and maintain the good socioeconomic order that formed each ruler's power base.[11]

Within this class of *shih,* there was a smaller group perhaps best called *shih idealists.* I believe a small group of *shih* idealists is responsible for the *Tao Te Ching.* The *Mencius,* a book roughly contemporary with the *Tao Te Ching,* gives us a fairly detailed picture of such men's conception of themselves and the leadership role to which they aspired. My picture of the group underlying the *Tao Te Ching* is largely drawn from what I think are parallels between the *Mencius* and the *Tao Te Ching* on this score. What the two groups have in common can be described roughly as follows.

They were alienated idealists. By *alienated,* I mean that they did not look upon traditional social life or the existing political order as a source of authoritative norms. Nor did they look on participation in ordinary sociopolitical life as something sufficient in itself to give meaning to one's life. They were idealists in that the quest for norms and sources of meaning superior to those of conventional society was a very central part of their lives. New norms they developed served as a basis for their claim to be *instructors* of those in authority, deserving (in the Laoist case at least)[12] the leadership status of new "Emperor," spiritual "Norm of the World."

They had a very strong sense of social responsibility. The *Chuang Tzu* puts the following words into the mouth of a *shih* idealist asking permission from his teacher to go "correct" the ways of a feudal lord:

> I have heard that the ruler of [the state of] Wei is very young. He...thinks little of how he rules his state, and fails to see his faults. It is nothing to him to lead his people into peril.... His people have nowhere to turn. I have heard you say, Master, "Leave the state that is well-ordered and go to the state in chaos!" I want to use these words as my standard, in hopes that I can restore his state to health.[13]

Even though *shih* idealists like this often have no official position and often are of lower-class origin, they feel that the burden of ensuring the health of the entire Empire rests on their shoulders alone. In their eyes, those in official positions of authority (many of them usurpers) for the most part are completely inadequate to this task. *Shih* idealists often travel from state to state, wherever they feel their services are needed and wherever they have some hope that they can influence local government, as either advisors or administrators in government service. In this they rely partly on an important element of Chou-dynasty (1122–222 B.C.) ideology: The Emperor must have wise counselor-"teachers" who constantly remind him of his moral responsibilities and correct him when they see him abusing his office or setting a bad tone for the people.[14] Formerly, however, such counselors were the highest ranking officials, drawn from the Emperor's noble kinsmen.

They accepted fully the present sociopolitical structure and their officially assigned place in it. Unlike idealist political reformers elsewhere, *shih* idealists did not advocate a change in the hierarchical structure of society. And, even though they regarded themselves as the true leaders of China, they did not aspire to topple those in power and personally take their place. Politically, their aspiration was to "rule from the middle," in their capacity as advisors and administrators at all levels of government, from the lowest level of inspector of wells and fields[15] to the highest level of "prime minister" just below the top feudal lord who was supreme head of state.

They offered a new foundation for Chinese culture and politics, but this foundation enters public life primarily in the person of the ideal shih. Here a contrast with John Locke (1632–1704) is helpful. Locke was an English philosopher who perhaps more than any other laid the foundations for modern secular democracy. The foundation Locke offered for this new kind of society consisted primarily of *philosophical theories*—theories about the natural freedom of human nature, theories about the basis for social organization and government, and so on. These theories in turn were based on more fundamental theories about the nature of reality and how we come to know reality. The new foundation Locke had to offer entered public life primarily as theory—as theory to be taught to and accepted by both government officials and the people they rule, as theory to be embodied in a constitution, as theory to be followed by judges in interpreting laws, and so forth. If we ask ourselves, How did Locke's thoughts and words insert themselves into concrete life? the answer is (a) his thoughts were the result of his conscious attempts to construct a rationally based philosophical system, and (b) he wanted his entire society to understand and accept these thoughts as a normative basis for social and political life.

Shih idealists also aspired to provide a new foundation for the crumbling sociopolitical order they saw around them. But the foundation they had to offer inserted itself into concrete life in a way fundamentally different from the way that Locke's philosophy did. They relied primarily on two ideas central to traditional Chou-dynasty thought: (a) Good social organization depends on the ruler gaining the voluntary respect and cooperation of the people. He does this by his personal good qualities and charisma (*te*[16] in Chinese) and by showing genuine care, concern, and competence in looking out for their needs. (b) The good ruler "sets the tone" for his society. The manner in which he conducts himself both privately and publicly establishes a certain atmosphere that subtly but powerfully influences the way the people conduct themselves. It is primarily this tone the ruler sets, rather than laws, teachings, or beliefs authorities teach to people, that is expected to produce a good peasant-citizenry and an orderly society. The *shih* idealists reflected in the *Mencius* and the *Tao Te Ching* regard themselves as the chief tone setters for society. The new "foundation" they have to offer inserts itself into public life primarily in their own person then. In whatever office they hold, they strive to set the proper tone for the social group in their charge, and in this they serve also as exemplars for the rulers whom they serve. And when these rulers ask for their advice about particular political problems, they advise them to address these problems in a way that will also set the proper tone for the larger society.

Because the personal character of ruler-administrators was so pivotal, shih idealists placed an extraordinary emphasis on character formation, "self-cultivation." Personal character formation, which Mencius calls *self-cultivation*,[17] is to the *shih* what philosophical theorizing is to John Locke. It is the source of his autonomy, his right to follow norms derived from within himself, rather than be bound by norms given externally. And it is the source of his critical leverage over against conventional society and its rulers, the basis on which he criticizes current practice and poses new norms to guide public policy. Good public policy in the *Mencius* and the *Tao Te Ching* is *defined* as that policy expressive of good character or the right state of mind of the ruler. Self-cultivation differs somewhat from the Western development of "virtuous character," in its strong emphasis on complete internalization, so that the personal qualities cultivated become part of one's instinctive impulses (not "convictions" one must hold oneself to). This is expressed in a famous saying attributed to Confucius: "At fifteen I set my heart on learning, at thirty I attained a firm position...at seventy *I followed my heart's desire without overstepping the line.*"[18]

Perhaps because the *shih* idealists as a class actually were the group with the best claim to moral respectability in Warring States China, they apparently gained considerable prestige (though probably their actual influence on politics fell very far short of their ambitions). Because the use of force and political manipulation increasingly came to replace hereditary title as a source of political power, rulers needed new sources of legitimation. Some may have looked to *shih* idealists as a source of this legitimation, wanting to appear at least to be associated with them and listening to their advice, or at least supporting them. (Mencius speaks[19] of a ruler who, although he rejects the advice of a particular *shih*, gives him material support anyhow, "Because I am ashamed to see him die of want in my territory.")

The very high respect with which some individual *shih* were regarded, led other *shih* to gather around them, to learn their ideas about good government and practice self-cultivation under their guidance, and by association with them to gain credentials that would get for them the government appointments they desired. This led to the formation of many small and informal *shih*-schools, groups of men gathered around one or more teachers, living with or near him, and often traveling with him as he went from state to state trying to influence rulers with his advice. This is the kind of group that gathered around the Confucian *shih* teacher Mencius, and this is the kind of group I believe also responsible for the *Tao Te Ching*. This latter was one among several groups sharing a common world-view opposed to Confucianism, groups that came later to be called by the general name *Taoist*.[20] Other roughly contemporary Taoist groups are known to us from an anthology of writings that goes under the name *Chuang Tzu*. Graham[21] recently suggested a new term, *Laoist* (after Lao Tzu, the legendary author of the *Tao Te Ching*) to refer to the specific thought of the *Tao Te Ching*, in contrast to the somewhat different ("Chuangist") Taoism represented in the *Chuang Tzu*.[22] I use *Laoist* as a term of convenience throughout this book, to make it clear that I am here dealing only with this brand of Taoism.

Note that my aim in this book is not to present a broad and balanced view of the cultural situation in ancient China, and reconstruct "the meaning" the *Tao Te Ching* had in the stream of history and in the development of Chinese thought. My aim is ultimately not to "place" Laoist thought in some broader framework, but to see the world as Laoists saw it. Because this means considering only those aspects of Chinese culture relevant to Laoism and seeing them from a Laoist perspective, my treatment of ancient Chinese culture as such is bound to have a narrow and lopsided cast. For broader intellectual history the reader should consult the two excellent recent books by Graham and Schwartz.[23]

The Composition of the Tao Te Ching: *What Kind of Writing Is It?*

We often approach ancient writings unconsciously under the sway of book-centered institutions common in our own culture. We forget that writing books, printing books, reading books, making books available in libraries and bookstores, and so forth are features very particular to our own culture, which were not always present. Like the Bible, the *Tao Te Ching* stems from a transition period between an oral culture and a culture centered on writing and reading. In the culture of late Warring-States China oral communication was still the overwhelmingly common means of communication, even among relatively educated *shih*. In all probability, few to none of the Classics that have come down to us from this period are the product of single thinkers who deliberately sat down to "write a book" to disseminate their ideas—this did not become a common custom in China until the Han dynasty (beginning 206 B.C.). Almost all of these works are collections of material put together by others.[24]

This background explains well some obvious features of the *Tao Te Ching* that are not easy to explain on the traditional view that this book is the product of a single author who sat down to write a book to disseminate his ideas. The book consists of eighty-one very brief, numbered "chapters," traditionally divided into "two books" (Chapters 1–37 and 38–81), but arranged in no evident order.[25] The chapters in turn typically consist of three or more short sayings, each of which could easily stand on its own. Often the sayings within a given chapter have no obvious relation to each other. These features give the chapters a discontinuous, somewhat jerky appearance, in contrast to the rather smooth continuity characteristic of compositions in which everything is written to go together. Most modern critical scholars are agreed that at least a good deal of the material in the chapters consists of individual sayings that once circulated independently of each other as oral tradition.[26]

The interpretation of the *Tao Te Ching* presented here results from a systematic analysis of the composition of each chapter, using the analysis of passages whose composition is relatively clear, to illuminate other passages where traces of the text's compositional history are more ambiguous. In this analysis I have made use of an approach developed in biblical studies to analyze some writings (like the Gospels) where significant amounts of material from early Christian oral tradition appears to have been incorporated into longer written compositions. This approach consists first of "form criticism," an analysis of the standard genres or "forms" (stories, songs, sayings, and so on) in which oral tradition is cast, and an attempt to interpret each unit of oral tradition in the context of some concrete life setting in which it was originally used. It consists secondly of "redaction criticism," an analysis of the techniques and intentions of those who wove the oral material into longer compositions.[27]

To spell out my hypothesis in more detail: The sayings we now have in the *Tao Te Ching* once circulated in the Laoist *shih* school as oral tradition. *Oral tradition* does not mean the sayings were memorized by students specifically to keep alive the authoritative words of a teacher. Rather, like common proverbs in any culture, they stuck in people's minds and were used frequently because they made some useful point about frequently recurring issues, and they made this point in a witty or otherwise memorable manner (many of the sayings are rhymed). The concrete situations in which they were used were, first, conversations among Laoist *shih* and between these *shih* and other visitors or rulers over the proper way a leader should conduct himself both in private and public life. Sayings used in these contexts are mostly proverb-like aphorisms. I call them *polemic aphorisms,* to emphasize the way that most of them are directed implicitly or explicitly *against* some views, assumptions, or tendencies Laoists oppose. A second context for sayings consisted of conversations within the Laoist school concerning the practice of self-cultivation, including instruction in self-cultivation given by teachers to students. Most of these sayings are "celebratory," celebrating the wonderful character of the quality of mind Laoists cultivate.

All of these sayings are very "context bound." Like sayings such as "It takes two to tango," the meaning of each Laoist saying is essentially connected to a very specific situation that it addresses. To miss this connection is to miss the meaning of the saying. At one ("form critical") level, then, to interpret the *Tao Te Ching* correctly is to place each individual saying in some oral context in concrete life and understand the point it makes about this situation.

A second ("redaction critical") level of interpretation is necessary, however. Despite the initial appearance of some chapters, I believe that the sayings are not thrown together randomly. A closer look reveals that the "chapters" of the *Tao Te Ching* are in fact artfully arranged collages of sayings, juxtaposed with some deliberate intentions and associations in mind, which are often suggested by brief additions and comments made by the person putting the collage together.[28] I call such persons the *composers* of the chapter-collages. My best conjecture is that these composers were teachers in the Laoist *shih* school in the second or third generation. At this stage, Laoist *shih* had begun reflecting on traditional oral sayings as repositories of group wisdom, and teachers began composing short collages of sayings to give to students as part of their training in the school. For us, this means that, in addition to the concrete oral setting, the chapters themselves form a second, *verbal* context; and each saying in a given chapter needs to be understood in some relation to this second context of which it is now a part.

My thesis that the chapters are artfully composed unities is based on (a) a study of standard techniques, visible in many chapters, aimed at bringing unity to the various sayings in a given chapter; and (b) a comparison of passages in which the same associations seem to guide the juxtaposition of sayings (for example, the same saying follows a criticism of "forcing" in both 33[55]:4–5 and 69[30]:4–5). Comparisons between the associations in various chapters are given in the commentary. My observations on the standard techniques are given in the Topical Glossary under Connective* Alteration, Framing*, and Take-Off*. Detecting the composer's additions to oral sayings is aided by the fact that Laoist oral sayings are generally highly unified and frequently exhibit recurrent patterns, like parallel grammatical construction, rhythm, and rhyme.[29] Words or lines that interrupt parallelism (like 69[30]:4) or rhymes (like 7[8]:2:1) or abruptly change the subject (like 27[10]:1:7–8, 57[68]:1:4) suggest alterations or additions to oral sayings. (See further under Framing*.)

I believe that there is evidence of deliberate composition in enough chapters to warrant the supposition that all chapters are deliberately composed, even though if one considers some chapters strictly by themselves, there is not enough evidence to warrant this conclusion. Careful study of the composers' techniques and associations gives some control over the "reading between the lines" we have to do to try to understand their intentions.

Form and redaction criticism are attempts to ground intepretive practice in some consistent general theory regarding the *formal* character of the text at hand, a corrective to the tendency to decide between intepretive choices mainly on the basis of substantive ideas we tend to find more congenial. Still, it should perhaps be emphasized that this approach is necessarily conjectural at many points. The Chinese text of the *Tao Te Ching* contains no quotation marks or other indications that it consists of various layers of material. My translation is printed in such a way (see p. x) as to show the reader how I reconstruct the composition of each chapter. But I would invite the reader to imagine different plausible ways of construing the composition of each. If my hypothesis is even plausible, this means there are no "safe" approaches to interpreting the *Tao Te Ching,* nothing to take as the "default" in the absence of certain and secure evidence to the contrary. To interpret the sayings outside of any concrete life setting is to conjecture that they are the particular kind of sayings that can be understood this way. To understand each chapter as the work of a single writer or a collection of unrelated sayings is to conjecture that this is their character. These approaches are ultimately based, like the present one, on educated guesses.

In the present view, the *Tao Te Ching* is probably an anthology of once independent chapter-collages. I take this as partial justification for my rearrangement of the chapters in an order I think better suited to introduce the modern reader to Laoist thought. In general this rearrangement proceeds from the personal to the political.[30] Chapters grouped together in Sections 1 and 2 concern two central facets of Laoist ideals, the cultivation of an unconventional and often negative-appearing kind of goodness (Section 1) and the cultivation of what we would perhaps call "mental or physical health" (Section 2). The chapters in Section 3 are more directly concerned with the practice of self-cultivation and the mental qualities cultivated. The chapters in Section 4 deal with teacher-student relations in the Laoist school and the kind of understanding of reality taught there. The chapters in Sections 5–7 are about ruling. The chapters in Section 5 express the principle Laoist ideals concerning the person and general role of the ruler-administrator. The chapters in Section 6 concern more particularly the "Soft" style of ruling Laoists advocate; and the chapters in Section 7 express Laoist ideals developed in opposition to contemporary social "improvement" programs. Further explanations of the rationale for the arrangement of chapters within each section will be found in the last paragraphs of the commentaries on Chapters 2[9], 5[45] 7[8], 9[79], 12[18], 15[11], 18[13], 21[12], 23[26], 24[33], 31[4], 34[40], 37[14], 39[25], 40[71] 45[70], 50[53], 53[72], 59[58], 61[54], 64[34], 66[74], 70[60], 74[76], 76[80], 81[37].

Analyzing Laoist Sayings: Nonliteral Interpretation

> They said, "You have a blue guitar,
> You do not play things as they are."
> The man replied, "Things as they are
> Are changed upon the blue guitar."
> And they said then, "But play you must,
> A tune beyond us, yet ourselves,
> A tune upon the blue guitar,
> Of things exactly as they are."
>   ...
> ...nothing changed except the place
> Of things as they are and only the place
> As you play them, on the blue guitar.
>
> —Wallace Stevens

The danger of "overanalyzing" a piece of writing is well known. Yet, when we are dealing with writing from a very distant era and culture, some kind of analysis takes place whether we like it or not. What we need in this case is not to analyze as little as possible, but to try to analyze most carefully and sensitively—to try to reconstruct and capture in our analysis the implicit structure of the words as they were heard by their original audience. Interpretive analysis should be like Wallace Stevens's "Blue Guitar." To analyze a saying is not to hear it as it was originally heard and understood, without analysis—inevitably, "things are changed" when analyzed. But our aim should be that the *only* change is the fact of analysis, making explicit exactly what was implicitly understood by the original author or audience. The meaning-structure of a saying merely makes a transition from being implicitly understood *in* the saying to being explicitly conceptualized. "A tune upon the blue guitar / Of things exactly as they are...Nothing changed *except the place* / Of things as they are and *only* the place."

The main danger in not being careful about analysis is that we will unconsciously tend toward what seems the "simplest" kind of analysis; that is, we will try to understand every statement as though it were trying to give us an accurate, literal picture of objective reality. For example, we will take the saying "One who knows does not speak" as the assertion of a fact or "general law" about the world, that "knowledge" and "speaking" are never found together. Similarly, we will take the saying "[Tao] is the origin of the thousands of things" as the assertion of a factual picture: There is an object, "Tao," that at some time in the past caused all the other objects in the world to come to be.

In trying to devise a controlled method for interpreting the *Tao Te Ching*, and not simply go by my own intuitions about its meaning, one of the things I have tried to do is work out some analytical models for interpreting Laoist sayings that are more in accord with the way they were (in my reconstruction) probably used in the Laoist community. Two of my basic presuppositions here are that (a) the many proverblike aphorisms in the *Tao Te Ching* have the same formal meaning-structure as proverbs in our own culture, and that (b) there is a large body of other sayings that have as their concrete background the practice of self-cultivation and experiences connected with this practice in the Laoist community.

Polemic Aphorisms

First, let me outline here my thesis about the meaning-structure of the proverblike polemic aphorisms, based on a careful analysis of the meaning-structure of proverbs implicit in the way we use them in our own culture.[31] This meaning-structure consists of three essential elements: the target, the image, and the attitude and the value orientation motivating it. These can be described as follows:

The Target. Aphorisms are essentially compensatory wisdom. They are always directed against some opposing human tendency, which they mean to correct or compensate for. "Slow and steady wins the race" is a common proverb although it is not reliable as a general law about who wins races. "The race usually goes to the swift" is more true, but is not a proverb. Why? People have a tendency to assume that being swift is *always the only* way to win races, and "Slow and steady wins the race" compensates for this tendency, to wake people up to a different possibility. This is its "point." But there is no tendency to think that fast people will not win. "The race goes to the swift" has nothing to compensate for. Although it is true, it has no useful "point" in everyday life. I will call this opposing human tendency the "target" of a given aphorism. Whoever does not understand the target of a saying does not understand its meaning. (Think of a foreigner trying to understand "It takes two to tango" without understanding what this saying is usually said to counteract.) Further, the meaning of any given aphorism is *exhausted* in making a point against its particular target. It is not a general truth to be applied consistently to all situations whatever nor does it necessarily have any additional relation to a further body of truths or principles. The unity of Laoist thought consists partly of the fact that it is directed against a relatively small number of targets. Positive Laoist ideals need to be understood by contrast to these "targets." These serve as the main basis for my rearrangement of chapters in topical groups in Sections 1–2 and 5–7 of the translation and commentary (see p. 199), and for grouping sayings together for discussion in the Topical Glossary. (See the topics Agitation*, Appearances*, Confucianism*, Desire*, Impressive*, Improvements*, Self-Promotion*, Strict*, Understanding*.)

The Image. An aphorism proposes not a general law, but an image. "A watched pot never boils" does not state a natural law about what always happens when one watches a pot. It means to suggest to us an image, that of a person anxiously watching a pot and feeling like it will "never boil." The image evokes a sensed connection, which does not always occur but sometimes occurs, between anxious waiting and the feeling that what is waited for will "never come." This feature of aphorisms often considerably narrows the meaning of the terms used. Here, not just any watching is intended, but anxious watching. And "never boiling" has a psychological rather than a physical reference (it *seems* to the anxious watcher that the pot will "never boil"). This means that aphorisms are never dogmatic, but mean to evoke an image in which the basis for connecting two ideas is clear to our minds. So, to understand the Laoist saying, "He does not show cff so he shines," we must try to conjure up some image in which the connection between the two terms would be clear, that is, we must try to imagine some *kind* of "not showing off" that could plausibly be expected *in some sense* to cause a person to shine. We must resist the temptation to reduce the image to a rule ("Don't show off"), or to purely practical advice ("If you want to shine, not showing off is the best strategy to use"). The purpose of such a saying is to encourage people to take attractive self-effacement as their ideal, rather than aggressive self-promotion. To put this another way, "The five colors make people's eyes go blind" (21[12]:1) does not state dogmatically that colorful things always dull one's senses and therefore should always be avoided. It means to warn one about colorful objects *when and insofar as* they dull the senses. The images offered by an aphorism are often *counter*images, intended to correct some human tendency (the saying's "target"), and for this reason images offered often (like the one about colors above) are deliberately exaggerated, paradoxical, provocative, "shocking." This is particularly true of Laoist sayings, known for their colorfulness. Their intent is not to present a sober, accurate, properly qualified general truth, but to "wake people up" to a perspective on the situation that they are ignoring. This should warn us against a literal-minded understanding, but neither should we regard hyperbole as a merely ornamental "figure of speech." Whoever compares his ideal ruler to a prostitute (56[61]:1) is deliberately trying to shock his moralistic contemporaries—this is part of the message of such a passage. (Note also that, for the sake of succinctness or wit, aphorisms sometimes depart considerably from logical or grammatical structure, as in "A miss is as good as a mile." This, rather than textual corruption, may explain some passages in the *Tao Te Ching* difficult to make sense of if one assumes normal Chinese usage.) Part of the unity of Laoist thought consists in the fact that several sayings directed against the same target present similar images (these are discussed in the Topical Glossary, under the topics listed at the end of the previous paragraph).

The attitude and the value orientation motivating it. The point an aphorism makes resides not in the contents of what is said, but in the implicit *choice* made to bring up this image rather than another. This choice in turn conveys the attitude of the speaker. When someone is deciding whether to take a risk, I might choose say "Better safe than sorry" or I might choose to say "Nothing ventured, nothing gained." The crucial issue behind this choice is not which saying is objectively more true, but which saying I think puts this particular situation in the right perspective. A child who says "Sticks and stones may break my bones, but names will never hurt me" is not explaining an objective truth but is "posturing"—assuming a certain posture or attitude toward a situation, insisting on seeing it in a certain perspective. Everyone saying an aphorism is "posturing"—assuming a certain posture or attitude toward the situation and inviting his or her addressee to share this attitude. In bringing up a particular aphorism, one is not primarily conveying information; one is primarily expressing an attitude. The ultimate basis on which an aphorism hopes to persuade is not the objective truth it directly states, but the attractiveness of the attitude or perspective it "acts out" toward the situation it addresses. Frequently this attractiveness lies in the particular value orientation underlying the saying. In my view, a relatively unified attitude underlies the entire body of Laoist polemic aphorisms, motivated by a particular value orientation. This attitude, cultivated as a "state or quality of mind," *is* the Laoist "Tao," the Laoist Way, the Laoist "approach" to life (see p. 214). This attitude is something "acted out" in a saying ("performed" by the saying, as J. L. Austin[32] might say), rather than explicitly spoken *about* in the saying. This is an important part of what it means to say (43[1]:1) that Tao cannot be named. In the present view, this point is immensely important to understanding the *Tao Te Ching*. Applying it to Laoist aphorisms reveals the *perspectival* and value-laden character of Laoist wisdom. Laoists neither teach a relativist skepticism of all values[33] nor is their advice based on a completely objective set of truths. They take a decisive stand in favor of one particular set of values and advocate adopting an attitude toward all situations based on this set of values. Attitude is important also when considering the problem of "consistency" in the *Tao Te Ching*. The "consistency" of Laoist wisdom is not based on a set of doctrines or moral-spiritual principles, which Laoists consistently apply to all situations. What is most consistent in the Laoist "system" (see pp. 213–214) is the attitude the aphorisms "perform." In un-Laoist fashion I have attempted to give an explicit account of the basic value orientation motivating the Laoist attitude, see p. 239 under "Organic* harmony."

Note that normally, none of the three elements outlined here is mentioned explicitly in a given proverb. And yet in every proverb these three elements are *essential* to its meaning, and highly *specific;* to guess wrongly about one of them is to misunderstand the proverb. In trying to understand a difficult proverb in the *Tao Te Ching,* it will not do to stare at the words and try to read directly off of them the meaning of the proverb. What we must do is make educated guesses—with the help of background information and parallel sayings in the *Tao Te Ching*—about the three essential meaning elements outlined earlier.

The kind of analysis of Laoist aphorisms this leads to can be illustrated by using the famous example: "One who speaks does not understand" (30[56]:1). It is incorrect to take this to mean that literally anyone who ever says anything must lack understanding. One could paraphrase its meaning rather as follows:

1. You might tend to be easily impressed by skillful speech and so assume that the eloquent speaker is a person of great understanding (this is the saying's "target").

2. To counter this, I want to call your attention to the image of empty-headed eloquence in which you can see a connection between skillful speech and lack of real knowledge.

3. As a reason for accepting this point, I invite you to adopt a value orientation and attitude in which substance is all-important even when not impressive and impressive show is of little importance (this is the attitude or "posture" the saying expresses).

I think reflection on our normal ways of making decisions in life would show that our processes approximate the "aphoristic" way of thinking illustrated here much more closely than they do the "logical deductions from consistent principles" we usually assume as an official ideal. In my view, attention to the meaning-structure of aphorisms is the single most important key to a proper understanding of the *Tao Te Ching*.

Sayings and Self-Cultivation

Besides the polemic aphorisms, there is another large group of sayings already mentioned, more directly related to self-cultivation, such as "The Abode of Mysterious Femininity is the Root of the World." As with polemic aphorisms, the common mistake is to take such sayings in the "simplest" way, that is, in the most literal-minded way, as teaching us some doctrines about cosmogony or metaphysics. But the first thing we must ask about such sayings is not, What truths do they teach us? but, How did these words insert themselves into the concrete lives of those who first spoke them? Doctrinal speculation and teaching doctrines of course represent one kind of concrete human activity connected with the use of words, but it is not the only kind.

My hypothesis on the issue of the concrete life setting for sayings like the one just quoted is based on paying careful attention first, not to the content of the sayings involved, but to their "form," as this term is used in an interpretive approach called *form criticism* (see pp. 196–198). *Form* here refers not directly to style, but to those features of oral sayings reflective of their concrete life setting. (For example, succinctness is a normal feature of the "form" of proverbs, reflecting the fact that they need to be inserted into conversation without interrupting its flow.) Doctrinal teaching arises out of speculative doctrinal thinking, and doctrinal thinking in turn typically expresses itself in a certain form of discourse—the kind we find in the writings of Aristotle and Kant, for example, or religious catechisms. If we look carefully at what the forms of expression used in the *Tao Te Ching* suggest about the background, the human activity, out of which they arise, what we find makes it unlikely that they arose out of speculative thought. The prevalent genres of sayings we find instead are for example, (a) instructions in meditation and self-cultivation, (b) sayings describing what it feels like to try to grasp mentally an elusive internal presence (see pp. 232 and 234 under Instruction* and Meditation*), and (3) a large number of sayings celebrating the great benefits that come to one who has internalized certain qualities called *Stillness, Femininity, Emptiness,* and so on (see p. 221, Benefits*). These genres are similar to the genres of sayings we find in another early writing called the *Nei Yeh*. (See p. 238) Both the nature of the genres and the context in which they occur in the *Nei Yeh* suggest a concrete background of self-cultivation (including here introspective meditation), rather than intellectual speculation.

In this view, for example, "Femininity" was among the qualities of mind Laoist *shih* cultivated in themselves. The saying "The [mental] Abode of Mysterious Femininity is the Root of the World" was used primarily among those who were familiar already with this quality, "Femininity," and had experienced it as something quite wonderful. The point of the saying is not to instruct people in something they do not know, but to celebrate the shared experience they already have, of Femininity as something of "cosmic" importance. In this respect, it is not unlike sayings such as "Love makes the world go 'round." This celebrates the experience of love. It does not answer the question, What makes the earth spin? but rather, How great is love?

In some sayings related to self-cultivation the point is not celebratory but instructional, as for example the simple directive, "Push [mental] Emptiness to the limit" (28[16]:1; see p. 232 under Instruction*). But *instructional* here always refers to *practical* instruction concerning the concrete practice of self-cultivation and its results in the way one lives (see p. 238, Normative*), not instruction in doctrines (see pp. 236 and 250, Naming* and Understanding*).

Laoists used a set of special terms to refer to the quality of mind they cultivated, which are always capitalized in my translation. Some of these words are descriptive: Softness, Stillness, Emptiness,

Steadiness, Clarity, Femininity, Harmony, The Merging, Nothing, Not Desiring, Not Doing. But this quality was also hypostatized, spoken of as though it were a quasi-independent entity or force, and this leads to the use of nonadjectival words like The One Thing, The Mother, The Uncarved Block, Tao, and Te. Each of these terms is a heading in the Topical Glossary, where the meanings are explained and references given to all their occurrences.

Origin Sayings

The group of sayings related to self-cultivation that probably will be most problematic for the modern reader are those that appear to describe the origin of the world. These also are the sayings whose interpretation in this book departs quite strongly from the dominant interpretive tradition. I would like to discuss my construal of the semantic structure of such sayings in a little more detail. These are sayings like

> I do not know of anything whose offspring it might be. It seems to precede God. (31[4]:5)
> Being is born of Nothing. (34[40]:2)
> The thousands of things gained the One Thing and so came to life. (35[39]:1)
> Tao produced the One, One produced Two, Two produced Three, Three produced the thousands of things (36[42]:1)
> Nameless, it [Tao] is the origin of the thousands of things. (43[1]:1)
> Tao produces them, Te rears them, events shape them, talents complete their development. (65[51]:1)

Beginning with early commentators like Wang Pi, sayings like this are most often interpreted as "doctrinal foundations" of Laoist thought, as though Laoists first arrived at some cosmogonic or metaphysical theories and then used these theories as a basic foundation on which to build the rest of their thought and their approach to practical problems. In my view, this approach to interpreting such sayings is the unfortunate result of some crucial differences between the situation and interests of later commentators and the situation of the Laoist *shih* who first used such sayings. What happened is a phenomenon common to many movements and traditions: At the beginning of a movement lies a small group of enthusiasts who are intensely moved, "carried away" by some experiences that transform both their personalities and their world as they perceive it. For early enthusiasts, this personal transforming experience is something one "must" be true to, simply because in it is revealed something directly experienced as more precious and important than anything else in life. Later people reading the words of these enthusiasts by and large have not shared this same experience. They are (a) members an organization, part of whose membership requirements is that one assent to certain doctrines or (b) philosopher-intellectuals who typically assume that "having theories," consciously formulated, is a form of knowledge superior in itself to unreflective experience of any kind. Both of these groups habitually distrust their own ("subjective") unreflective experience of the world as a guide to normative truth and are seeking for some authoritative and "objective" external foundation that will provide a critical standard distinguishing their "true" from their false perceptions, their "good" from their bad impulses. They come to writings like the *Tao Te Ching* looking for such authoritative foundational doctrines. Not surprisingly, they find there what they came looking for.

The tendency described here is shared both by many traditional Chinese commentators on the *Tao Te Ching* and many modern scholar-intellectuals, Eastern and Western, among whom there is an unspoken assumption that treating any writing as "philosophy" is a precondition for taking it seriously. Western scholars often come to the *Tao Te Ching* additionally burdened by the quest to discover "absolute foundations" for knowledge that has preoccupied philosophical thought from the time of Descartes up until the "antifoundational" thinkers of very recent times.[34] Finally, the acknowledgement and respect for cultural diversity beginning in the nineteenth century raised for many the threat of "relativism,"[35] and a consequent search for transcultural "universal" absolutes to overcome it. This, too, has greatly affected the concerns and interests with which twentieth century readers approach the *Tao Te Ching*.

My view is that the approach to the interpretation of origin-sayings in the *Tao Te Ching* guided by these interests is fundamentally misguided, because these interests did not motivate those who composed the *Tao Te Ching*. The "point" of Laoist origin sayings is not instructional, but celebratory, celebrating the *existentially* "foundational" character of Tao as concretely experienced in the self-cultivation practice of the ideal Laoist, experienced both as an internal personal center and a foundation for meaning in a transformed world.

A major problem for us moderns in understanding origin-sayings is that they reflect certain imaginal and linguistic habits common among ancient Chinese (and ancient peoples generally) that are no longer common. One of the closest analogies, I believe, though still only approximate, is some of the ways we still speak about the "transforming" experience of falling in love. Consider, for example, the love song which begins:

> The first time ever I saw your face,
> I thought the sun rose in your eyes,
> And the moon and stars were the gift you gave,
> To the dark and the empty skies.

This song celebrates the "cosmic" significance that the loved one takes on for the lover. The significance of the cosmic images seems roughly this: One thing that makes falling in love different from ordinary experiences is that ordinary experiences take place within a "world" that is the stable backdrop for our lives. Falling in love strongly affects the backdrop itself, making it seem as though the world itself is radically changed ("I felt the earth shake under my feet, and the sky come tumbling down"). It is now a *fundamentally* different place, a place in which love and the loved person have a central place on the "largest" possible scale. Compare the eulogy of *li*/Etiquette:Ceremony in the Confucian* *Hsün Tzu:*

> By this Heaven and Earth join
> By this sun and moon shine,
> By this the four seasons proceed,
> By this the stars take their course,
> By this the Yangtse and the Yellow River flow,
> By this the myriad things flourish.[36]

We could diagram the semantic structure implicit in the last two lines of the love song above in the following way:

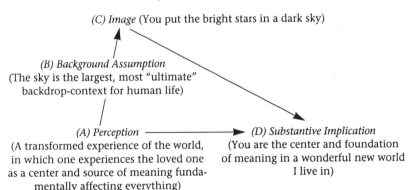

(C) Image (You put the bright stars in a dark sky)

(B) Background Assumption
(The sky is the largest, most "ultimate"
backdrop-context for human life)

(A) Perception ⟶ *(D) Substantive Implication*
(A transformed experience of the world,   (You are the center and foundation
in which one experiences the loved one   of meaning in a wonderful new world
as a center and source of meaning funda-   I live in)
mentally affecting everything)

The perceptual basis (A) here is the foundation for everything. Neither the background assumption that the sky is the "ultimate context" for human life (B), nor the idea that the loved one put the stars in the sky (C) are doctrinal "beliefs" on which anything is based. The image of the stars' origin (C) is a celebratory expression of the perception (A). It does not represent something one knows in addition to it, nor is it a separate basis for the substantive implication (D), which is wholly grounded in the perception (A).

Of course, there are significant differences between this love song and Laoist sayings about Tao as origin. Being in love often is a temporary phenomenon, whereas Laoist self-cultivation aimed at keeping life centered on Tao. Being in love is strictly personal, whereas Laoists posed their Tao as the foundation for a new "world" order (in their naive ethnocentrism, of course "the world" meant the Chinese Empire).

Some differences between Laoist and modern thought habits that also are important here lie in the area of what were called in the diagram *background assumptions*. Of principal importance here is the tendency of ancient Chinese to use chronological imagery, images of "ancient time" and "original source," to express ideas for which we tend to use spatial imagery, images of "depth," "foundation," and so on. This can be illustrated by a number of examples:

• Contemporary *shih* were in the habit of presenting the policies they considered ideal as the policies of legendary ancient kings and sages. Usually, the semantic structure of such statements is the same as that pictured above. That is, they usually have no reliable independent knowledge of ancient policies on which to base their recommendations. Ascribing a policy to the ancients is a conventional way of *expressing* its ideal character. (See p. 220, Ancient*.)

• Graham points out that the Chinese word *ku*/ancient is related etymologically to another *ku* that means "a reason," "a basis," used for example by Mohist logicians to refer to the factual assertion that is the "basic core" of a sentence's meaning.[37]

• In speaking of the single unifying spirit underlying all Laoist wisdom, two passages in the *Tao Te Ching* use the image of a parent: This spirit is the "ancestor of my words" (45[70]:2), the "father of my teaching" (36[42]:6). Because Tao also is called the *ancestor of the thousands of things* (31[4]:2) one could say: Tao is to the thousands of things what the single Laoist approach is to the multiplicity of Laoist sayings.

• A passage from the *Chuang Tzu* says: "You have only to rest in inaction and things will transform themselves. Smash your form and body, spit out hearing and eyesight, forget you are a thing among other things. [This is] the Great Merging [*ta t'ung*], deep and boundless. Undo the mind, slough off spirit, be blank and soulless, *and the ten thousand things one by one will turn back to the Root.*"38 As in 28[16]:2, the image of "things turning back to the Root" here describes not an objective event, but a shift in the way one *experiences* the world (see p. 242, Shift*). There is one state in which one's own mind is very active, and it experiences the world as full of a multiplicity of active things. As one's own mind calms down, the world seems to calm down, too, until one begins to experience the multiplicity of the world as though it has its source-foundation in a single Still Root. Here we can see the relation of the image of Tao as Root-Origin to the transformed experience of the world brought about in Laoist self-cultivation.

• 29[52]:1–2 pictures the hypostatized quality of mind one cultivates as the source-Mother of the empirical world, called here the *children*. The saying says "Once you get the Mother, then you understand the children." The key to understanding the true meaning of things in the world is understanding them in relation to a certain source-foundation of meaning, identical with the quality of mind one cultivates. This is the probable meaning also of the sayings "understanding the *ku*/ancient source is the main thread of Tao" (37[14]:6) and "[Tao's power] allows us to see the beginnings of everything" (38[21]:3). The expression *seeing the ancient beginnings* of something *means* seeing it in its true light.

Finally, we should remember that the distinction we customarily make between "bare objective facts," on the one hand, and the "meanings" these facts have for humans is a thoroughly modern distinction, wholly dependent on the development of the modern scientific idea of a "bare objective fact." "The world" that prescientific peoples refer to when they speak of "the origin of the world" does not consist of bare physical facts and objects, but the meaning-filled world of their ordinary experience. Because for most the meaning of the world is the preeminent question, the question about the origin-foundation of the world is a question about the origin-foundation of meaning in the world.

With these observations in mind about the "background assumptions" underlying origin imagery, we can diagram the semantic structure of Laoist origin sayings roughly as follows:

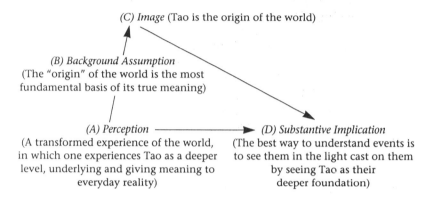

(C) Image (Tao is the origin of the world)

(B) Background Assumption
(The "origin" of the world is the most fundamental basis of its true meaning)

(A) Perception ⟶ *(D) Substantive Implication*
(A transformed experience of the world, in which one experiences Tao as a deeper level, underlying and giving meaning to everyday reality)   (The best way to understand events is to see them in the light cast on them by seeing Tao as their deeper foundation)

The perceptual basis (A) here is the foundation for everything. Neither the background assumption equating origins with what is existentially fundamental (B) nor the idea that Tao is the origin of the world (C) is a doctrinal "belief" on which anything is based. The image of Tao as world origin (C) is an expression of the perception (A). It does not represent something one knows in addition to it, nor is it a separate basis for the substantive implication (D), which is wholly grounded in the perception (A). "Tao-originated" is adjectival, describing the character of the world as seen from a Laoist perspective.[39]

To interpret Laoist origin sayings in this way is not to deny that some Laoists may have taken these primarily celebratory sayings *also* as literal pictures of the world's origin. In the absence of any competing, scientifically based picture of world origins, this would be a very easy and natural thing to do. But (a) there is still no indication that they took literal facts of this kind as the *basis* for their thought. And (b) one indication that literal interpretation was not *foremost* in their minds is the lack of any visible attempt in the *Tao Te Ching* to harmonize the many different, sometimes conflicting images of world origins contained in the sayings. (See, for example, comments on 35[39]:1.) This is what one would expect of someone seriously interested in constructing a consistent set of literal beliefs or doctrines about how the world began. What we have instead are a series of overlapping images.

Some may see this analysis as reductionist, reducing Laoism to something less than it would be if it were a philosophical doctrine based on objective and absolute metaphysical truths. This is so only on the assumption that absolute metaphysical truths are the sole desirable, possible, and adequate foundations for a well-founded world-view. My own assumptions on this matter (spelled out in the longer edition of this work) are quite opposed to this.

The Laoist "System"

Laoist thought forms a coherent "system" of mutually defining elements, each of which can be properly understood only in relation to a structured whole. The discussions earlier in this chapter can be summarized here by giving a brief account of the formal structure of this system as I understand it. This account is approximate, schematic, and very simplified. I offer it to counterbalance the natural tendency to structure Laoist thought in more familiar ways, for example as a set of doctrines or rules or as a description of goals and of means to achieve them.

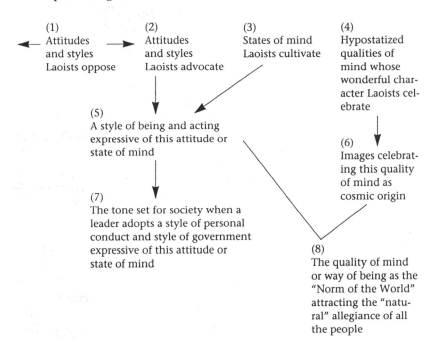

(1)
Attitudes and styles Laoists oppose

(2)
Attitudes and styles Laoists advocate

(3)
States of mind Laoists cultivate

(4)
Hypostatized qualities of mind whose wonderful character Laoists celebrate

(5)
A style of being and acting expressive of this attitude or state of mind

(6)
Images celebrating this quality of mind as cosmic origin

(7)
The tone set for society when a leader adopts a style of personal conduct and style of government expressive of this attitude or state of mind

(8)
The quality of mind or way of being as the "Norm of the World" attracting the "natural" allegiance of all the people

This sketch uses several English phrases—*attitude, state of mind, style, setting a tone*—to describe different aspects of something spoken of in the *Tao Te Ching* as a *single* reality, what it is that Laoists "cultivate." Aspects (2), (3), (4), (5), (7), and (8) are all called *Tao*. The center of the system is the attitude or state of mind cultivated, valued for its own sake. Styles of acting are valued insofar as they express this attitude, and social "tone setting" is valued insofar as it spreads the spirit of this attitude to the society as a whole. Celebratory sayings, including origin sayings, celebrate the wonderful character and fundamental importance this attitude or state of mind is directly experienced to have. The positive images presented in polemic aphorisms give representative examples (not rules) of ways of being and acting expressive of this attitude. These aphorisms are also "speech acts" acting out this attitude (see p. 204).

A Note on Translation

This translation is based on the standard traditional Chinese text of the *Tao Te Ching* given in the commentary of Wang Pi, as printed in Ho Shih-chi's *Ku pen tao te ching hsiao k'an*. When I accept a reading not from Wang Pi, I always mention this in the textual notes. Most of these other readings are from the newly discovered Ma-wang-tui manuscripts, as printed and discussed in Henricks.[40]

This translation was done over a period of eighteen years, during which I went carefully through the Chinese text a number of times, comparing it to the principal available scholarly translations in Western languages, especially those of Paul Carus, Wing-tsit Chan, Ch'en Ku-ying, Ch'u Ta-kao, J. J. L. Duyvendak, Carmelo Elorduy, Robert Henricks, Bernhard Karlgren, D. C. Lau, James Legge, Victor von Strauss, Arthur Waley, and the translations of Chinese commentators given in Erkes (1950), Julien, and Rump (see References). Phrases in my translation and ideas in my commentary too numerous to mention are borrowed from these previous works. On matters having to do strictly with the meanings of individual words I often give special weight to the very literal translation by Bernhard Karlgren, a scholar with little interpretive expertise but a foremost expert on ancient Chinese language and lexicography and the author of a standard dictionary of ancient Chinese. Ninety-five percent of the time, my basic understanding of the text is found in at least one of these translators. (I have been somewhat cautious in this matter as I am self-taught in Chinese.) In cases where I am consciously departing from all these authors in my basic understanding, I mention either in the commentary or the textual notes that this is a "new" translation or interpretation of the text and try to give some reasons. The designation *new* signals only a departure from the previously mentioned translations—other translators whom I have not read of course also may have arrived at the same understanding. My intention is not to claim credit for original opinions, but to alert the reader when I depart from the opinion of learned sinologists and perhaps strike out into more shaky territory.

My method of translation is a compromise between two main principles. The first principle is, where possible, to give a fairly literal translation, approximating one English word for one Chinese word and approximating also the Chinese word order. (The first goal is rendered difficult because the Chinese of the text is so succinct. The latter goal is often made relatively easy because Chinese syntax resembles English in many respects.) This literal approach yields translations like "not Tao, soon gone" (69[30]:5).

Literal translation sometimes, however, would give the wrong impression in English, read too awkwardly, or be too succinct to make sense to an English-speaking reader.[41] Where this seemed to be the case I have drawn on a different approach to translation: One ought to try first to get a concrete sense of what the Chinese probably means, keep this concrete sense without words, and then try to think how one would express this sense in contemporary English today. So for example in 3[67]:1 a very literal rendering would read something like,

I great seem not resemble...
if resemble long-time the insignificance.

I translate

I am 'great—but not normal'...
if I were 'normal,' I'd have been of little worth for a long
time now.

I have deliberately avoided the somewhat formal style characteristic of older translations, considering more colloquial English closer to the Laoist spirit. I have especially tried to maintain the colorful, sometimes "shocking" character of the Chinese, which is sometimes smoothed out by other translators.

This entire work is an *interpretation* of the *Tao Te Ching*. That is, both in the translation and in the commentary I have construed everything in some way that I can make some sense of. I have strongly resisted forcing the text to say what I would like it to say—the theories discussed earlier about this book's composite character and complex origins provide many options for solving difficulties for which others often propose solutions I tend to adopt only as a very last resort, like textual emendation without manuscript support.[42] On the other hand, even where the text is difficult to make sense of, I have generally chosen some conjectural rendering that makes some sense, rather than giving a literal translation and leaving the reader to make sense of it however she can. For the sake of brevity, I have also generally given only one interpretation of each passage, rather than discussing several other plausible ones, even where this means choosing on the basis of rather slight probabilities inclining in one direction rather than another. Where I am conscious that my translation is more than usually conjectural, I have tried to mention this fact either in the commentary or the additional textual notes.

I am more confident in the questions I have asked and the general lines of interpretive method I have tried to follow than I am about all the details of this particular interpretation. Considering especially the limitations of my sinological knowledge, the probabilities are that I have often guessed wrong on details. I hope this interpretation will stimulate others to proceed to further improvements in our understanding of this great book.

Topical Glossary

This glossary contains brief discussions of some topics that recur frequently in the Tao Te Ching or in the commentary. The topics are listed alphabetically under key-words marked with an asterisk in the commentary. (All forms of a word are listed under one heading; for example, references to desiring*, desirable*, and desireless* will all be found under Desire*.) These key-words are primarily a reference device—many are chosen merely because of the ease with which they could be worked into the commentary. This means that often key-words themselves cannot be used as an accurate clue to Laoist thought; primary attention needs to be paid to the discussion following each word. (For example, the discussion under Self-promotion* makes it clear that Laoists were not against seeking promotions. The discussion under Metaphorical* is not an essay on Laoist use of metaphor.)

Agitation.   The target of one group of polemic aphorisms* is the human attraction to exciting things and stimulating activities, which Laoists criticize on the grounds that they agitate the mind. Among "agitating" things are included colorful clothes, fine foods and music, horse racing and hunting (21[12]:1), luxurious living (22[50]:1-2, 51[75]:1-2), excited conversation (16[5]:3, 14[23]:1-2, 30[56]:1-2), and the pressures of one's job (29[52]:4). Desire* and desirable things are also mentally agitating. We tend to regard our lives as dull when nothing especially exciting or desirable "stands out" against our ordinary existence. But when something that stands out stimulates us, this causes our being to strain to align itself around this, losing the organic* order it has when all the parts are allowed to align themselves naturally with each other in a harmony arising from within. Our being can stand this only so long, and this is why prolonged stimulatation eventually reduces the sensitivity of our senses (21[12]:1), causes internal agitation (21[12]:1:4, 23[26]), makes us vulnerable to disease (22[50]:1-2), wears us out (29[52]:4), and is bound to be short lived (14[23]:1-2, 69[30]:5). In contrast, Laoists cultivate an extraordinary internal Stillness* that deepens and enhances the organic harmony toward which our being tends when left to itself. This gives us an inexhaustible source of energy (16[5]:2, 32[6]:4), an internal Steadiness*, a lasting* way of being as opposed to constant ups and downs, and preserves whole a capacity for deep satisfaction (21[12]:2). One who cultivates this Stillness and Harmony* on a deep level can engage in intense activity without becoming agitated or wearing herself out (33[55]:2:6–7). See 5[45]:3, 14[23]:1,2, 16[5]:2,3, 21[12]:2–3, 22[50]:2, 23[26]:1–3, 29[52]:4, 32[6]:4, 33[55]:5 (= 69[30]:5). Section 2 of the translation groups together chapters that center on mental excitement/ desire/agitation and the opposite ideal of Stillness* and contentment. These are the chapters in which Laoist thought comes closest to that attributed to Yang* Chu and also to the emphasis on physiological self-cultivation in some later forms of Taoism (see comments under 22[50]). See also Desire*.

Ancient*.   Contemporary Chinese frequently invoked the image of idealized kings and their perfectly wise advisors who ruled in a legendary ancient Golden Age. To attribute a particular policy to these ancient worthies was a conventional way of putting forth this policy as an ideal, often with no appeal to any historical evidence that the ancient sages actually practiced it. (See p. 210, and the analysis of origin* sayings, pp. 207–213.) See 4[22]:7, 6[15]:1, 11[38]:4, 12[18]:1, 37[14]:5, 38[21]:3, 48[62]:6, 57[68]:2, 80[65]:1.

Aphoristic*.   A word I use to describe the meaning-structure of the proverblike polemic aphorisms in the *Tao Te Ching*. Aphorisms are not rules to be applied literally and consistently, but are corrective, "compensatory" wisdom, counterbalancing some tendency in the opposite direction (see p. 201). The polemic thrust of these aphorisms describes one kind of thrust Laoist sayings have, the other two kinds being instructional* and celebratory*. The analysis of polemic aphorisms on pp. 201–205 is the single most important set of guiding principles underlying the present interpretation of the *Tao Te Ching*.

Appearances*.   The target of one group of polemic aphorisms* is the tendency to admire most and cultivate in oneself the appearances of good qualities that will impress others—qualities like uprightness (4[22]:2, 5[45]:2), competence, (5[45]:2), knowledge (8[81]:1), eloquence (8[81]:1, 5[45]:2, 30[56]:1), and Te (11[38]:1, 44[41]:3). These qualities would have been especially attractive to *shih** anxious to further their careers by making a good impression, as well as to rulers who wanted to impress* their people. Some of these sayings hold up ideals that would be commonly admired, but are not very strikingly impressive; for example, sincere speech in contrast to eloquent speech (8[81]:1). Others are more extreme, holding up for admiration qualities that would conventionally be regarded as positively bad or undesirable (for examples, *compromised* [4[22]:2], *disgraceful* [17[28]:1]). Social admiration tends to make certain personal qualities stand out, and we experience them then as especially desirable and solid*, in contrast to other qualities cast into the shade as Empty*, Nothing*, even disgraceful. But seeing things this way and working* to develop impressive qualities and repress disgraceful ones ruins the organic* harmony, the goodness including the whole of each person's unique being, toward which it tends when this external influence does not interfere. Such working, typically motivated by self-promotion*, "cuts up the Uncarved* Block" (17[28]:2). Laoist self-cultivation aims at developing and enhancing this organic and holistic goodness, less impressive externally but more genuinely satisfying to the possessor ("useful" 5[45]:1, 11[38]:7, 15[11]:2). This means counterbalancing our tendency to emphasize socially desirable qualities, by deliberate attempts to develop and integrate the "shadow" side of ourselves (Jung): the qualities of our being we ignore or repress because in the eyes of conventional society they seem worthless or "bad." These ideas account for much of the paradoxical character of Laoist thought, in contrast to Confucians*, who tended to see their ideals as more continuous with conventional standards. See 3[67]:1, 4[22]:2, 5[45]:2, 7[8]:2, 8[81]:1, 11[38]:1, 14[23]:4, 17[28]:1, 30[56]:1, 44[41]:3, 48[62]:3. Section 1 of the translation groups together chapters that criticize admiration of impressive appearances and propose Laoist ideals that contrast with this. See also Self-promotion*.

Benefits. A large group of celebratory* sayings celebrate the wonderful powers or benefits that result from cultivating Tao and conducting government and personal life accordingly. The benefits described are usually based on relatively realistic experiences, but the descriptions extrapolate from this to highly exaggerated and utopian images. For example, one could easily see that the Still* state of mind Laoists cultivated might be more even and lasting* than the ups and downs in the life of one who likes excitement. But some sayings extrapolate from this to a utopian image of "inexhaustible" energy (16[5]:2, 29[52]:4, 32[6]:4), even perhaps to "lasting" beyond death (24[33]:3). I think the exaggerated and utopian imagery reflects the Laoist experience of being "saved" by Tao (48[62]:6, 49[27]:3): Something that solves so wonderfully the *main* life problem, the problem of meaning, is easily taken to have the potential of bringing about a perfect state. Sometimes the utopian images in these sayings have some *specific* connection to words or phrases describing the quality of mind being celebrated, for example, the connection between the not-desiring* ruler and the *p'u*/Simple people in 77[57]:5:8–9. But often the connection is very loose; for example, in 26[59]:3 there seems no specific connection between the connotations of the phrase *Mother of the State,* on the one hand, and the benefit *lasting long* on the other. "Possessing the Mother of the State" counts here as just one more description of the single state of mind Laoists cultivate, and this state of mind allows one to "last long." This observation should caution against emphasizing specific connections; for example, the connection between "not desiring" and understanding things truly in 43[1]:3.[1] The celebratory* character of these sayings means that they assume a primary audience who already experienced Tao as something wonderful, and the exaggerated images in these sayings express this shared experience of Laoist *shih**. See 3[67]:3–4, 14[23]:3, 16[5]:2, 22[50]:3, 25[48]:2–3, 26[59]:2–3, 29[52]:2:1–2, 31[4]:3, 32[6]:4, 33[55]:1, 37[14]:5, 38[21]:1 and 3, 43[1]:3, 46[35]:1,3, 47[43]:1, 48[62]:2 and 6, 49[27]:3, 52[77]:2, 56[61]:3, 61[54]:1,2, 63[32]:2, 70[60]:2,4, 72[64]:5, 75[78]:1, 77[57]:5, 81[37]:1.

Celebratory*. A word I use to describe the intent or thrust of many Laoist sayings, in contrast to a polemic (see Aphoristic*) or instructional* intent. See pp. 197, 206, 208–209. Discussions of the main types of celebratory sayings will be found under Benefits* and Cosmic*, and in the treatment of origin sayings pp. 207–213.

Ch'i*. *Ch'i* means literally "breath, air," but the word is often used to refer to one's bodily energy as felt internally. As Mencius[2] says, "Stumbling or rushing—[the way] this [feels] is *ch'i.*" Hence "the mind controlling the *ch'i*" (33[55]:4) probably refers to attempts to directly control the quality of this felt energy by will power, and "Empty *ch'i*" (36[42]:3) refers to an Empty* quality of mind Laoists cultivate. Although *ch'i* was beginning to be used by some[3] as a technical theoretical term, I believe that in the *Mencius* and the *Tao Te Ching* it is still an unsystematized term of folk psychology, similar in use to words like *feelings* in colloquial English.[4] *Ch'i* occurs in 27[10]:1, 33[55]:4, 36[42]:3.

Chuang* Tzu. Laoists share a general approach to life characteristic of several other groups, which later came to be known collectively as *Taoist*.[5] A roughly contemporary book, called the *Chuang Tzu*,[6] is an anthology of writings from various other Taoist groups[7] and the principal source of our knowledge of early Taoism in addition to the *Tao Te Ching* (see p. 195). Quotations from the *Chuang Tzu* will be found on pp. 192, 211, and 234.

Clarity*. *Ming*/Clarity is one of the names for the quality of mind Laoists cultivate, probably referring to the mental clarity experienced when the mind is at rest. Mental *ch'ing*/clarity is the result of gradually Stilling the mind in 6[15]:3. In 27[10]:1, *ming*/Clarity is a quality of reality as experienced by one in a meditative state. See 6[15]:3, 24[33]:1, 27[10]:1, 28[16]:3, 29[52]:5,6, 33[55]:3, 49[27]:3, 73[36]:1. *Ming* also can mean "bright" (44[41]:2), "shine" (4[22]:5), or "to enlighten [= to educate]" (80[65]:1).

Composers*. The term I use for the Laoist teachers whom I believe composed the collages of oral sayings that constitute the "chapters" of the *Tao Te Ching* (see p. 198).

Confucianism*. The target of one group of polemic aphorisms* is the approach of other contemporary *shih** teachers with a Confucian bent. Confucius (551–479 B.C.) was one of the earliest, and the most famous of the *shih** teachers. Several later teachers, including Mencius*, claim to be following "the Tao of Confucius." At a later time, Confucianism and Taoism became the two principal rival movements in China (Buddhism being a third upon its arrival in the first century A.D.) Commentators generally agree that, in Laoist sayings, *jen*/Goodness, *i*/Morality, *li*/Etiquette, and *hsüeh*/Learning serve as code words, referring to the focus of self-cultivation for contemporary Confucian *shih*-schools.[8] *Goodness*, which might also be translated "benevolence," "humaneness," or "empathy," often functions as a summary reference to the Confucian ideal. *Morality* means doing what is right according to a refined version of conventional norms, especially those regarding conduct proper to one's station in life. *Etiquette* is a very approximate translation of *li*: It refers to elaborate religious and court ceremony, but Confucian ideals tended to picture refined social interaction as a kind of ceremony as well.[9] *Learning* refers primarily to character formation and only secondarily to the study of traditional customs and exemplars that were to serve as a guide.[10] Polemic aphorisms against Confucian self-cultivation are related to Laoist thought against impressive appearances*, against self-promotion*, and against working*. Laoist sayings against naming* probably have at least partly in mind the Confucian project of "rectifying names." Laoist criticisms caricature their Confucian rivals and should not be taken as accurate representations of Confucian thought. See 11[38]:3,4,5, 12[18]:1, 13[20]:1,2, 16[5]:1, 42[2]:1, 72[64]:7, 78[19]:1. I believe 7[8]:2, 25[48]:1:1, and perhaps 13[20]:3:1, are Confucian sayings.

Connective*.   I believe that composers of the chapter collages often have altered or added to an oral saying to connect it to other sayings included in the same chapter (see p. 198). The main criteria I use for conjecturing that this has probably happened are (a) a word or line interrupts a pattern (such as rhyme or parallelism) in the saying where it occurs, and in addition (b) this same word or line connects this saying to another nearby. I list examples here in three groups, explained under Framing*: (a) 27[10]:1:7–8; 35[39]:1:26; 51[75]:1:4–6; 56[61]:2:2; 57[68]:1:4; 67[31]:7:2; 69[30]:4:3. (b) 6[15]:2:9; 7[8]:2; 28[16]:5:6; 30[56]:3:5; 44[41]:3:9; 77[57]:5:6–7; 79[3]:2:1 and 4:2. (c) 11[38]:4:2; 38[21]:2:1–2; 55[66]:3:4–5; 58[73]:5:5.

Conquest* cycle.   Some ancient texts make reference to a kind of primitive physics-psychology in ancient China comparable to the "four elements" theory of ancient Greece.[11] In the Chinese version there was an attempt at a hierarchical ordering of certain hypostatized* elements or energies, expressed by saying that the superior energy *sheng*/overcomes ("conquers") an inferior one, as in the following excerpt from the *Shuo Wen:* "Joy injures the heart, but fear overcomes joy. Heat injures the breath, but cold overcomes heat, and bitterness injures the breath, but salt overcomes bitterness.... Fear injures the kidneys, but desire overcomes fear...cold injures the blood, but dryness overcomes cold."[12] Graham[13] calls this the *cycle of conquests*. Several Laoist sayings borrow the formula "X *sheng*/overcomes Y" to express the superiority of the internal "energies" they cultivate over their opposites, as in "Softness overcomes hardness" (75[78]:2). This is further evidence for my thesis that Laoists hypostatized* the quality of mind they cultivated. I believe Laoists have no genuine interest in this speculation as such. These sayings are purely celebratory* in intent. See 5[45]:3, 56[61]:2, 73[36]:2, 75[78]:2, and perhaps 23[26]:1 and 47[43]:1.

Contending*.   *Cheng*/contend means both "to strive, compete" and "to quarrel" (see 57[68]:2). It is a negative term in the *Tao Te Ching,* referring especially to competition with others for higher status and reputation, so this term is related to the Laoist polemic against self-promotion* and against admiring only impressive appearances*, and to the positive Laoist ideal of "being low*" (see 57[68]:1–2). *Not-contending* describes an attitude or state of mind that is the contrasting Laoist ideal. See 4[22]:6 (= 55[66]:4), 7[8]:1,3, 8[81]:4, 57[68]:2, 58[73]:5, 79[3]:1.

Content. Resting "content" within oneself as opposed to reaching out for desirable* and exciting things is a Laoist goal mentioned in 19[44]:3, 20[46]:2,3, 24[33]:2.

Cosmic. Some sayings celebrate the foundational importance of Tao in the life of the ideal Laoist, by ascribing to it a foundational role in the cosmos, as in the origin* sayings (see pp. 205–213). Other "cosmic" sayings frequently use the formula *X wei t'ien hsia Y*, "X is the Y of the World" (as in "Stillness is the Norm of the World," 5[45]:4). This formula probably draws on the tradition of the Chou Emperor* as one of the pillars of the cosmic order (see 35[39]:1) and the Laoist idea that the ideal Laoist is the spiritual heir to this role. See 4[22]:4, 5[45]:4, 17[28]:1, 28[16]:5, 30[56]:5 (= 48[62]:7), 32[6]:2, 35[39]:1:13, 39[25]:4, 48[62]:1, 65[51]:2:2.

Desire. The target of one group of polemic aphorisms* is reaching out for "desirable" things, especially material goods and fame (21[12]:1, 18[13]:1–3, 19[44]:1, 72[64]:7), and things regarded as improvements* (20[46]:1, 43[1]:3, 76[80]). These desires are not criticized primarily on moral grounds, that is, as something egotistical. Rather desire causes mental agitation*, disturbing mental Stillness* and contentment, and because of this causes social disharmony. See 18[13]:1–3, 19[44]:1, 20[46]:1,2, 21[12]:1, 43[1]:3, 72[64]:7, 76[80], 79[3]:1,3, and comments under Agitation*. *Yü*/desire also is a recurrent term with a somewhat specialized meaning in Laoist thought. *Yü* is a negative term in 20[46]:2, 79[3]:1, 81[37]:2, and *wu yü*/"not desiring" describes the opposite, ideal Laoist state of mind in 43[1]:3, 64[34]:4, 72[64]:7, 77[57]:5, 78[19]:2, 79[3]:1,3, 81[37]:2. As with not working*, this should not be taken literally, as a ban on all desires. "Desire" is negative *when and insofar as* it interferes with Laoist goals. "Ambitious" (lit. *yu yü*/"having desires") is a positive term in 1[24]:4.

Doing. See Working*.

Dwelling. Several sayings use spatial imagery to describe maintaining a certain frame of mind, as though there are several mental "spaces" where one can "dwell." For example, the saying "Achieves successes but does not *dwell* in them" (42[2]:5 = 52[77]:3), seems to envision a kind of floating "I" that can choose whether or not to "dwell in" (identify with) external successes. Similarly, 11[38]:7 speaks of "residing in" truly substantial personal qualities rather than in "thin" external show. See 1[24]:4 (= 67[31]:2), 42[2]:3,5, 67[31]:7,8, 42[2]:3,5 (= 52[77]:3). Sayings 24[33]:3 and 72[64]:7 also seem to envision a mental "place" one should return to or not leave. It is partly on the basis of this imagery that I translate *men*/gate:dwelling as "abode" in 32[6]:2 and 43[1]:5, where others usually translate "gate." *Men* seems to mean "abode" rather than "gate" in a phrase found in the *Chuang Tzu* "take Tao as your *men*."[14] *Shih** gathered around a teacher are sometimes called *men jen*/"house men," that is, men of the master's house. The idea of a mental "abode" is frequent in the *Nei** *Yeh,* although a different word is usually employed.

*Embrace**. A verb describing self-cultivation. See Use*.

*Emperor**. Traditional Chou-dynasty (1122–222 B.C.) thought conceived of the Emperor as someone representing in his person the symbolic Norm of the World. This tradition is reflected in the *Tao Te Ching* (35[39]:1 and 39[25]:4), showing that, on one level, Laoists did not question this idea. On another level, however, Laoists regarded the person well advanced in self-cultivation as having the most valid spiritual claim to this symbolic normative "cosmic" role in Chinese culture, in contrast to actual contemporary claimants to the "Emperor" title (see pp. 191 and 192). This is the background for many phrases in Laoist sayings that implicitly evoke the spiritual role of Emperor as an image of the cultural leadership role one deserves who is accomplished in Laoist self-cultivation. Some of these phrases, like "take over the world" (25[48]:3,4) probably refer on a literal level to the ambitions of the heads of various Chinese states to reunite the Empire under their leadership. From the early fourth century onward, the title of *wang*/Emperor began to be claimed by many rulers of feudal territories,[15] and accordingly I translate *wang* as "king." The Emperor image is evoked by phrases in 4[22]:4, 17[28]:1, 18[13]:4, 25[48]:3,4, 28[16]:5, 55[66]:1, 57[68]:2, 75[78]:4, 77[57]:1.

*Empty**. This is one designation of the quality of mind Laoists cultivate in themselves, conveyed by three Chinese synonyms *ch'ung, hsü,* and *wa. Hsü*/empty has the connotation "worthless," as can be seen in 4[22]:7, "Is this an empty saying?" I believe this negative connotation of Emptiness is important throughout. It refers to our tendency to experience qualities that are not socially admired—this includes the most important qualities for Laoists—as somehow lacking full reality. They feel like nothing*, a word with similar meanings in the *Tao Te Ching.* See 4[22]:2, 5[45]:1, 16[5]:2, 28[16]:1, 31[4]:1, 36[42]:3, and "vacant

Valley" in 6[15]:2. The opposite word, *ying*/fullness connotes a solidly felt, substantial presence in the world; for example, 6[15]:4 characterizes "cautious, timid, hesitant" ideal men as "not full." Because the English word *full* does not have these connotations, I translate *ying* as "solid." *Solid* occurs in this meaning in 4[22]:2, 5[45]:1, 6[15]:4, 31[4]:1. See also Appearances*.

Etiquette. See Confucian*.

Excellent. *Shan*/good:excellent is very common in Chinese, meaning both "morally good," and "competent" ("good at..."). Like the English word *good* it is a "generic" concept; that is, it refers to something the *speaker* approves of, although different people have different ideas about what actually is "good." *Shan* is used very frequently in the *Tao Te Ching* to refer to the ideal Laoist way of being. In several passages it seems to refer to a *very high degree* of Laoist "goodness"; for example 49[27]:3–4 speaks of the Taoist teacher as a *shan jen*/"good man" and his pupil as a *pu-shan jen*/"not good man." It is unlikely that the latter phrase means a "no-good man"; it means rather one who is not highly advanced in goodness like the teacher: hence my translation "Excellent man" and "not excellent man." This understanding of the word is supported by three other passages (22[50]:3, 49[27]:1–3, 61[54]:1), which attribute wonderful and quasi-magical effects to actions done "Excellently." Saying 7[8]:1 describes the important Taoist ideal of lowness as "high Excellence." *Shan*/Excellent occurs with this meaning in 6[15]:1, 7[8]:1,2, 8[81]:1, 22[50]:3, 49[27]:1,2,3,4, 55[66]:1, 58[73]:5, 61[54]:1, 69[30]:4.

Femininity. One designation of the quality of mind Laoists cultivate, conveyed by the synonyms *p'in* and *tz'u*. The parallel with "disgraceful" in 17[28]:1 makes it clear that this conventionally was considered a negative characteristic, in the male-dominated society of ancient China. See also Mencius's[16] disparaging comparison of other *shih** to women—the point being that the role of women is to be compliant, but the role of *shih* is to stand up against bad rulers, which these *shih* failed to do. The *Chuang* *Tzu* occasionally mentions[17] women students and one woman teacher, but otherwise I know of no evidence suggesting that the Laoist valuing of Femininity led them to advocate upgrading the social position of women. See 17[28]:1, 27[10]:1, 32[6]:1,2, 56[61]:2.

Forcing. *Ch'iang*/force is a negative term in 33[55]:4, 69[30]:1,4, and 36[42]:6 (translated "violent" in this last passage). *Ch'iang* also means "hard, strong," the opposite of Laoist "Softness" in 73[36]:2; 74[76]:1,2,3,4; 75[78]:1,2. *Ch'iang*/strength is used in a positive sense in 24[33]:1; 29[52]:5; 6[15]:2; and 39[25]:2.

Framing*. I believe that sometimes the composers, instead of juxtaposing closely related sayings, will try to unify their chapter collages by placing closely related sayings at the beginning and the end of a collage, or before and after other material, "framing" these intervening sayings. Methodologically, support for this hypothesis about composition entails making a distinction between (a) those passages that can be used as *evidence* the composers used this device, and (b) those passages that probably ought to be *construed* this way, once one has discovered evidence for the presence of this device by means of examples of type (a).[18] Accordingly, I use three rough distinctions in grouping examples of this device here: (a) clear examples, where the conscious use of this device would seem the most likely explanation of the text, even if we looked at each example in isolation; (b) probable examples where, in isolated examination of each, the presence of the device would seem somewhat likely; and (c) examples where we would not know whether this device was being used consciously if we did not already know it was in common use elsewhere in this book. (These are rough and relative distinctions, of course. *Clear* means "relatively clear.") Where there are easily mentioned catchword connections between sections, I indicate this in parentheses in the listing given here. (a) 4[22]:1 and 7; 7[8]:1 and 3 (contend); 22[50]:2 and 4 (death spot); 23[26]:1 and 3 (agitated/root/master); 28[16]:1 and 3:1 (Stillness); 31[4]:2 and 4; 65[51]:1 and 3; 76[80]:2 and 4. (b) 9[79]:1 and 4 (good); 11[38]:1–2 and 4 (Te); 29[52]:2 and 6 (turn back); 32[6]:1 and 3–4; 44[41]:1–2 and 4 (Tao); 48[62]:1 and 5–6 (Tao), 2 and 6–7 (treasure); 50[53]:2 and 6 (display/boast), 1–3 and 6 (Tao); 58[73]:1–3 and 6 (Heaven); 63[32]:1 and 3; 67[31]:1 and 4 (weapons), 3 and 7, 6 and 8; 72[64]:4–5 and 8 (not working); 79[3]:1 and 3 (wise/clever), 2 and 4 (govern); 80[65]:1–3 and 5. (c) 6[15]:1 and 5 (beyond-understanding/concealed); 14[23]:1 and 4; 35[39]:1 and 3, 2 and 4; 43[1]:1 and 4 (names), 3 and 5 (hidden essences); 59[58]:1 and 4; 60[49]:1 and 3.

Get*.   A verb describing self-cultivation. See Use*.

Good*. See Confucian*.

Harmony*.   One designation of the quality of mind Laoists cultivate. In 33[55]:2, the ideal mental quality of *ho*/Harmony is illustrated by the image of the "harmonious" working of bodily forces that allows an infant to "scream all day without becoming hoarse." A felt internal organic* harmony probably is meant, a state in which all the forces of one's being seem to be working smoothly together, rather than at odds with each other. Ho/Harmony is associated with mental Steadiness* and Clarity* in 33[55]:3, and with Emptiness* in 36[42]:3. In 30[56]:3 (= 31[4]:3), ho/harmonize is used as a verb in the phrase "make the flashings harmonious," that is, smooth out those things experienced as exciting or jarring about the world. See 30[56]:3 (= 31[4]:3), 33[55]:2,3, 36[42]:3. See also shun/harmony:submission in 80[65]:5.

Heaven.   In Chou-dynasty thought, t'ien/Heaven was a general name for the highest divinity, sometimes pictured as a personal being and sometimes as an impersonal principle or force similar to our Fate. Traditional religious beliefs like this play no central role in the thought of Laoists (or that of most other contemporary shih, who in this respect resemble modern secular "intellectuals."[19]) At times some traditional ideas associated with Heaven are indirectly alluded to or invoked in the Tao Te Ching, but this is always to make some other point, not to teach some Laoist doctrines about Heaven. There are none, as shows in the contradictory notions invoked at times (for example, 16[5]:1 and 58[73]:3 contradict 9[79]:4 and 8[81]:4.) Heaven is sometimes pictured as a cosmic principle or force—sometimes alongside "Earth" (e.g. 10[7]:1), or the Emperor (28[16]:5, 39[25]:4). The phrase "Heaven's Tao/Way" is a conventional designation of "the right way," which Laoists sometimes use to describe the Laoist way. Heaven's Way occurs in 2[9]:2, 8[81]:4, 9[79]:4, 41[47]:1, 52[77]:1, 58[73]:5. Other occurrences of Heaven are 3[67]:4, 10[7]:1, 14[23]:2, 16[5]:1,2, 26[59]:1, 27[10]:1, 28[16]:5, 32[6]:2, 39[25]:1,4, 48[62]:5, 57[68]:2, 58[73]:3,6, 63[32]:2. T'ien hsia/"Heaven under" is the normal Chinese expression for "the world," usually meaning the Chinese Empire.

Hurt.   Laoists stress the way that an impressive* and strict* ruler is felt by the people as someone trying to put them to shame by comparison and so is experienced as burdensome and "hurtful," sparking resentment. This theme is explicit in 46[35]:1, 55[66]:3, 59[58]:4, 81[37]:2, and implicit in 54[17]:1, 60[49]:3.

Hypostatize.   To hypostatize something is to speak of it as though it were an independent entity or force. "The weather is acting strangely today" is an hypostatization of the weather. "Let the music flow through your fingers" is an hypostatization of music. "I got in touch with my anger" or "a wave of anger came over me" is an hypostatization of anger. I believe that Laoists hypostatized the quality of mind they cultivated, for instance speaking of "bringing about Stillness*" as a mental state or quality, but also of Stillness* as an independent force that is "the Norm of the World" (5[45]:4). Among other indications like this, formulas borrowed from speculation about the "conquest cycle" also support the thesis that Laoists assimilated the internal "energies" they cultivated—Softness, Femininity, and Stillness—to the hypostatized energies, or *hsing*/agents, that others[20] used to explain physical and psychological phenomena. (See further under Conquest*.) I believe Tao, The Mother, and The One Thing are hypostatizations of this quality of mind as well. Hypostatization is part of the Laoist *imaginal and linguistic* style. In my view the *Tao Te Ching* makes no attempt to develop a system of doctrines about Tao as an independent entity (see pp. 207–213). Compare the hypostatization of Wisdom in the biblical books of *Proverbs* (Chapters 1 and 8), *Sirach* (1 and 24) and *Wisdom of Solomon* (6–9).

   Impressive.   The target of one group of polemic aphorisms* is the tendency of rulers to project an impressive presence, inspiring awe in their people, for example, by speaking to them in a haughty manner (55[66]:2) or by insisting on recognition of their privileged status by imposing high taxes and setting aside royal lands where peasants cannot live (53[72]:2). But for Laoists, even the Confucian* ruler who strives to impress people with his high moral qualities (16[5]:1) is a ruler trying to emphasize the way that he personally stands out over against the "ordinary" and inferior masses. This polarization ruins the organic* harmony of society and causes people to resent the ruler (54[17]:1) as burdensome and tiring (55[66]:3, 53[72]:2), hurting* them by making them feel inferior. He is someone engaging in personal and quarrelsome contention* for social status, provoking his subjects to contend/quarrel with him to defend their own sense of worth. He thus loses the respect and cooperation of the people, a central basis for social order. The ideal organic* social harmony envisioned by Laoists *includes* the central figure of the ruler as symbolic norm setting the tone for the society, on the model of the traditional Chou Emperor*. Organic harmony for them still depends on the allegiance and cooperation that the people "naturally*" and spontaneously accord to a true ruler. (See Graham's enlightening remarks[21] on "hierarchic anarchism" in ancient China.) But for them the preeminent characteristic of a true ruler is that, in his style of ruling, he strives mightily *not* to stand out. In transactions with his subjects, he adopts the manner of one lower in social standing than they (55[66]:1–2, 35[39]:2). He works hard and competently at administration, but keeps such a low profile that his work goes unnoticed and people think good order came about spontaneously (54[17]:3, 81[37]:3). He quietly nips in the bud bad social tendencies (72[64]:1–2) or defeats his opposition by indirect and nonconfrontational tactics (73[36]:1), so he will not be forced into dramatic personal confrontations. He has no principles that stand in opposition to the general character of his society (60[49]:1). What he stands for and what he tries to foster and draw out is just the ideal goodness incipiently inherent in the way social groups spontaneously tend to structure their relationships to each other (72[64]:8). This kind of goodness radiates from his person and his style of governing, as extremely subtle but powerful Te*, setting a tone and producing a perfectly harmonious and prosperous society. (This Te is not a *substitute* for effective administrative work, law enforcement, and so on, but radiates from the *style* in which the ideal ruler carries out these routine tasks.) Sayings directly targeting the "impressive" ruler are 35[39]:2, 36[42]:5, 46[35]:1, 53[72]:1, 54[17]:1,3, 55[66]:1,2,3, 59[58]:4:5. Section 5 of the translation groups together chapters that center on criticism of the impressive ruler or propose contrasting Laoist ideals. See also Strict* and Hurt*. Like all "advice for rulers" these sayings are intended both (a) for *shih** in the Laoist school, advising them on how to conduct themselves as administrators; and (b) for top rulers whom Laoist *shih* would like to advise. See further on this under 78[19].

*Improvements**. Some polemic aphorisms* are directed against programs proposed by other *shih** schools designed to introduce what Laoists see as fundamental changes in the "natural*" social order. Such fundamental "improvements" include the use of ("Mohist*") utilitarian rationality in deciding government policy and encouraging this kind of rationality among the people (79[3]:1–2, 80[65]:1–3). They include the program of rectifying names*, "carving up" implicit organic* social norms into codified legal prescriptions (63[32]:3, 77[57]:3:1–2 and 4). They include deliberate attempts to provide incentives for ambitious people to educate themselves and improve their administrative or work skills, thereby improving public administration and general living standards (79[3]:1–2, 78[19]:1:5–6, 77[57]:3:5–6). Even the Confucian program of trying to spread consciously conceived "virtues" among the people is looked upon by Laoists as an attempt to fundamentally alter and replace people's organic, "natural*" goodness (78[19]:1:1–4). In Laoist eyes, these programs spread to the society those very things they struggle against personally in themselves in their self-cultivation practice. They bring about a general populace full of disquieting desires* destructive of social harmony, conducting personal and public business under the guidance of rational-conceptual (naming*) knowledge and replacing their natural goodness with the artificial appearances* of virtue. Laoists explicitly acknowledge (80[65]:5, 36[42]:2) that people left to themselves often will want to proceed in this "improving" direction, destructive of the "natural" organic* harmony of society that the ("conservative") Laoist administrator-advisor wants so much to protect and foster. Sometimes therefore he must set himself "in opposition to things" (80[65]:5). This of course also is a dilemma for the Laoist administrator, who would like as much as possible to let the mind of the people be his mind (60[49]:1) and avoid confrontation with the people. The basic Laoist solution: "I will restrain them with the Nameless One's Simplicity...caus[ing] them no disgrace...[then] they will be Still*." (81[37]:2) *P'u*/simplicity: "Uncarved* Block" is a name for the quality of mind the Laoist cultivates, which governs the style in which he rules and therefore the tone he sets for his society. These "improving" trends must be opposed, but the hope is that this can be done in a manner that the people will not feel as a humiliation, so that it will result in a Still* people, content with a simple life (76[80], 77[57]:5, 79[3]:2–3). *Not working** also is a common term used for a style of ruling that does not try to "work over" (or allow others to work over, 79[3]:3) the society by implementing "improvements," but tries to maintain its organic harmony (72[64]:8). Laoist thought on this subject is contained mainly in chapters in Section 7, "Against Disquieting 'Improvements.'" See the sayings in 62[29]:1, 76[80]:2,3,4,5,6, 77[57]:3,4,5, 78[19]:1, 79[3]:1,2, 80[65]:1,2,3.

Infant*. A frequently recurring metaphorical* image representing one aspect of the state of mind Laoists cultivate. See 13[20]:4, 17[28]:1, 27[10]:1, 33[55]:1,2, 74[76]:1.

Instruction*. *Instructive* is one kind of thrust Laoist sayings have, the other two major kinds being *polemic* (see Aphoristic*) and *celebratory*. Besides those instructive sayings listed under Meditation* and Normative* another small group of sayings give instruction in Laoist self-cultivation, typically by using several favorite Laoist terms or phrases: See 28[16]:1,2, 29[52]:4, 71[63]:1, 72[64]:7, 78[19]:2:4–5.

Laoist*. A term of convenience I use, following Graham,[22] for the thought of the *Tao Te Ching* and the *shih** school out of which it arose, to distinguish it from other ancient and later forms of Taoism. See p. 195 and *Chuang* Tzu.*

Lasting*. Some passages speak of lasting as a benefit* of Laoist self-cultivation. Such lasting is contrasted with the "exhausting" effects of agitated*, short-lived excitement. In contrast to this, Laoists experienced the Feminine*/Still*/Empty* state of mind as an inexhaustible source of energy (32[6]:4, 16[5]:2). See 10[7]:1, 14[23]:2, 19[44]:5, 24[33]:3, 26[59]:3,4, 28[16]:5:6, 32[6]:4, 33[55]:5 (= 69[30]:5) 61[54]:2, and Agitation*. Chapters 24[33]:3 and 32[6] suggest that some Laoists may have extrapolated from this experience to an expectation of surviving death (which became a major goal in some later Taoist movements).[23] I believe a utilitarian interpretation of this theme in the *Tao Te Ching* is mistaken, however: Lasting is one among many utopian "marvelous benefits*" one might hope for from Laoist self-cultivation in its perfection, not the main purpose for undertaking it.

Learning*. See Confucian*.

Life*. *Sheng*/life:living has a negative sense in 51[75]:1–2 and 22[50]:1–2, referring to the high living of the "life-loving" aristocracy, which wears them out. Attempts by others to "increase *sheng*/vitality" by direct meditation* techniques is also criticized in 33[55]:4. But "fostering *sheng*/life Excellently*" describes a positive Laoist goal in 22[50]:3. And 38[21]:2 and 33[55]:2 mention *ching*/"vital energy" as something Laoists cultivate—in 33[55]:2 this is exemplified in the vitality of a young infant*, an image of positive, Soft* "life" also in 74[76]:1–2. See Graham's discussion[24] of the close relation between the etymologically cognate *sheng*/life and *hsing*/"[human] nature" and the use of both words by Yangists* expressing their concern to "keep life/nature intact."

Link*. One genre of Laoist sayings celebrates the way that cultivating one quality of mind is linked to the achievement of other qualities as well. For example, "Experiencing Steadiness* is Clarity*" (28[16]:3:4.) See also 29[52]:5, 33[55]:3, 36[42]:3.

Low*. *Hsia*/"[being] low" is a term used frequently to describe one aspect of the Laoist ideal. It describes a deferential manner in dealing with others, as well as a more general willingness to accept being one whom others look down upon—the consequence sometimes of cultivating qualities and practicing a Tao* that is not impressive. This is different from Western "humility," if humility is understood to reflect an acceptance of one's place as someone not very important or deserving. The cultivation of Laoist lowness on the contrary gives one the spiritual status of Emperor*, "Norm of the World." Laoists hoped that people would actually feel the subtle greatness of the "lowness" they cultivated and would want to make such a low person the leader he deserves to be. See 35[39]:2, 55[66]:1,2, 56[61]:1,2,3,4,6, 57[68]:1. (Lowness is implied also in 7[8]:1 and 63[32]:4.) *Hsia*/low is also used sometimes in its ordinary negative sense to designate something of inferior quality, translated "poorest" in 11[38]:1 and 44[41]:1. A related word is *hsiao*/small:insignificant, also used sometimes in its usual negative sense referring to someone of "small" worth or significance (for example, 3[67]:1:6), but also sometimes used paradoxically to characterize "great" Tao (for example, 29[52]:5, 63[32]:1, 64[34]:4).

Meditation*. Two sayings, 27[10]:1 and 6[15]:3, are fairly clearly meditation instruction, and this is probably true of 28[16]:2 and 30[56]:2-3 as well. The entire chapter collages 28[16], 29[52], and 30[56] probably have this intention. (Saso describes[25] meditation practices of a modern Taiwanese Taoist group that appears to me very similar to those suggested in the *Tao Te Ching*. *Meditation* here of course does not mean meditating *on* some ideas, but introspective exercises aimed at changing the quality of consciousness.) I believe four other sayings (30[56]:4, 37[14]:3-4, 38[21]:2, 46[35]:3) describe the experience of trying to mentally grasp the elusive quality of mind Laoists cultivated. These follow a sayings form common in the *Nei* Yeh* as well. Saying 39[25]:1 may represent a vision seen at meditation. The mention of "Heaven's Gate" in 27[10]:1 may indicate that Laoists, like other Taoists represented in the *Chuang Tzu*, integrated into their meditation practice elements of earlier Chinese shamanism, involving mental "spirit journeys." The following passage from the *Chuang Tzu* illustrates this. I have slightly revised Watson's translation here, and inserted asterisks to highlight the connection of the overall spirit journey theme with the achievement of mental qualities cultivated by Laoists:

The Extreme of Perfect Tao* is mysterious and hushed in silence. Let there be no seeing, no hearing; embrace* the spirit in Stillness* and the Form[26] will become correct by itself. You must be Still*, you must be pure. Do not labour your Form, do not churn up your vital energy [*ching*], and then you can live a long life. When the eye does not see, the ear does not hear, and the mind does not know, then your spirit will watch* over the Form. With this Form will come long-lasting* life. Be cautious of what is inside; block off what is outside.... Then I will lead you up above the Great Clarity*, to the source of Perfect *Yang;* I will guide you through the Dark and Mysterious Gate, to the source of the Perfect *Yin*.... I watch* over this One* Thing, so as to reside in this Harmony*.... So I will take leave of you, to enter the abode of the Inexhaustible and wander in the limitless fields, to form a triad with the light of the sun and moon, to partake in the Steadiness* of Heaven and Earth.[27]

Mencius*. Mencius was a Confucian* *shih** teacher (c. 370–300 B.C.) known to us from a large book bearing his name (but probably written by his pupils) consisting mainly of stories about him and lectures given by him. This book is the principal contemporary source I rely on for understanding the social position of Warring States' *shih* teachers and the nature of *shih*-schools.

Merging*. One name for the mental state or quality that Laoists cultivate, occurring in 30[56]:3 and 43[1]:4–5. See discussion in 30[56]:3, and the occurrence of *t'ung*/Merging in the quote from the *Chuang Tzu* p. 211.

Metaphorical* Images. Some sayings use images, mostly nature images like the behavior of water, as metaphors illustrating some particular Laoist idea or combination of ideas. Sayings in this genre are often taken[28] as an indication that Laoists strove to "imitate nature," giving the mistaken impression that they first neutrally observed nature and then formulated human ideals based on this objective inquiry. The *selection* of images represented makes it clear that the opposite is the case: Laoists first formed ideals based on their own values and perspective, and then selected natural phenomena that could serve as metaphorical images for these ideals. (The projection of their ideals onto nature of course resulted in a world-view felt to be "in accord with nature" so perceived.) It is noteworthy that in 69[30]:5 and 14[23]:2, natural phenomena serve as *negative* images of what is to be avoided. And, on the other hand, not all the images used are taken from nature; for example, the image of a gentleman traveling in a caravan (23[26]:2), and the images of a wheel, a pot, and windows and doors (15[11]:1). See 7[8]:1, 10[7]:1, 14[23]:2, 15[11]:1, 16[5]:2, 23[26]:2, 33[55]:1,2, 33[55]:5 (= 69[30]:5), 44[41]:3:5–8, 47[43]:1, 52[77]:1, 55[66]:1, 56[61]:1, 63[32]:4, 74[76]:1,3, 75[78]:1.

Mohists*. Followers of a *shih** teacher, Mo Tzu (c. 480–390 B.C.). According to Graham[29] and Schwartz,[30] Mohist political thought was based largely on utilitarian rationality; that is, analyzing situations in terms of conscious goals and calculating the means best suited to achieve these goals. Mohists were also among the few ancient Chinese who reflected systematically on questions of formal logic.[31] Mohist or Mohist-like thought is probably one of the targets of Laoist polemic aphorisms* against Improvements* and Naming*.

Morality*. See Confucian*.

Mother*. *Mu*/Mother is one hypostatization* of the quality of mind Laoists cultivate. This partly reflects the theme that this quality is envisioned as the origin* ("Mother") of the world. But as the origin image conveys the idea of something fundamental, this "Mother" one cultivates internally is also called the *Mother of the State*, that is, the foundation of Chinese culture (26[59]:3). (The idea that Laoists found a foundation for their thought in the physical universe, as opposed to human culture, in my view is a mistake.) *Mother* is also related to the idea that the hypostatized quality cultivated is internally nourishing (13[20]:5) and Feminine* (a contrast with the challenging Father Gods central to many religions). See 13[20]:5, 26[59]:3, 29[52]:1–2, 39[25]:1, 43[1]:2.

Naming*. For Laoists, *ming*/naming is generally a negative term referring to the use of conscious concepts to try to understand the world. Laoists may have lumped together several different groups here: Some early Chinese "Sophists" who concerned themselves with logic were later labeled the *School of Names*.[32] Some Mohists* were also concerned with logic, and they may be included here. "Legalist"[33] thinkers, who advocated written codification of customary law, may be the target of Laoist criticism of naming in 63[32]:3. Included, finally, is the program advocated by some Confucians* called *rectifying names*—attempts to fix social norms by carefully defining moral terms.[34] Such naming "cuts up the Uncarved* Block" (63[32]:3); that is, true normative goodness perceived through unconceptualized experience.

In my view, *unconceptualized* here only refers to the absence of *conscious and explicit* concepts. *Unconceptualized experience* does not mean perception of "objective raw data," completely uninfluenced even in an *implicit* way by cultural influences and subjective concerns. A multitude of implicit cultural assumptions, and personal concerns and values, entered into what Laoists considered a "true understanding*" of the world. (I often in these pages try to make explicit assumptions and concerns they left implicit, see especially comments under Organic* harmony.) This is why (contrary to Hansen[35]) it is perfectly consistent for Laoists (a) to reject some *conventional* evaluative naming, and (b) to reject the emphasis placed on explicit *conceptual* naming by other *shih**, and yet also (c) clearly to do some evaluative "naming" themselves, as when they name some attitudes *Soft* (good) and others *hard/forcing** (bad). The *focus* of Laoist thought remains however on an unconceptualized "state of mind" and the experience one has of the world when in this state of mind. "Names" like *Softness* only partially describe a state of mind which would be destroyed if one thought of sayings about Softness as a set of "truths" to be understood intellectually and deliberately "applied" to life.

This is also why Laoists are so "inconsistent" in their use of words—verbal consistency is important only to one whose worldview is centered on a conceptualized doctrinal system. (See comments on *shen*/self in 10[7], on *sheng*/wisdom in 78[19], on *yü*/desire p. 225, *ch'iang*/strong:forcing pp. 227 and 243, *t'ien*/Heaven p. 229, *sheng*/life p. 233, *hsia*/low p. 234. *Ming*/name itself has a positive use in 43[1]:1, 41[47]:3, and 38[21]:3; in the last passage Tao's "name" stands positively for its power.) See comments on Laoist "consistency," pp. 202, 204, 213, and further discussion under Understanding*.

Criticism of conceptual naming is related to criticism of self-assured knowledge of norms and the laws that govern events (58[73]:1–3, 59[58]:2, 62[29]:3). Passages critical of "naming," or presenting namelessness or wordlessness as an ideal, are 42[2]:1–4, 43[1]:1 and 4, 47[43]:2, 63[32]:3, 77[57]:3:1–2 and 77[57]:4. "Namelessness" as a characteristic of Laoist Tao occurs in 37[14]:3, 39[25]:2, 43[1]:1,2, 44[41]:4, 63[32]:1, 81[37]:2. It is relevant to this last usage that *ming*/name can also mean "fame, reputation" (for example, 19[44]:1:1).

Natural*. Being "natural" is a modern ideal that bears some similarity to a central Laoist ideal. Modern thought on this topic, however, has been greatly affected by the concept of nature developed in modern science: The idea that "Nature" is what we learn about through objective and impersonal scientific research and is the only solid foundation for true knowledge of any kind. This leads, for example, to a quest to discover human "nature" as it would be apart from the overlay of any particular "culture." Such assumptions and concerns are foreign to Laoist thought. I believe the concept of "organic harmony" comes closer to the aspect of the Laoist ideal often called *naturalness*. (See Organic* harmony.) "Naturalness" as organic harmony (a) assumes normal human acculturation and (b) is an ideal state that must be worked at and cultivated, not something that happens by itself. See Graham on "nature" in other *shih** schools.[36] The only *term* in the *Tao Te Ching* that comes close to our word *natural* is *tzu-jan*, (lit. "self-like"), occurring in 14[23]:1, 54[17]:3, 72[64]:8, 65[51]:2, and 39[25]:4 (translated in the last passage "things as they are").

Nei Yeh.* Nei-Yeh/"Inward Training" is the name of Chapter 49 of an ancient anthology of miscellaneous material called the *Kuan Tzu*. The *Nei Yeh* probably dates from the fourth century B.C. and is a valuable source of information about early self-cultivation and meditation practices in China.[37] Many sayings in it are similar in form or content to sayings in the *Tao Te Ching*, including sayings using the word *Tao** to refer to an hypostatized* quality of mind that one cultivates; one such saying is quoted under Tao*.

Normative Description.* Some instructional* sayings give a normative description of what one is like who embodies Laoist Tao or Te. The main thrust of such sayings is to specify what true Laoist Tao/Te consists in, by describing ways of being or acting expressive of these qualities. They function in effect as definitions of Laoist "orthopraxy." See 6[15]:4, 9[79]:3, 20[46]:1, 31[4]:1, 34[40]:1, 37[14]:6, 60[49]:2, 64[34]:1, 69[30]:1, 80[65]:1.

Nothing.* One designation of the quality of mind Laoists cultivate. On my view, "Nothing" (*wu* or *wu yu*), and its contrast "being" need to be interpreted not philosophically, but experientially. This is evident in passages like 47[43]:1, where *wu yu*/"non-being" parallels "Softness" as a description of a style of personal interaction. That is, it refers to a very subtle influence one person has on another, an influence that *feels* like "nothing" because it is so indirect and intangible. Thus the contrasting pair Nothing/being is very similar in meaning to the pair Empty*/solid. *Nothing* refers to a quality of mind in 15[11]:1–2, 34[40]:2, and 47[43]:1.

One Thing.* One name for the hypostatized* quality of mind Laoists cultivate. The *Tao Te Ching* gives little clue as to the connotations of *yi*/One. I tentatively translate *yi* as "The One Thing," based partly on a passage in the *Doctrine of the Mean* (20/8–18) that speaks of "nine standard rules," "five duties," and "three virtues," and says that the key to all of these is *yi*/"one thing"—apparently referring to "genuineness" (20/18), a central focus of self-cultivation in the *Doctrine of the Mean*. A possible connection between 35[39]:1 and 35[39]:3 may suggest that *yi*/One there refers to a single feeling that seems to pervade the universe when one is in an ideal state of mind (see further comments on 35[39]). The contrast with "divided" in 27[10]:1 suggests that *yi* might also describe a *unified* state of mind, as opposed to one of inner conflict. (Compare the mental quality or state described in 37[14]:2, in which everything blends and *wei yi*/"becomes one.") *Yi*/"One Thing" occurs in 4[22]:4, 27[10]:1, 35[39]:1, 36[42]:1.

Oracle*. The *Yi Ching,* an ancient Chinese divination manual, sometimes uses a formula exemplified in, "Not acting the robber [but] intent on marriage, in the end [there will be] no fault [*wu yiu*]."[38] Some Laoist sayings seem to borrow this "oracle" formula, as for example 7[8]:3, "Do not contend, then [there will be] no fault [*wu yiu*]." The chief implication of this observation for interpretation is that no *specific* importance should be given to the phrases *no fault, no trouble,* and so on in sayings using this formula. These phrases are merely conventional ways of designating something as "lucky," an action or event that will bring good fortune. See 7[8]:3, 13[20]:1, 19[44]:3,4 (= 63[32]:3:4), 28[16]:6 (= 29[52]:3), 50[53]:2.

Organic*. The Laoist view of the world is remarkably unified (45[70]:1), but this unity is suggested and "performed" (p. 204) rather than explicitly spelled out. Among my own attempts to spell out explicitly the single thing that Laoists value most, forming the basis for the Laoist perspective on the world, the concept I have found most satisfactory overall is that of "organic harmony."

Organic harmony in a social group is exemplified in the case of a harmonious family or a group of friends or coworkers who have been together for a long time. In such cases the unity and harmony of the group is "organic," a spontaneous and integral part of the way members instinctively relate to each other. The identities, roles, and modes of relating have been formed in the context of this group, hence it is not a question of trying to *impose* unity and organization from without, on a group of isolated and independent individuals. "Organic" social harmony and organization stands in contrast to organization that results from formulating a conscious plan as to how each person in the group should act—a plan that needs then to be consciously and deliberately implemented. It is also opposed to that kind of organization that happens when one dominating person, "standing out" from the organic group, imposes his ideals, his plans and his will on the others. This kind of organic harmony is the underlying value motivating the Laoist attitude toward ruling. (See Impressive*, Strict*, Forcing*, Improvements*, and Sections 5–7 of the translation and commentary.)

One can also speak, by analogy, of an "organic harmony" within a person's being. This might be (a) an organic harmony characterizing a person's "personality"—she has developed a kind of goodness arising from a unique, organic integration of all the good potentialities of her own being. She does not let certain personal qualities "stand out" and ruin this harmony, merely because these qualities make her "stand out" socially in the admiration of her fellows. Nor is she trying to live up to some ideals consciously conceived in her mind as intellectual convictions, which she "works*" to directly impose on her being. This kind of organic harmony is the value that motivates the Laoist attitude toward personal character formation and interaction with peers. (See Appearances*, Self-Promotion*, and Section 1 of the translation and commentary.)

Organic harmony might also characterize (b) a person's psychobiological being: All the parts and forces of her psychobiological makeup work harmoniously and healthily together. This kind of organic harmony is disrupted when something external, standing out" in contrast to everyday life, "excites" one's being, stirs it up to move in one particular direction. The strain this places on one's being as a whole is manifest in the fact that an excited state cannot last a long time; eventually the tug of other parts of one's being pulls everything back toward an *internally* balanced, homeostatic state. This kind of organic harmony is the value motivating the Laoist attitude toward mental-physical health. (See Agitation*, Desire*, Stillness*, and Section 2 of the translation and commentary.)

Finally, organic harmony might characterize (c) one's conscious awareness of the world as a whole perceived by a participant concerned with and involved in the ongoing processes of the world. This kind of organic harmony is disrupted by attempts to replace holistic experience with clear, conscious concepts, "standing out" in contrast to unreflective experience, as the main way of grasping reality and directing one's dealings with the world. The reality that abstract conceptual thought can capture is only pale and partial compared to the richness of the world perceived holistically. This kind of organic harmony is the value motivating the Laoist attitude toward attempts to understand the world. (See Understanding*, Naming*, and the first four chapters in Section 4 of the translation.)

In all these cases, organic harmony tends to be a taken-for-granted "background," against which certain things stand out as a "foreground" in our awareness, a phenomenon to which modern Gestalt psychology calls attention. Laoists emphasize the way attending to and developing this out-standing foreground causes us to neglect, and also damage, the taken-for-granted background, which is a necessary sustaining basis (a "Mother*") for our personal and social life. Although it needs to arise from within, organic harmony does not always and necessarily come about of its own accord. The high level of organic harmony Laoists desire must be cultivated, but this can only be done indirectly. For example, cultivating organic harmony in one's psychobiological being is primarily a matter of cultivating a deep Stillness* that is a prime *condition* fostering the harmonious integration and functioning of all parts of our being. Hence, Stillness is the kind of thing Laoist sayings explicitly speak *about,* because these sayings are centered on the *practice* of self-cultivation and use rhetorical devices to *induce* the attitudes they advocate. Laoists did not develop an explicit *concept* of organic harmony because they had no interest in a theoretical explication of their values such as I attempt here.

Origins*. Some sayings celebrate* the cosmic importance of Tao by picturing it as a cosmic origin. This genre, important but difficult for us moderns to understand, is discussed at length pp. 207–213. See 29[52]:1, 31[4]:2, 32[6]:2, 34[40]:2, 35[39]:1, 36[42]:1, 39[25]:1, 43[1]:2, 65[51]:1,3.

Self-promotion.* The target of a large group of polemic aphorisms* is the tendency of people to try to achieve recognition by direct and conscious "boasting" efforts to impress others as someone who stands out above others. This must have been a common tendency among *shih** anxious to draw attention to themselves to further their careers. These sayings offer several closely related images to counter this tendency: There is first the negative image of the self-defeating show-off who turns off other people by obvious self-promotion (for example, 1[24]:2). And there are several contrasting positive images: (a) the image of attractive self-effacement that wins admiration from others on this basis (like 4[22]:5); (b) the image of the competent and successful *shih* who does not treat success primarily as a means to enhance his own prestige (like 42[2]:5); (c) the image of the *shih* in office who works selflessly for the good of others in society rather than competing with others for higher personal status (like 7[8]:1, 8[81]:3); (d) the image of the person, selfless and secure in himself, who can be generous to others even when they do not reciprocate (9[79]:3, 60[49]:2); (e) the image representing a hyperbolic extreme of this, the person willing to accept the lowest position in society (7[8]:1), and "fall like a stone into oblivion" (35[39]:4). One must not turn the aphoristic* thought here into a literal rule against seeking promotions of any kind. In my view, Laoists wanted to influence their society from positions of highest leadership and hence must have wanted ultimately to "get promoted" to high government posts. And on the other hand, a utilitarian interpretation of Laoist thought here probably also is mistaken—the view that self-effacement is merely a tactic adopted to further egotistic ambition. Being self-effacing is part of a certain posture and "style" of relating to the world that Laoists value for its own sake (see pp. 213–214). Their hope is that the true hidden worth of the good but self-effacing person will subtly shine through and win public admiration and influence. Sayings on this topic "sublimate" the desire of *shih* for reputation and influence, substituting the subtle ideal of attractive self-effacement for the crass ideal of aggressive self-assertion. See further comments under Appearances*. See 1[24]:2, 2[9]:2, 3[67]:2, 4[22]:5,6 (= 55[66]:4), 6[15]:2, 7[8]:1,3, 9[79]:3, 10[7]:1,2,3, 18[13]:4, 27[10]:2, 35[39]:4, 42[2]:5, 50[53]:2, 52[77]:3, 53[72]:3, 62[29]:4, 64[34]:3,5 (= 71[63]:5), 65[51]:4, 69[30]:3.

*Shift**.   Some passages reflect an experience in which a shift in one's state of mind causes a shift also in the world as perceived. The *Chuang* **Tzu* has a good example of this (quoted more fully p. 211), which I believe also illuminates 28[16]:2: "Be blank and soulless, and the ten thousand things one by one will return to the root." That is, one first experiences the world as a place of bewildering multiplicity. As one manages to clear ("blank") one's mind, one begins to experience the world differently, as though this multiplicity springs from a single root. See also 30[56]:3 (= 31[4]:3), 42[2]:1, and comments on origin* sayings, pp. 207–213.

*Shih**.   The name of the social class to which the authors of the *Tao Te Ching* probably belonged, discussed on pp. 191–195. The word *shih* occurs in 6[15]:1, 44[41]:1, and 57[68]:1 (in the last passage it means "soldier").

*Softness/Weakness.**   *Jou*/Softness and *jo*/Weakness often occur together as descriptive terms referring to the quality of mind Laoists cultivate (the opposite of *ch'iang*/hard:strong:forcing). This quality is a kind of energy one can cultivate internally (27[10]:1, 74[76]:1). But this quality of mind also expresses itself in a certain "Soft," nonconfrontational way of dealing with the world. *Judo*, the name of a Japanese martial art, is taken from the Chinese *jou-Tao*/"Soft Way," and 73[36] makes it clear that, like judo, "Softness" describes a nonconfrontational *style* by which one hopes to defeat opponents when necessary. *Jo*/Weakness is not of course to be taken literally. It is a term with ordinarily negative connotations that refers paradoxically to a positive quality (which can also be described as an inner *ch'iang*/strength, 29[52]:5). See 27[10]:1, 29[52]:5, 33[55]:2, 34[40]:1, 47[43]:1, 73[36]:2, 74[76]:1,2,3,4, 75[78]:1,2. See also Forcing*.

*Solidity**. See Empty*.

*Steady**. *Heng*/Steadiness[39] is another descriptive name for the quality of mind Laoists cultivate. Some translate *heng* as "eternal," but I think this mistakenly evokes the concerns of Hindu and Greek thinkers to grasp eternal metaphysical truths. Laoism is more practically oriented, so I believe this term refers to a concretely felt steadiness of mind, able to remain centered in itself in the midst of disturbing and distracting events in the world. (*Mencius**[40] uses *heng* to describe the "steady" mind of a good *shih**, able to keep his integrity even in the face of strong pressures from difficult life situations.) See 28[16]:3,4, 29[52]:7, 33[55]:3. In 43[1]:1 and 17[28]:1 *heng* serves as an adjective describing "true" Tao/Te on which one can always rely as an unchanging internal standard. In these passages I translate "invariant." *Heng* also has a very common use meaning "always, invariably." In this use, it sometimes has a very weak sense as an introductory (43[1]:3, 64[34]:4, 80[65]:4) or concluding (42[2]:2) particle, similar to the use of *fan* in the *Nei** *Yeh*[41]. (This is important in 43[1]:3, where commentators often mistakenly emphasize this word.)

*Still**. *Ching*/Stillness is another descriptive term referring to the quality of mind Laoists cultivate. Stilling a "stirred up" mind is a goal of meditation in 6[15]:3. Mental Stillness is contrasted with "agitation" in 23[26]:1 and 5[45]:3, and with *tso*/activity in 28[16]:2–3 and 81[37]:2. See 5[45]:3,4, 6[15]:3, 23[26]:1, 28[16]:1–3, 56[61]:2, 77[57]:5, 81[37]:2. *Ching* also means "pure."

*Strict**. A target of some polemic aphorisms* is the ideal of the ruler as a model and enforcer of strict moral norms. Laoists dislike the confrontational, "hurting" stance such a ruler takes toward his people and reject his underlying assumption that he has full and certain understanding* of the norms that ought to be enforced (58[73]:1–3, 59[58]:2, 62[29]:3). Some passages pose the counterimage of a ruler who actually does enforce high standards, but does so in a tactful and nonconfrontational way that does not make the people feel hurt (for example, 55[66]:3:3, and see Hurt*. Chapter 58[73] makes it clear that literally *not* enforcing laws is not the issue: a "Soft" *style* of law enforcement is the ideal). Also relevant here is (a) the counterimage suggested in 60[49]:1: the ruler who imposes standards that are just an idealized version of the organic* harmony already inherent in the society. And one should also consider (b) the kind of understanding* Laoists take as their ideal: They reject the use of concepts that incline us to impose fixed standard categories on fluid and always different situations. The direct experience on which they rely instead is better able to adapt itself to new and unique circumstances. These seem to be the positive ideals underlying several other, highly exaggerated counterimages: The ruler who simply "drifts" to and fro (64[34]:1), who is like a prostitute devoid of standards (56[61]:1), who appears "dull and incompetent" (59[58]:1), and "keeps his mind muddled" (60[49]:3). See further discussion under Impressive*. See 56[61]:1, 58[73]:5, 59[58]:1,4, 60[49]:1,3,4, 64[34]:1.

*Superstitious**. Some situations make people uneasy for not quite rational reasons: Things have been going too well too long, someone is getting much too rich much too easily, a pridefully self-assertive person is stepping all over other people with impunity so far, someone is introducing radical changes in a very stable traditional community, and so forth. The kind of uneasy expectation we have in such circumstances that something bad is going to happen for not quite accountable reasons—this is what I call in the commentary a *quasi-superstitious* feeling. Such a feeling underlies many Laoist sayings, especially those against war and violence grouped together at the beginning of Section 6. Part of this feeling is due to Chinese ideas about the close connection between proper ruling and good order in the world of nature. (A passage from the *Mo Tzu*[42] describes some of the effects of a bad ruler: "Phantom women came out after dark...a woman turned into a man, flesh rained down from heaven, brambles grew on the state roads." See further comments at 70[60].) "Quasi-superstitious" Laoist sayings are half rationalized, in that (a) things said to bring misfortune are always things rejected on the basis of Laoist values expressed elsewhere; and (b) there is a continuity between the Laoist world-view and the general sense of things which underlies "superstitious" thinking: That is, in both cases the underlying sense is that there is a certain "natural*" way the world runs, and things that appear strange, novel, or individually self-assertive against this background are felt to be vaguely "dangerous." Self-assertive people acting with hubris put themselves in a "precarious" situation. See 1[24]:4 (=67[31]:2), 19[44]:2, 36[42]:6, 66[74]:2, 67[31]:1,2,6, 69[30]:2–3, 70[60]:2, 77[57]:3. See also Oracle*.

*Take-off**. Sometimes the composer of a chapter seems to quote a saying not for its own sake, but simply to use as a take-off point for some other comment he wants to make. See 9[79]:1, 25[48]:1:1, 34[40]:2:1, 40[71]:1:1, 58[73]:1, 66[74]:1:1, 77[57]:1. In 29[52]:2 and 81[37]:3 the composer's comments reverse the point of a Laoist saying commented on.

*Tao**. Along with Te*, Tao is the predominant term Laoists use to refer to the hypostatized* quality of mind they cultivate, and these two terms give the book its name.[43] Tao has a variety of meanings in the *Tao Te Ching,* due partly I believe to the fact that the meaning of the term had not yet been systematized. Sometimes Tao is used in a way common to ancient Chinese generally, and sometimes it is used in a way more specific to Laoism. Its main uses in the *Tao Te Ching* can be summarized under the following three points:

(a) The basic meaning of *tao* is "road, way," and its most basic metaphorical meaning is best captured in the English phrase *the right way.* Tao was a *generic* concept, designating something that the speaker regards as normative, but the content fluctuated as there was no general agreement among ancient Chinese about what exactly *is* the right way of doing things. Like others, Laoists use *Tao* to mean *their* version of "the true Way" (the phrase "*this* Tao" [6[15]:4] implicitly recognizes there are others). *Tao* can also refer to *teaching* about the right way, and "assisting people's rulers with Tao" (69[30]:1) describes the activity of a *shih** counselor giving advice to rulers on the right way of governing. Because the Laoist way does not consist of a set of rules, "the right way" for them was a kind of internal spirit that expresses itself in a certain style of relating to the world (see p. 214). This is the connection between this meaning and the meanings in (b) and (c) that follow.

(b) For some *shih* involved in self-cultivation, Tao is an hypostatization* of the spirit or quality of mind one is cultivating internally. The following passage from the *Nei** Yeh illustrates this usage:

> Tao is what perfects the [mind's] Form,
> But men cannot make it stand fast.
> [Sometimes] it goes and does not return,

> [Sometimes] it comes and does not stay...
> Tao has no [fixed] place.
> It will peacefully settle in a good mind.
> The mind still, the *ch'i** right,
> Then Tao can stay.[44]

In a similar fashion, 44[41]:4 and 14[23]:3 in the *Tao Te Ching* speak of Tao as being a "supporting" or "welcoming" internal presence. This hypostatization of Tao paved the way for picturing it as a cosmic* force, the origin* of the world (see pp. 207–213).

(c) Although other schools also call their Way *Tao*, Taoists seem somewhat unique in taking it as the predominant summary reference to the quality of mind they cultivate, and particularly in taking it as the distinctive name that describes their self-cultivation project *in contrast* to that of others. Thus 25[48]:1 contrasts "doing Tao" with "doing [Confucian] Learning," a contrast Confucians would not have agreed to.[45] In accord with this, *Tao* seems in some sayings to be a shorthand designation for Laoist self-cultivation itself, as in 11[38]:6, "Foreknowledge is the flower of Tao [= one result of Laoist self-cultivation]" or 34[40]:1, "Turning back is Tao movement [= the internal movement characteristic of Laoist self-cultivation]." See also 37[14]:6. Related to this is an "adjectival" use of *Tao* in 69[30]:5: The seasonal flourishing and dying of plants is used as a metaphor for short-lived human excitement, and this is called "un-Tao-ish"[46]—it is an image of the lack of Tao as a mental quality or spirit that Laoists cultivate internally, which is something steady and lasting. See 1[24]:3, 6[15]:4, 7[8]:1, 11[38]:4,6, 12[18]:1, 14[23]:3, 20[46]:1, 25[48]:1, 28[16]:5, 31[4]:1, 33[55]:5, 34[40]:1, 36[42]:1, 37[14]:5,6, 38[21]:1,2, 39[25]:2,4, 43[1]:1, 44[41]:1,2,4, 46[35]:2, 48[62]:1,5,6, 52[77]:2, 63[32]:1,4, 64[34]:1, 65[51]:1,2,3, 69[30]:1,5, 70[60]:2, 80[65]:1, 81[37]:1. I translate *Tao* as "Way," in 2[9]:2, 9[79]:4, 26[59]:4, 41[47]:1, 50[53]:1,3,6, 52[77]:1, 58[73]:5. See also *Heaven's Way* under Heaven*.

*Te**. "Virtue" is a rough equivalent for the Chinese word *te*, if we include the older meaning of "virtue," which also referred to the powers of something or someone emanating from their innate character (as when Medieval people spoke of the "virtues" of certain herbs or gems). Like the Greek word for virtue, *aretê*, and the Latin *virtus*, *te* had an early stage in which the meaning of "power" was emphasized—in this case it is perhaps closest to what we now call personal "charisma." But during the Warring States period it took on a more ethical coloring. Thus Mencius* uses *te* often as a general word referring to good character. Like Tao*, *te* was in this period a generic word, whose content could vary, according to varying conceptions of what "good character" consists in. This is why Laoists can use the word as a summary designation for their conception of the highest kind of human goodness, sometimes hypostatized* as a quasi-independent energy or force that one "accumulates" internally through self-cultivation (26[59]) and that can be envisioned as a cosmic force, the origin* of the world (65[51]). Laoists probably liked the word partly on the basis of its older connotations of "power/charisma," because of their emphasis on the subtle but powerful influence that the ideal ruler or administrator exerts on those under him (this meaning is evident in 57[68] and 26[59]:2. See also the story of Ch'i Tzu, included under the topic This*).

Three passages (9[79], 60[49]:2, 71[63]:3) emphasize the association with Te as self-forgetting generosity, able to "be good to those who are not good." In 61[54]:2, Te refers to the good character or spirit of larger social units (family, village, state). See 9[79]:3, 11[38]:1,2,4, 14[23]:3, 17[28]:1, 26[59]:2, 27[10]:2, 33[55]:1, 38[21]:1, 44[41]:3, 57[68]:2, 60[49]:2, 61[54]:2, 65[51]:1,2,3,4, 70[60]:4, 71[63]:3, 80[65]:4,5.

Teaching.* Some sayings reflect directly on what it is like to be a teacher in the Laoist school, both the difficulty of this because of the subtlety and unconventional nature of the "wordless" Tao one is trying to teach and the supreme importance of what one has to offer the world. See 3[67]:1, 36[42]:6, 42[2]:3, 45[70]:1,2,3, 46[35]:2, 47[43]:2, 48[62]:4,5, 49[27]:3,4,5, 75[78]:3,5. Chapters dealing mainly with this topic are grouped together as the last six chapters in Section 4 of my translation.

*Things.** *Wu*/thing(s), and *wan wu*/"the thousands of things" are common phrases in the *Tao Te Ching,* with a meaning I believe close to the colloquial use of *things* in English, as in "don't let things get to you." *Wu* refers not only to individual objects, but to many other kinds of realities, as for example the *reputation or influence* of a king (36[42]:5) or *problems* a teacher resolves (49[27]:3). Although sometimes the "thousands of things" are contrasted with "people" (for example, 74[76]:1), very often it is clear that "things" or "thousands of things" refers primarily to people (36[42]:2, 80[65]:5, 81[37]:2.) Compare Mencius' statement,[47] "[The rulers] correct themselves and *wu*/things are corrected" (Legge translates "*others* are corrected"). This usage probably reflects the fact that Laoists look on the world primarily from the perspective of the ruler-administrator: The world at large—consisting of lands, crops, people, political cohesion, social tendencies, and so on—constitutes a field of "things" that it is his job to manage well. *Wu*/thing can also mean "substance," as in 38[21]:2, where Tao is called a *wu*/thing, inside of which there is *wu*/"something substantial." Finally, in 1[24]:4 (= 67[31]:2) *wu*/things refers to normative reality as seen from the Laoist perspective—the reality with which one's actions ought to be in accord.

This*. I believe the Laoist saying "Leave 'that' aside, lay hold of 'this'" (11[38]:8 = 21[12]:3 = 53[72]:4), uses *this* and *that* in a special sense (not, as some think, to mean simply "the former...the latter"). The key to this saying's meaning is found in a passage where it is quoted in the *Huai Nan Tzu*, a passage reporting Confucius' comments on the case of a ruler with such strong Te* (invisible influence) that fishermen threw back small fish of a size below the limit he set even when no one was looking, merely because they knew that he wanted them to.

> How perfect is the Te of Ch'i Tzu. He causes men to act even in private as though there were going to be stern punishment for any infraction. How did Ch'i Tzu achieve this? Confucius said, "I have heard...it said, 'Sincerity in this is [equivalent to] enforcement in that.'" So Lao Tzu said, "Leave 'that' aside, take hold of 'this.'"[48]

Huai Nan Tzu here takes *this* in both the Confucian and the Laoist sayings to refer to the cultivation of Te in one's own person, whereas *that* refers to attempts to affect others by external means (here, through punishment). This is confirmed by a variation of the above Confucian saying that appears in the *Great Learning*,[49] which substitutes "inside/outside" (*chung/wai*) for "this/that" ("Sincerity on the *chung*/inside [is equivalent to] enforcement on the *wai*/outside"). This meaning fits the context well in 11[38]:8 and 53[72]:4. I think the meaning is extended somewhat in 21[12]:3, where the parallel of "this/that" with "belly/eye" suggests that *that* refers to eye-catching things "out there" in the world, and *this* refers to something truly satisfying internally—or perhaps to the mind itself, in a state capable of quiet satisfaction.

Three other sayings using *this* which need comment are those using the formula, "How do I know...? By this" in 38[21]:4, 61[54]:4, and 77[57]:2. My conjecture is that this formula is a favorite Laoist reply to questions from others demanding reasons or evidence supporting their opinions. The Laoist reply appeals simply to *this*—meaning either (a) the reality right in front of you, intuitively understood and evaluated in the right state of mind, or (b) your mind itself, in a cultivated state able to understand* things rightly by intuition. The latter use of *this* occurs in a passage from the *Kuan Tzu* quoted by Waley: "What a man desires to know is *that* (i.e. the external world). But his means of knowing is *this* (i.e. himself). How can he know *that*? Only by the perfection of *this*."[50]

Turn back*. This is one designation of the activity of self-cultivation, conveyed by three words with similar meanings, *fan, kuei,* and *fu*. Fan (39[25]:3, 34[40]:1) connotes "reversing direction" and is used in the *Mencius** to mean introspective "turning inward."[51] Mencius also uses *fan pen*/"turn back to the root" to mean "get back to fundamentals."[52] *Kuei* connotes rather "returning *home*" and is found in connection with self-cultivation in 4[22]:7, 17[28]:1, 28[16]:2, 29[52]:2. Two Laoist notions condition the meaning of this term in the *Tao Te Ching:* the idea of an original and superior, "natural*" state of mental Stillness* we ought to "turn back to," and the idea of an unfortunate human tendency to become mentally active and direct energy outward—in this context Laoist self-cultivation involves a "reversal," "turning back to the place all others have gone on from" (72[64]:7). See 4[22]:7, 17[28]:1, 28[16]:2,3, 29[52]:2,6, 34[40]:1, 37[14]:3, 39[25]:3, 64[34]:4, 72[64]:7, 78[19]:1, and comments on "knowing to stop" in 63[32].

Uncarved Block*. *P'u*/"Uncarved Block" is one name for the quality of mind Laoists cultivate. *P'u* can also mean "Simplicity" (see 81[37]:2 and 77[57]:5), but it is used in two passages in the *Tao Te Ching* that then speak of "cutting [it] up," evoking the word's concrete reference to a block of wood on a carver's shelf, prior to its carving. For Laoists, this is an image of "natural*" human goodness before it is "carved up" into socially determined good and bad qualities (17[28]:1–2) or before rulers attempt to define it by "naming*" it in definite legal rules (63[32]:3). The *Mencius**[53] uses a similar image, attributing to a rival *shih** teacher (Kao Tzu) the idea that making a person's character Good and Right is like carving a block of willow to make a cup or bowl. (Mencius also rejects this model of self-cultivation, as implying that cultivating virtue does violence to our nature.) Note that the Laoist "Uncarved Block" is not the same as a "bare" human nature completely uninfluenced by culture. In the absence of the modern preoccupation with "bare objective reality" as opposed to human culture (see Natural*), we should assume that Laoists spoke of reality as they perceived it. *Natural* meant what feels natural, in contrast to what one feels socially imposed. *P'u/*"Uncarved Block" occurs in 6[15]:2, 17[28]:1,2, 63[32]:1, 77[57]:5, 78[19]:2, 81[37]:3. See also Appearances*, Naming*.

*Understanding**. Some polemic aphorisms* are directed against ideas of other *shih** about the right way to go about understanding the world. The claim to have a superior understanding of things was central to the leadership role that *shih** wanted to play in their society. But of course what is primarily to be "understood" here are not the abstract natures of individual objects, but sociopolitical situations and forces; and to "understand" these rightly meant to be able to *evaluate* them well and propose an analysis that would serve as a *practical* guide to dealing effectively with problems. The targets of Laoist criticism here are primarily (a) the emphasis others give to broad learning (8[81]:1:5–6, 41[47]:1–2); (b) emphasis on conceptual "naming*" (42[2]:1,2, 63[32]:3); and (c) their confidence based on this that they know the universal norms and laws governing every possible situation (62[29]:3, 58[73]:1–3, 59[58]:2).

This kind of knowledge gives the knower a sense of being in possession of something special, something more clear and more valuable, "standing out" against the unreflective perception of the world given in plain experience. But plain experience of the world has a valuable "holistic" character—in it the world is directly perceived as an organic* whole in which things are all interrelated and interpenetrate each other in subtle and complex ways. This perception is organic also in that the world perceived is directly colored by the values, concerns, and feelings of the perceiver, who is not a separate theoretical observer. This holistic character of unreflective experience is destroyed when one tries to relate to the world primarily through the medium of deliberately learned ideas and conceptual categories. In addition, because the reality of any given social situation can never be completely grasped by analytical thought, a ruler-administrator who acts on the basis of rational analysis runs the danger of neglecting some important facets of the situation that the categories of his thought are inadequate to grasp.

Laoist *shih** do not want to rely on plain *conventional* experience—situations have a mysterious, deep and subtle dimension (6[15]:1, 43[1]:3), which the conventional minded cannot grasp.

But neither do they want to "improve" on unreflective experience by developing rational-conceptual thought. Their view is that the personal transformation achieved in self-cultivation also causes a shift* in the world as perceived, *deepening* the organic wholeness found in ordinary unreflective experience. To perceive the world in this new, ideal state of mind *is* to see the truth about events. One image for this: The "nondesiring*" mental abode in which one now rests, where all particulars are Merged* into an organic whole—this is the abode where the *miao*/"hidden essentials" of situations reside (43[1]:3,5). Another image: To get in touch with the quality of mind Laoists cultivate is also to get in touch with a deeper level of reality, the source or foundation of the true meaning of events. Once you get in touch with this foundation, you understand the events (29[52]:2:1–2, 37[14]:6, 38[21]:3; and see p. 211).

In the absence of any other likely candidates for the "hidden essence" of situations that Laoists see, I think we ought to assume that this is identical with the view of various situations expressed by Laoist polemic aphorisms*. (See the use of *miao*/"hidden essence" to refer to a "hidden" truth about how to view teacher-student relationships in 49[27]:5.) See 4[22]:3, 6[15]:1, 8[81]:1:5–6, 29[52]:2:1–2, 30[56]:1, 37[14]:6, 38[21]:3,4, 40[71]:1, 41[47]:1,2,3, 42[2]:1,2,4, 43[1]:1–5, 58[73]:1–3, 59[58]:2, 61[54]:3, 62[29]:3, 75[78]:3. See also Naming* and comments on the formula "How do I know...by this?" under This*. Chapters on this topic are grouped together as the first four chapters under Section 4 of the translation. *Knowledge* is a negative term in 12[18]:1, 27[10]:1, 78[19]:1, 79[3]:3, 80[65]:2,3, probably referring primarily to conceptual (naming*) knowledge others pride themselves on. *Chih*/know:understand can also refer to direct experience of something, as in "*chih*/experiencing Steadiness" 28[16]:3.

Use. *Yung*/use is one of several words to describe the action of cultivating or internalizing certain internal qualities in self-cultivation. Contemporary English terms better expressing the idea might be *practice, internalize, act in accordance with*. In 46[35]:3, "using"/internalizing this quality is contrasted with trying to grasp it with one's mind. See 17[28]:2, 31[4]:1, 32[6]:4, 34[40]:1, 46[35]:3. Other terms constituting a special vocabulary related to self-cultivation are (a) *shou*/"watch over" (16[5]:4, 17[28]:1, 28[16]:1, 29[52]:2 and 5, 63[32]:2, 81[37]:2, Mencius uses this term similarly[54]); (b) *pao*/embrace (4[22]:4, 27[10]:1, 61[54]:1, 78[19]:2 (see also "embrace *yang*" 36[42]:2); (c) *te*/get (29[52]:2, 35[39]:1, 37[14]:1). See also Turn* back.

Valley*.   An image associated with the ideal Laoist state of mind in 6[15]:2, 17[28]:1, 32[6]:1 (see comments on 32[6]).

Watch* Over.   See Use*.

Weakness*.   See Softness*.

Wise* Person.   *Sheng jen*/"Wise Person" is often used in contemporary literature, to designate the very highest human ideal. (For example, *Mencius*[55] quotes Confucius as saying that being a *sheng jen* was beyond his capacity.) *Wise* does not capture the full meaning of *sheng*, which some translate "holy" or "saint." *Sheng jen* figures in the *Tao Te Ching* mainly in a standard formula that the composers use to introduce sayings.

Working*.   *Wei*/working:doing is used often as a negative term. It describes an attitude rather than an activity: The attitude of one who thinks of reality as inert raw material on which to impose her plans and make her mark. All the importance is given to her ideas and efforts and none to the innate character of what she is working on. The contrasting Laoist ideal, *wu wei*/"not working" should not then be taken literally. It also describes an attitude, the attitude opposite that of the "worker," one who aims to draw out the inherent goodness of what is given and who is willing to subordinate herself to the demands of the material and the task, with subtle attention and extreme care. See especially comments on 71[63] and 72[64]. *Work* is used in this special sense in 11[38]:2–3, 25[48]:1,2,3,4, 27[10]:1, 41[47]:3, 42[2]:3, 47[43]:1,2, 51[75]:1,2, 62[29]:1,2, 71[63]:1, 72[64]:4,5,8, 77[57]:1,5, 79[3]:3,4, 81[37]:1. Some of these passages (like 71[63]:1, 77[57]:1,5) use not *wei* but a somewhat synonymous term, *shih*/serve:work, commonly used to refer to "service" in a government post. *Working* is used predominantly in sayings against "improvements*," but there is also a tendency to apply this key term to other areas of life as well, like self-cultivation (11[38]:2,3), gaining knowledge (41[47]:3), and even "working" at luxurious living (51[75]:2). Note that *wei*/work is used in a positive sense, to refer to administrative tasks the *shih** ought to undertake, in 8[81]:3,4, 27[10]:2 (= 52[77]:3, 65[51]:4), and 72[64]:2.

Yang* Chu.   A shadowy figure who came to stand for an attitude probably common to many others in Warring States China: the rejection of government service to care for one's own personal well being and peace of mind.[56] The Laoist polemic against mental agitation*, contained mostly in Section 2 of my translation, has something in common with the "Yangist" concern for peace of mind. See further comments under Life*. I believe 18[13]:1 is probably a Yangist saying—"reinterpreted" however by the Laoist composer to fit with the Laoist acceptance of public service as an ideal.

Yin*. Some thinkers in ancient China were beginning to develop schemes for categorizing forces in the world. One of these schemes centered around the polar opposites, *yin* and *yang* (originally terms meaning "shady" and "sunny," respectively). Under *yin* were grouped such things as femininity, darkness, passivity, moisture. Under *yang* were grouped such things as masculinity, brightness, action, heat.[57] Some later Taoist groups advocated deliberately trying to *balance yin* and *yang,* but Laoist aphoristic* wisdom emphasizes cultivating *yin* qualities as opposed to *yang* ones (see comments in 17[28]). The terms *yin* and *yang* occur only once in the *Tao Te Ching,* 36[42]:2.

Notes

How to Read This Book

1. See Hansen 1983: 52 n. 1.

Introduction

1. Mair 1990: xi.

2. This was the principal meaning of *hermeneutics* until recently. Many thinkers skeptical of this traditional goal now use *hermeneutics* to refer to interpretive practice with different goals. For my critique of recent skeptical hermeneutics see LaFargue 1988b. For a brief history of hermeneutics, see Mueller-Vollmer (1988: 1–53); and for a longer account of recent developments, see Palmer (1969).

3. See, for example, Hansen (1983: 1–29) and Hall and Ames (1987: 1–9 and passim). I regret I that I am not able to read or comment on the considerable body of modern Chinese and Japanese scholarship on the *Tao Te Ching.*

4. This is a central principle put forth by by Friedrich Schleiermacher, one of the pioneers of modern hermeneutics, in the new approach to interpreting Christianity he introduced in his 1801 *Lectures on Religion.*

Hermeneutics

1. On the meaning of *hermeneutics,* see the Introduction p. xv and note 2.

2. *Tao and Method: A Reasoned Approach to the Tao te ching.* Forthcoming from SUNY Press. I have developed other aspects of a theory of hermeneutics in LaFargue 1985: 1–9, 206–217; 1988a; 1988b.

3. See Baker and Hacker 1980: 47–79.

4. Extant sources give us no reliable direct accounts of the *Tao Te Ching*'s origin. All attempts to discover this are based on indirect and fragmentary evidence. Chan (1963: 35–93) gives a lengthy discussion of the main evidence and traditional attempts to provide an account of the *Tao Te Ching*'s origin.

5. Hsu 1965. I am also grateful to Professor Hsu for his personal help, commenting on this aspect of my work.

6. My heavy reliance on the *Mencius*—and on the *Nei Yeh* (see p. 238)—in this book does not represent an informed judgment that other ancient works have little relevance to an interpretation of the *Tao Te Ching*. I am sure the opposite is the case. After a cursory survey of many such works early in my research it seemed that these two held the most promise for the kinds of questions I wanted to ask, and I concentrated the limited time I had on a systematic study of them.

7. The similarities and differences between medieval European and ancient Chinese feudalism are discussed at length in Creel 1970a: 317–387.

8. Hsu 1965: 24–52.

9. Ibid.: 89.

10. This is the term Hsu uses to describe this class, and the *Mencius* uses the term this way sometimes but not always. The Chinese word *shih* has a somewhat broader usage in the *Mencius* and other ancient Chinese texts. Creel (1970a: 331–334) gives a discussion of older usages.

11. Hsu 1965: 34–37, 51–52, 88–106.

12. This is true of Mencius, too, if we interpret *cheng* as "normative, norm giving" in the phrase *t'ien hsia chih cheng wei*, "[stands in the] norm-giving position of the world" (3B/2,3). This is the meaning translators usually give to *cheng* in the *Tao Te Ching*. Many stories in the *Mencius* (e.g. 2B/2, 5B/7) center on Mencius's claim that he is superior in status to all feudal "kings."

13. Watson 1968: 54. In the probably legendary story, the pupil is Yen Hui and the teacher is Confucius.

14. The *Chün Shih* chapter of the Shu Ching (Karlgren 1950: 59–62) gives a good picture of this important and exalted role of counselor, in what may be a genuine speech given by a very early great counselor, the Duke of Chou, later considered a model for those aspiring to this role. (See Creel 1970a: 71–80, and 453, n. 34.)

15. See *Mencius* 5B/7,1.

16. See p. 246 under "Te*."

17. The phrase *hsiu-shen*/"self-cultivation" occurs, for example, in 7A/1,3; 7A/9,6; 7B/32,2. The last passage brings out the implied agricultural metaphor of *hsiu* by comparing the "cultivation" of self to "weeding fields." *Hsiu* also has a more general meaning of "repair," as in "repair the walls of my house," *Mencius* 4B/31,1.

18. *Analects* 2:4.

19. 6B/14,4.

20. For the subsequent history of Taoism, see the article "Taoism" in the Encyclopedia Brittanica.

21. 1990: 118, 124. Creel also (1929: 47) once suggested the term *Laoism* to refer to ancient Taoism in general.

22. For Graham's view on how the *Tao Te Ching* came to be attributed to "Lao Tzu," see Graham 1990: 111–124. Chan (1963: 35–59) gives a broader survey of the evidence and older discussions of this issue. Graham (1989: 170) points out that the earliest sources mention the *Tao Te Ching* and the *Chuang Tzu* separately. The Han court historiographer Ssu-ma T'an (d. 110 B.C.) is the first extant source to have classified both works as "Taoist." Creel (1970b: 5–6, 43–47) describes the differences between what he sees as the "contemplative" Taoism of the *Chuang Tzu* and the "purposive" Taoism of the *Tao Te Ching*.

23. Graham 1989; Schwartz 1985. The interpretation of the *Tao Te Ching* in both these books however is very different from the present one.

24. See the discussions of authorship in ancient China in Waley (1958: 101–105) and Lau (1963: 149–165).

25. The earliest commentary on the *Tao Te Ching*, contained in the *Han Fei Tzu*, comments on the chapters in a very different order than the traditional one. Manuscripts of the *Tao Te Ching* from the second century B.C., recently found at Ma-wang-tui, also arrange the chapters in a slightly different order.

26. See, for example, Karlgren (1932: 25 n. 1), Waley (1958: 97), Lau (1963: 163–174), Kaltenmark (1965: 13–15), Creel (1970b: 6). The only serious exception I am aware of in recent times is R. G. Wagner (see also p. 228 n. 18), who has tried to show the existence of an elaborate pattern in the book ("interlocking parallelism") that could have come about only through the careful work of a single author in complete control of the material.

27. The pioneering and now classic work on form criticism applied to the Synoptic Gospels is Rudolf Bultmann's *History of the Synoptic Tradition*. I learned form criticism from a pupil of Bultmann, Dieter Georgi. For a brief account, see McKnight. For a more detailed account of the development of this method, see Rhode or, for the Old Testament, Rast.

28. This is contrary to Lau's view (1963: 51–52, 163–174), who thinks it a mistake to try to find connections between the sayings in a given chapter. Some think that the sayings originally were presented in an organized fashion, but that at some point this organization was lost. Taking this view, the Chinese scholar Ma Hsü-lun attempted to reconstruct what he thought was the original order. His work has influenced the translations of Ch'u, Duyvendak, and Karlgren. The view taken in this book is close to that expressed by Waley (1958: 96–98). The Japanese scholar Kimura Eiichi also has a theory about the deliberate ordering of sayings in the chapters and analyzes the entire work accordingly (Kimura's analysis is translated, with an introductory explanation, in Hurvitz). But Kimura's analysis is quite different from mine and assumes several successive redactions of the *Tao Te Ching*.

29. For rhyme schemes in the *Tao Te Ching*, I rely on Karlgren's (1932) reconstruction of rhymes in this book, based on the phonetic values of the words in ancient Chinese.

30. Although completely unintentional, it is perhaps noteworthy that, in the traditional "first book" (Chapters 1–37) only three (3, 17, 19) of the first twenty-eight chapters fall into my

"political" Sections 5–7, and only two (33, 35) of the remaining nine chapters fall into my "personal" Sections 1–3. Likewise in the traditional "second book" (Chapters 38–81) only four of the first nineteen chapters (49, 51, 53, 54) fall under my "political" Sections 5–7, only four (59, 67, 79, 81) of the remaining twenty-five chapters fall under my "personal" sections.

31. In addition to the longer treatment of this topic in *Tao and Method,* see the fuller discussion of the semantic structure of aphorisms in LaFargue (1990).

32. Austin 1962: 4–11.

33. This is a common view, two different versions of which have been put forth by Hansen (1981) and by Schwartz (1985: 196–213), respectively. Schwartz, however, also acknowledges that the *Tao Te Ching* has a "moralistic torque" that stands in contradiction with this relativism (203–204, 213).

34. See for example Bernstein (1983); Rorty (1982). The impact of antifoundationalist thought on Christian theology is illustrated in Schüssler-Fiorenza (1985: 285–311).

35. Gardiner (1981) gives a good account of the relation between the rise of cross-cultural study and the perceived threat of relativism.

36. Quoted in Graham 1989: 243.

37. Graham (1989) 161 and footnote reference to pp. 124 and 154.

38. Watson 1968: 122, slightly altered.

39. Those familiar with biblical scholarship will recognize here the influence of Rudolf Bultmann's "demythologizing" approach to comparable themes in the New Testament. I reject, however, Bultmann's tendency to think that philosophy is a superior mode of representing what myths represent indirectly and inadequately.

40. Henricks's work appeared during the last stages of preparation for this book. His detailed discussions of the differences between these manuscripts and the traditional text made possible for the first time a close comparison and evaluation of these differences for persons like myself who are not specialists in pre-standardized Chinese writing and lexicography. More work evalu-

ating these differences certainly needs to be done. My own impression so far is that the earliness of Ma-wang-tui texts (c. 200 B.C.) is counterbalanced by the fact that they contain many more surely corrupt passages than the traditional Wang Pi text. See the introduction to "Additional Textual Notes."

41. The reader wishing to consult a more literal translation can consult the recent translation of Yi Wu (1989), or the older work of Paul Carus (1913), each of which gives the Chinese text and places English equivalents next to the Chinese characters.

42. Compare, for example, my comments on 50[53]:2 with those of Duyvendak.

Topical Glossary

1. For example, Hansen 1981: 236, 238.

2. 2A/2,10.

3. See Graham 1989: 351–354.

4. See Schwartz's comment on the colloquial usage of *ch'i* (1985: 181).

5. See Graham 1989: 170–171.

6. Watson 1968.

7. See Graham 1989: 172–211; Schwartz 1985: 215.

8. Compare *Mencius** 7A/21,4.

9. See especially Fingarette.

10. For further discussions of these terms, see the references to them in Graham's (1989) index.

11. See Forke 1925: 235, 251–254, 286.

12. Quoted in ibid.: 235.

13. 1989: 326.

14. Watson 1968: 362.

15. Bodde 1981: 105.

16. 3B2,2.

17. Watson 1968: 72, 82.

18. Failure to observe this distinction is the main methodological failing of Wagner's (1980) thesis about the *Tao Te Ching*'s composition (see p. 196 n. 26). He simply uses a certain pattern as an *analytical device* to analyze many passages. Such analysis in itself cannot serve as *evidence* that the author worked according to this pattern.

19. See Maspero 1981: 23–25.

20. See Graham 1989: 340–356.

21. 1989: 299–311.

22. 1990: 118, 124.

23. See Maspero 1981: 413–421 and 446–553; and Kohn passim.

24. 1989: 53–59; also Schwartz 1985: 175.

25. Saso 1983.

26. See note on *hsing*/form and *ching*/"vital energy" in 38[21]:2.

27. Watson 1968: 119, lightly revised.

28. See, for example, Needham 1962: 46–52.

29. 1989: 39–41.

30. 1985: 136–172.

31. See Graham 1989: 137–170.

32. See Graham 1989: 75–95.

33. Ibid.: 267–292.

34. See Ibid.: 23–25, 261–267, 283–285; Hansen 1983a: 72–82.

35. 1981: 237–244.

36. 1989: 56, 118–125.

37. Translated in Rickett 1965: 158–168. See the discussion in Graham: 1989: 100–105. Waley (1958: 43–50) also discusses some parallels between this book and the *Tao Te Ching*.

38. Hex. 22, line 4, "Great Symbol" commentary. Compare also hex. 23, line 5, and hex. 39, line 2.

39. The Ma-wang tui text has *heng* where Wang Pi generally has the synonym *ch'ang*. Henricks (1989: xv) says that Wang Pi represents a change in the original text, to avoid the taboo name of an Emperor Liu Heng (179–156 B.C.).

40. 1A/7,20.

41. Rickett 1965: 158 A, opening line.

42. Watson 1963: 57.

43. *Ching* in *Tao Te Ching* means "sacred book." According to Welch (1957: 104), the book first acquired this status under the Emperor Ching Ti (156–140 B.C.).

44. Rickett 1965: 158–159 A, my translation.

45. The *Mencius* (3B/4,4) describes the specific occupation of *shih* generally—in contrast to, say, carpenters—as *wei tao*/"doing Tao."

46. *Pu tao. Pu* is an adverbial negative preceding an adjective or verb, in contrast with the verbal *wu* which is used with nouns.

47. 7A/19,4.

48. Morgan 1969: 132–133, my translation.

49. 6/2.

50. 1958: 47; parenthetical remarks are Waley's. The quote is from a writing similar to the *Nei Yeh*, found in chapter 36 of the *Kuan Tzu*.

51. For example, 1A/7,9, 2A/2,7.

52. For example, 1A/7,23.

53. 6A/1.

54. 2A/2,6. The basic meaning of the word is "to guard" something (as in "guarding gold and jewels," 2[9]:1), but it has a more general meaning "to take care of," as in "take care of parents," contrasted with "neglecting" them. (*Mencius** 4A/19,1.)

55. 2A/2,19.

56. See Graham 1989: 53–64.

57. See further in ibid.: 330–340.

References

Austin, J. L. 1962 *How to Do Things with Words*. Oxford: Clarendon Press.

Baker, G. P., and P. M. S. Hacker. 1980. *Wittgenstein: Meaning and Understanding*. Essays on the Philosophical Investigations, Vol. 1. Chicago: Chicago University Press.

Bernstein, Richard J. 1983. *Beyond Objectivism and Relativism: Science, Hermeneutics, and Praxis*. Philadelphia: University of Pennsylvania Press.

Bodde, Derk. 1981. *Essays on Chinese Civilization*. Ed. and introd. Charles LeBlank and Dorothy Borei. Princeton: Princeton University Press.

Bultmann, Rudolf. 1963. *History of the Synoptic Tradition*. New York: Harper and Row.

Carus, Paul. 1913. *The Canon of Reason and Virtue—Being Lao-tze's Tao Teh King. Chinese and English*. Chicago: Open Court.

———. 1973. *The Canon of Reason and Virtue*. Chicago: Open Court.

Ch'en, Ku-ying. 1981. *Lao Tzu: Text, Notes, and Comments*. Trans. Rhett Y. W. Young and Roger T. Ames. Republic of China: Chinese Materials Center.

Ch'u, Ta-kao. 1973. *The Tao Te Ching*. New York: Samuel Weiser.

Chan, Wing-tsit. 1963. *The Way of Lao Tzu (Tao te ching)*. Chicago: University of Chicago Press.

Creel, Herrlee G. 1929. *Sinism: A Study of the Evolution of the Chinese Worldview*. Chicago: Open Court.

———. 1970a. *The Origins of Statecraft in Ancient China Vol. I.* Chicago: University of Chicago Press.

———. 1970b. *What is Taoism?* Chicago: University of Chicago Press.

Duyvendak, J. J. L. 1954. *The Book of the Way and Its Virtue.* London: J. Murray.

Elorduy, Carmelo, S. I. 1961. *La Gnosis Taoista del Tao Te Ching: Análisis y Traducción.* Oña (Burgos) Spain: Facultad de Theologia S.I.

Erkes, Eduard. "Arthur Waley's Laotse-Übersetzung." *Artibus Asiae* 5: 288–307.

———, trans. 1950. *Ho–Shang-Kung's Commentary on Lao-Tse.* Ascona Switzerland: Artibus Asiae Publishers.

Fingarette, Herbert. 1972. *Confucius: The Secular as Sacred.* New York: Harper and Row.

Forke, Alfred. *The Cosmo-conception of the Chinese.* New York, 1925.

Gardiner, Patrick. "German Philosophy and the Rise of Relativism." *Monist* 64 (1981):138–54.

Graham, A. C. *Disputers of the Tao: Philosophical Argument in Ancient China.* LaSalle, Ill: Open Court, 1989.

———. *Studies in Chinese Philosophy and Philosophical Literature.* Albany, New York: State University of New York, 1990.

Hansen, Chad. 1981. "Linguistic Skepticism in the Lao Tzu." *Philosophy East and West* 31 (July) pp. 231–246.

———. 1983a. *Language and Logic in Ancient China.* Ann Arbor: University of Michigan Press.

———. 1983b. "A Tao of Tao in Chuang Tzu." In *Experimental Essays on Chuang-tzu,* ed. Victor H. Mair, 24–55. Asian studies at Hawaii. Honolulu: University of Hawaii Press.

———. 1989. "Language in the Heart-mind." In *Understanding the Chinese mind,* ed. Robert E. Allinson, pp. 75–124. Oxford: Oxford University Press.

Hawkes, David, trans. 1985. *Songs of the South.* New York: Penguin.

Henricks, Robert G. 1989. *Lao-Tzu Te-Tao Ching*. New York: Ballantine.

Ho, Shih-chi. 1936. *Ku pen tao te ching hsiao k'an*. Beijing: National Peiping Academy.

Hsu, Cho-yun. 1965. *Ancient China in Transition: An Analysis of Social Mobility, 722–222 B.C.* Stanford, Calif.: Stanford University Press.

Hurvitz, Leon. 1961. "A Recent Japanese Study of Lao-Tzu." *Monumenta Serica* 20 311–367.

Julien, Stanislas. 1842. *La Livre de la Voie et de la Vertu*. Paris: L'Imprimiere Royale.

Kaltenmark, Max. 1965. *Lao Tzu and Taoism*. Trans. Roger Greaves. Stanford, Calif.: Stanford University Press.

Karlgren, Bernard. 1932. *On the poetical parts in Lao-tsi*. Göteborgs Högskolas Arsskrift 38, 1932: 3. Göteberg: Elanders Boktryckeri Aktiebolag.

Karlgren, Bernard, trans. 1950. "The Book of Documents." *Bulletin of the Museum of Far Eastern Antiquities* 22.

———, trans. 1957. "Notes on Lao Tze." *Bulletin of the Museum of Far Eastern Antiquities*.

Kimura, Eichi. 1959. *Roshi No Shin-kenkyu*. Tokyo: Sobunsha.

Kohn, Livia, ed. 1989. *Taoist Meditation and Longevity Techniques*. In collaboration with Yoshinobu Sakade. Michigan monographs in Chinese studies. Ann Arbor: Center for Chinese Studies, University of Michigan Press.

LaFargue, Michael. 1985. *Language and Gnosis: Form and Meaning in the Acts of Thomas*. Philadelphia: Fortress Press.

———. 1988a. "Socio-Historical Research and the Contextualization of Biblical Theology." Ed. J. S. Frerichs, R. Horsley, P. Borger, J. Neusner. In *The social world of formative Christianity and Judaism: Essays in honor of Howard Clark Kee*, pp. 3–16. Philadelphia: Fortress Press.

———. 1988b. "Are texts determinate? Derrida, Barth, and the Role of the Biblical Scholar." *Harvard Theological Review* 81, no. 3: 341–357.

———. 1990. "Interpreting the Aphorisms in the *Tao Te Ching.*" *Journal of Chinese Religions* 18 (Fall): 25–43.

———. Forthcoming. *Tao and method: A reasoned approach to the Tao Te Ching.* Albany: State University of New York Press.

Lau, D. C. 1963. *Tao Te Ching.* Baltimore: Penguin Books.

Legge, James, trans. 1885 (Delhi: Motilal Banarsidass, 1964). *The Sacred Books of China: The Texts of Confucianism. Part IV The Li Ki [Li Chi].* Oxford: Oxford University Press.

——— trans. 1891 (New York: Dover, 1962). *The Texts of Taoism, Part. 1.* In *Sacred Books of the East* Vol. 39. Oxford: Oxford University Press.

———, trans. 1893 (New York: Dover, 1971). *Confucian Analects, The Great Learning, and The Doctrine of the Mean.* In *The Chinese classics* Vol. 1. Oxford: Clarendon Press.

———, trans. 1895 (New York: Dover, 1970). *The Works of Mencius.* In *The Chinese classics.* Vol. 2. Oxford: Clarendon Press.

Lin, Paul J., trans. 1977. *A Translation of Lao Tzu's Tao Te Ching and Wang Pi's Commentary.* Michigan papers in Chinese studies. Ann Arbor: Center for Chinese Studies, University of Michigan Press.

McKnight, Edgar V. 1969. *What is Form Criticism?* Philadelphia: Fortress Press.

Mair, Victor H., trans. 1990. *Tao Te Ching.* New York: Bantam Books.

Maspero, Henri. 1981. *Taoism and Chinese Religion.* Trans. Frank A. Kierman Jr. Amherst: University of Massachusetts Press.

Morgan, Evan, trans. 1969. *Tao the Great Luminant: Essays from Huai Nan Tzu with Introductory Articles Notes Analyses.* New York: Paragon Book Reprint.

Mueller-Vollmer, Kurt, ed. 1988. *The Hermeneutics Reader.* New York: Continuum.

Needham, Joseph. 1962. *Science and Civilization in China.* Vol. 2. *History of Scientific Thought.* Cambridge, England: The University Press.

Palmer, Richard E. 1969. *Hermeneutics: Interpretation Theory in*

Schleiermacher, Dilthey, Heidegger and Gadamer. Northwestern University Studies in Phenomenology and Existential Philosophy. Evanston Ill.: Northwestern University Press.

Rast, W. E. 1972. *Tradition and History in the Old Testament.* Philadelphia: Fortress Press.

Rhode, J. 1968. *Rediscovering the Teaching of the Evangelists.* Philadelphia: Fortress Press.

Rickett, W. Allyn. 1965. *Kuan-tzu: A Repository of Early Chinese Thought.* Hong Kong: Hong Kong University Press.

Rorty, Richard. 1982. *Consequences of Pragmatism.* Minneapolis: University of Michigan Press.

Rump, Ariane, trans. 1979. *Commentary on the Lao Tzu by Wang Pi.* In collaboration with Wing Tsit Chan. Monographs of the Society for Asian and Comparative Philosophy, no. 6. Honolulu: University of Hawaii Press.

Saso, Michael. 1983. "The Chuang-tzu Nei-p'ien: A Taoist Meditation." In *Experimental essays on Chuang-tzu,* ed. Victor H. Mair, pp. 140–157. Asian Studies at Hawaii. Honolulu: University of Hawaii Press.

Schleiermacher, Friedich. 1801. *Lectures on Religion: Speeches to Its Cultured Despisers.* New York: Harper and Row.

Schüssler-Fiorenza, Francis. 1985. *Foundational Theology.* New York: Crossroad.

Schwartz, Benjamin I. 1985. *The World of Thought in Ancient China.* Cambridge, Mass.: Harvard University Press.

Strauss, Victor von. 1959. *Lao-Tse Tao Te King.* Zurich: Manesse Verlag.

Stryk, Lucien, ed. 1969. *World of the Buddha: A Reader—From the Three Baskets to Modern Zen.* New York: Doubleday.

Wagner, R. G. 1980. "Interlocking Parallel Style: Laozi and Wang Bi." *Asiatische Studien* 34 no. 1: 18–58.

Waley, A. 1958. *The Way and Its Power.* New York: Grove Press.

Watson, Burton, trans. 1963. *Mo Tzu: Basic writings.* New York: Columbia University Press.

————, trans. 1968. *Chuang Tzu.* New York: Columbia University.

Welch, Holmes. 1957. *Taoism: The Parting of the Way.* Boston: Beacon Press.

Wu, Yi. 1989. *The Book of Lao Tzu (the Tao Te Ching).* San Francisco: Great Learning Publishing Co.

List of Chapters in the Traditional Arrangement

Old Number	New Number	Page	Old Number	New Number	Page
[1]	43	p. 94	[31]	67	p. 146
[2]	42	p. 92	[32]	63	p. 136
[3]	79	p. 172	[33]	24	p. 54
[4]	31	p. 68	[34]	64	p. 138
[5]	16	p. 34	[35]	46	p. 100
[6]	32	p. 70	[36]	73	p. 158
[7]	10	p. 22	[37]	81	p. 176
[8]	7	p. 16	[38]	11	p. 24
[9]	2	p. 6	[39]	35	p. 76
[10]	27	p. 60	[40]	34	p. 74
[11]	15	p. 32	[41]	44	p. 96
[12]	21	p. 46	[42]	36	p. 78
[13]	18	p. 40	[43]	47	p. 102
[14]	37	p. 80	[44]	19	p. 42
[15]	6	p. 14	[45]	5	p. 12
[16]	28	p. 62	[46]	20	p. 44
[17]	54	p. 118	[47]	41	p. 90
[18]	12	p. 26	[48]	25	p. 56
[19]	78	p. 170	[49]	60	p. 130
[20]	13	p. 28	[50]	22	p. 48
[21]	38	p. 82	[51]	65	p. 140
[22]	4	p. 10	[52]	29	p. 64
[23]	14	p. 30	[53]	50	p. 110
[24]	1	p. 4	[54]	61	p. 132
[25]	39	p. 84	[55]	33	p. 72
[26]	23	p. 50	[56]	30	p. 66
[27]	49	p. 106	[57]	77	p. 168
[28]	17	p. 36	[58]	59	p. 128
[29]	62	p. 134	[59]	26	p. 58
[30]	69	p. 150	[60]	70	p. 152

Old Number	New Number	Page	Old Number	New Number	Page
[61]	56	p. 122	[72]	53	p. 116
[62]	48	p. 104	[73]	58	p. 126
[63]	71	p. 154	[74]	66	p. 144
[64]	72	p. 156	[75]	51	p. 112
[65]	80	p. 174	[76]	74	p. 160
[66]	55	p. 120	[77]	52	p. 114
[67]	3	p. 8	[78]	75	p. 162
[68]	57	p. 124	[79]	9	p. 20
[69]	68	p. 148	[80]	76	p. 166
[70]	45	p. 98	[81]	8	p. 18
[71]	40	p. 88